GW00385472

Praise for *Asian Brand Strategy*

"Building successful global brands is – and will be – critical for the rapidly increasing number of Asian champions on the global stage. Martin Roll provides a compelling and practical roadmap on how to do this, based on his extensive experience advising Asian corporations."

–Dominic Barton, Global Managing Director, McKinsey & Company

"Building brands have become a C-suite topic in Asia as Asian firms seek to globalize. Martin Roll provides a compelling framework, clear guidelines, and multiple insights into successfully brand marketing. A 'must-read' for anyone interested in the rise of Asia from the leading expert."

–David Aaker, Vice-Chairman, Prophet; author of *Aaker on Branding*

"Martin Roll's *Asian Brand Strategy* provides superb motivation and substance into Asian brands and branding. It offers invaluable inspiration and guidance into one of the hottest areas of marketing."

–Kevin Lane Keller, Professor of Marketing, Tuck School of Business

"Branding is the hottest topic in marketing! Martin Roll describes all the key opportunities and challenges that Asian firms need to further challenge their Western competitors. As the leading expert on Asian brands, Martin Roll brings a unique knowledge and experience that make his book a 'must-read' for all global marketers!"

–Dominique Turpin, President, IMD Business School

"An insightful look into branding as a strategic tool for Asian companies – *Asian Brand Strategy* by Martin Roll is a brilliant, incisive read. A treasure of ideas and case studies, this compelling new book discusses the challenges Asian corporations face to stay relevant in today's dynamic, global market."

–N. R. Narayana Murthy, Founder, Infosys

"*Asian Brand Strategy* is an important handbook for Asian executives aspiring to build strong brands. It provides a solid foundation for future success in the global market place."

–John A. Quelch, Charles Edward Wilson Professor of
Business Administration, Harvard Business School

"The 21st century will be the Asian century. Asian corporations will naturally attain greater global prominence. However, they can achieve global recognition much faster if they pay greater attention to their brand strategies. Martin Roll's book could not be more relevant and timely. Asians should heed his advice."

–Kishore Mahbubani, Dean, LKY School of Public Policy (NUS),
author of *The New Asian Hemisphere*

"*Asian Brand Strategy* is a brilliant publication with valuable in-depth analysis of the current Asian Branding Platforms that are shaping the retail and consumer perceptions of products and services in a highly dynamic and competitive Asia. The market place today has many established and emerging brands and the key to a successful brand with sustainable growth and customer loyalty is a total approach and a detailed 360-degree strategy. Martin Roll has done an excellent job in giving readers great insights and has demonstrated clearly the challenges ahead for all stakeholders of Asian Brands to be accomplished performers in the global stage! Highly recommended!"

–Sudhitham Chirathivat, Chairman of Advisory Board, Central Group of Companies

"Branding has become a hot topic for Asian companies which are no longer able to compete purely as contract manufacturers and now need to directly 'own' the end consumer. As shelf space in bookstores get filled with myriad books on branding as the next best thing, Martin Roll's book *Asian Brand Strategy* stands out above the pack. It has the serious theoretical framework which underpins any real understanding of the role of branding in business. And it has the practical pointers which make it useful for anyone wanting to implement a brand strategy. Roll's five major messages – that branding can enhance shareholder value; that it must be led by the top person in a company; that it is not simply slick advertising and PR but a holistic integration of many business functions; that Asian companies must embrace branding to move up the value chain, and that branding strategies can be measured through metrics – resonate strongly within my own company and have been the key factors for Banyan Tree's own success in branding. I would strongly recommend this book as compulsory reading for anyone who wants to understand the power of branding and how to implement a practical, no-gimmicks brand strategy."

–Ho Kwon Ping, Executive Chairman, Banyan Tree Group

"Martin Roll provides clear, insightful strategies for Asian firms seeking to globalize their brands, and for global brands -aspiring to succeed in Asia. A brilliant guideline!"

–Michael Aagaard Andersen, Senior Advisor and Vice President, ONLY (Bestseller, China)

About the Author

Martin Roll
Business & Brand Strategist
Martin Roll Company

Martin Roll is the founder of Martin Roll Company, a global advisory firm. The company seeks to empower clients to succeed through better business performance and to become enduring, leading enterprises.

Martin Roll delivers the combined value of an experienced global business strategist, senior advisor, and facilitator to Fortune 500 companies, Asian firms, and family-owned businesses on how to build and manage strong, global brands as well as leadership of high-performing, marketing-oriented businesses.

Martin Roll is very experienced in engaging and advising clients at all management levels from business owners and C-suite leaders to functional staff across multiple industries and cultures.

Martin Roll is a keynote speaker at global conferences, an experienced conference moderator, and executive workshop facilitator. He also teaches MBA, EMBA and Executive Education programs at Nanyang Business School (Singapore), and is a frequent guest lecturer at INSEAD and other leading, global business schools.

Martin Roll is the author of global bestseller *Asian Brand Strategy*, a business columnist with INSEAD Knowledge, a prolific management writer, and a regular commentator in global media. He holds an MBA from INSEAD.

Martin Roll is currently writing on four new global management books.

He is a Danish citizen, a Singaporean permanent resident, and divides his time between East and West.

Specialities: Branding, Marketing, Strategy, Leadership, Change & Transformations, Business Family Transition, Business Coaching, Asia & Emerging Markets.

Martin Roll can be contacted at: **www.martinroll.com**

Building and Sustaining Strong Global Brands in Asia

Asian Brand Strategy (Revised and Updated)

Martin Roll

Business & Brand Strategist, Senior Advisor,
Martin Roll Company, Singapore

First edition published 2005 by
PALGRAVE MACMILLAN
9781403992796 hardback

Second edition published 2015 by
PALGRAVE MACMILLAN

Palgrave Macmillan in the UK is an imprint of Macmillan Publishers Limited,
registered in England, company number 785998, of Houndmills, Basingstoke,
Hampshire RG21 6XS.

Palgrave Macmillan in the US is a division of St Martin's Press LLC,
175 Fifth Avenue, New York, NY 10010.

Palgrave Macmillan is the global academic imprint of the above companies and
has companies and representatives throughout the world.

Palgrave® and Macmillan® are registered trademarks in the United States,
the United Kingdom, Europe and other countries.

ISBN 978–1–137–35916–2

This book is printed on paper suitable for recycling and made from fully
managed and sustained forest sources. Logging, pulping and manufacturing
processes are expected to conform to the environmental regulations of the
country of origin.

A catalogue record for this book is available from the British Library.

Library of Congress Cataloging-in-Publication Data
Roll, Martin, 1967–
Asian brand strategy : building and sustaining strong global brands in Asia /
Martin Roll. —2nd edition.
pages cm
ISBN 978–1–137–35916–2 (hardback)
1. Brand name products—Asia—Management. 2. Brand name products—
Asia—Marketing. I. Title.
HD69.B7R65 2015
658.8′27095—dc23   2015003633

Typeset by MPS Limited, Chennai, India.

To Mads, Jens, Leah, Camilla, Emma, Oskar, Erik, and Nicklas. May you find journeys where you can make differences that matter.

In memory of Sue Blake, my book publicist, who sadly passed away too early and could not be part of the second journey. You will be missed forever.

Contents

List of Figures and Tables

Figures

Tables

Consulting and Speaking Enquiries

Martin Roll Company, a global advisory firm, seeks to empower clients to succeed through better business performance and to become enduring, leading enterprises. The advisory firm has wide knowledge and experience within a broad range of management topics, industries, and markets. The company engages with businesses, government, and associations all over the world.

Clients can also engage Martin Roll as a moderator for conferences, seminars, workshops, and in-house meetings.

Martin Roll delivers the combined value of an experienced global business strategist, senior advisor, and facilitator to Fortune 500 companies, Asian firms, and family-owned businesses on how to build and manage strong, global brands as well as leadership of high-performing, marketing-oriented businesses.

Martin Roll is very experienced in engaging and advising clients at all management levels from business owners and C-suite leaders to functional staff across multiple industries and cultures.

Martin Roll is a regular visitor to all continents where he passes on his experience, foresight and comprehensive toolbox on global leadership, strategy, business development, branding, and marketing. With his global consultancy business based in Singapore, Martin Roll is also in great demand for his insights into Asia, Asian affairs and business and leadership issues in Asia.

Martin Roll represents a flexible business approach including consulting, advisory services and mentoring assignments, and he is available on an ad hoc basis or for longer-term projects. His global customers often establish long-term agreements with him to secure continuity and close dialogue on the numerous challenges and opportunities facing their companies.

If interested in exploring further about how to engage Martin Roll Company anywhere in the world, please contact us on contact@martinroll.com

Thanks for your interest in Martin Roll Company.

www.martinroll.com

Foreword

A strong brand can differentiate a company from its rivals, make it stand out from the competition, successfully influence consumer purchase decision, build customer loyalty, and boost the company's financial performance.

Asian Brand Strategy explores these issues, with a focus on the Asian market environment and on attempts to build Asian brands.

Brand management is essential if a firm desires sustained success, especially during intense periods of competition and difficult product differentiation. This situation is observed in many parts of Asia and in many product categories, and has often led to market commoditization, in which pricing is the only applicable rule of the game.

Branding is one way out of commoditization and its consequent profit erosion. Strong brand building requires long-term commitment, and the sacrifice of short-term profits. Unfortunately, many Asian companies traditionally favor investment in tangible assets such as manufacturing capacity and property. Intangible assets such as intellectual property, proprietary technologies, and products, systems, and brands have generally been given lower priority. This is reflected in the percentage of companies' market value accounted for by intangible assets – less than than 50 per cent and sometimes as low as one-third, even in the case of large Asian companies recognized as brand leaders. In contrast, it is more than 75 percent for Western branded consumer goods companies, which own the most prominent brands.

Furthermore, Asian firms tend to use price to push sales, thereby undermining both the implicit guarantee of the consistency of the offer and the quality perception essential to brand building. As a result, few Asian brands are considered globally strong and those in the top league come mainly from Japan and Korea. The first Chinese companies like Lenovo and Huawei are in the process of joining them.

The overall weakness of Asian brands in international markets does not mean that local brands do not exist or are not preferred in some Asian countries. The Chinese computer market is dominated by Lenovo and the beer market by three domestic brands, despite the major efforts of global leaders like Budweiser, Carlsberg, and Heineken. In the Philippines, local brand Jollibee has a dominant share of the domestic fast-food market, beating the established global brand McDonald's. In the 2014 BrandZ Top 100 Most Valuable Chinese Brands rankings, China Mobile enjoys the first rank, followed by ICBC and Tencent in second and third places respectively.[1]

The real challenge for many of these local brands comes when they try to sell to foreign consumers. Very few have succeeded, and attempts to build regional brands in a global marketplace have proved difficult. The immense population, increasing base of middle-class consumers, and unexploited market territories make Asia a thriving marketplace. Additionally, diverse cultures, disparity between rich and poor, infrastructural changes, and evolving mind-sets represent enormous challenges.

Branding in Asia is often wrongly referred to as an exercise that involves changing the company logo, design style, and colour scheme. It is often accompanied by a new corporate slogan, and everyone expects immediate results. Naturally, these are important elements to consider and potentially change once the strategy has been decided upon, but strategy development must precede this. Branding is a serious, long-term undertaking involving more skills and activities than the mere production of an updated glossy marketing facade with meaningless jargon.

In the Asian context, this is less evident. Branding is often seen as costly and is driven tactically at a low organizational level. Very often, advertising and promotion are the core activities driving brand-building efforts. Branding, as Martin Roll discusses vividly, is still not fully appreciated at boardroom and senior management level. Beyond that, the inherent cost- and volume-driven characteristics of Asian companies have resulted in a short-term view on return on branding investments. Such a view will not help companies to build trust in brands that come from a part of the world that became famous (or infamous) for cheap products and low-quality fakes. While Japanese and Korean products have long overcome this country-of-origin disadvantage, Chinese brands will have to work hard and smart to overcome this negative image when competing in the international arena.

Companies need to realize the strategic importance of branding. This call for Asian boardrooms and management teams to take charge of the branding domain themselves. A strong brand strategy can add significant value in helping the entire corporation and the management team to implement the long-term vision, create unique positions in the market, and unlock leadership potential within the organization.

Successful brands are managed by the top management level and implemented by the entire organization through multiple actions, behaviors, and customer touch points. Few publications in the past have detailed the strategic aspects of branding in Asia. In *Asian Brand Strategy*, Martin Roll has successfully tackled head-on many of the challenges illustrated and critical factors in the Asian environment such as culture and corporate structure. *Asian Brand Strategy* demonstrates how successful brands are helping top-tier Asian companies penetrate the global stage and how some aspiring Asian companies are beginning to make their mark against larger Western players. These brands share the same common denominator – a strong commitment to branding by their boardrooms and senior management teams.

Asian Brand Strategy provides insights, tools, and practical step-by-step guides that demystify the process and delivery of brand development and management. It demonstrates clearly why Asian boardrooms and management teams must begin to improve their competitiveness through branding. Martin Roll provides a very compelling framework and a winning formula for this process. *Asian Brand Strategy* is solid proof that there is no excuse for not building strong Asian brands and delivering better shareholder value across the region.

Prof. Dr. Hellmut Schütte
Dean Emeritus of CEIBS
Professor Emeritus of International Management – INSEAD

Preface and Acknowledgments

Strategic brand transformation: From nice to have, to need to have

My first encounter with Asia goes back to September 1992 when I flew into Tokyo Narita Airport in the early morning. The sun was shining brightly on Mount Fuji, a breathtaking scene for an Asian first-timer, a classic and picturesque scene taken from a leisure travel guide. I was in Asia for the first time with an open mind and eager to learn about the region. What made a great impression on me that early morning in Japan became the start of a journey that grew deeper and deeper into the Asian region with a fascination for all her myths, ancient histories, and blend of cultures, people and traditions. A region which combines low and high tech like no other, the past is sometimes part of the present and the future – where one has to expect the unexpected – all fast-paced, Asian style.

I have been intrigued since that defining moment. When I settled in Singapore in 2001 as a management advisor after leaving the global advertising industry and graduating from INSEAD, Asia was characterized by local companies like the South Korean Hyundai and Samsung, and the Japanese Shiseido and Sony, but none of them were anywhere near the global versions of today. The huge imbalance between East and West in terms of branding led me to write *Asian Brand Strategy*.

The first edition of this book, published in 2006, was a recipe for Asian brand challenges in management, strategy, branding, and internationalization. To successfully globalize means to build brands and avoid competition on the basis on low-cost production and price. This path has indeed increased the business value of many brands.

Since 2001, many more local brands have expanded regionally and globally, to face new competition. With increasing opportunities and further deregulation, home markets are opening up to global brands whether local incumbents like it or not. Hence, branding is no longer something nice for Asian brands to have – it is mandatory.

Some brands that have become hugely successful since I last wrote this book now face new challenges. Arrogance and complacency have hit many successful organisations, weakening their leadership power and leading to a danger of succumbing to the "victory disease" of hubris.

A large part of the findings and recommendations has been drawn from my many years working with global management teams and business owners. Through innumerable consulting projects with global boardrooms and corporate management teams, including several Fortune 500 companies, I have made observations and gained insights which shaped the arguments in the book. Additionally, delivering keynote speeches, panelling at many international conferences, and hosting many annual boardroom workshops globally have further distilled the ideas presented. The audiences attending these events have served as valuable sounding boards and discussion partners.

Asian Brand Strategy is written for boardrooms and corporate management teams. The book is aimed primarily at Asian business leaders and Western observers. Firstly, Asian boardrooms are facing defining moments for enhancing shareholder value. This is where comprehensive, consistent, and truly committed brand building comes in, with all its intricacies and challenges. Branding done right is not easy – yet it seems simple.

Secondly, Western business leaders are looking toward Asia like never before. The region not only provides cheap manufacturing and new growth opportunities, but also represents important potential threats from tough Asian competition, whether non-branded or branded. *Asian Brand Strategy* offers first-hand insights into Asian consumers, markets, and companies' efforts to build strong brands. The book details the strategies and activities in building, managing, and leveraging stronger Asian brands. I also hope the book will inspire researchers, students, and anyone else interested in the world's most fascinating and fast-paced region.

I have been inspired by many friends and business associates throughout my career in Asia. Without these wonderful people, this book could not have been written. One particular person has contributed significantly to the profound interest in Asia that later led me to live and work there: Professor Hellmut Schütte, Vice President, Dean and Distinguished Professor of International Management, CEIBS. Hellmut introduced me to and inspired my interest in Asia with his brilliant classes at INSEAD. He remains an inspiring mentor and a good friend, for which I am grateful.

I want to thank researcher Marc Bauche for his invaluable contributions to Martin Roll Company and this book. Insights director Sandeep Das is a great source of inspiration and contributed immensely to the book. I also want to thank Dora Chan and Riko Mulia for excellent work in editing and completing the manuscript.

I want to thank the following people for their contribution to the second edition: William M. Booth, Eric Booth, Steve M. Benhar, Choon Phong Goh, Nicholas Ionides, Wilson Heng, Lisa Bovio, Nicholas Priest, Sue Shim, Kevin Cho, Joy Tan, Ralph Ahrbeck, Margaret Des Gaines, Ho Kwon Ping, Samantha Burgess-Allen, Jessie Chong, Ravi Thakran, Wendy Chan, Grace Ng, Rebecca Chia-Rodrigues, Susan Kim Tsui, Kyung-Bae Suh, Brian Lee, Sunghae Kweon, Dae Ryun Chang, Michael Aagaard Andersen, Rhoda Yap, Pat Liew, Lindsay Beltzer, Kasper Leschly, Michael Hobson, Rita Lam, Sebastian Koschel, Ivy Boon, Sarah Smith, Luca Deplano, Carolina Arraiza, Maranda Barnes, Lewis Lim, Anja Wittrup, JP Kuehlwein, Victoria Great, Yukiko Shimomura, and Colin D'Silva.

Several other people made great contributions to the first version, and it would take too much space to mention them all. Special thanks to Abhijith Holehonnur, Pierre Chandon, Amitava Chattopadhyay, Jill Klein, Peter Williamson, Ziv Carmon, Julien Cayla, Mike Sherman, Lily Lou, Aaron Lau, Michael Backman, Mervin Wang, Susan Fournier, Anil Thadani, Maisy Koh, Lay Cheng Teo, Roshini Prakash, Kosuke Tomita, Mutsumi Takahashi, William Yue, Abel Wu, Gaurang Shetty, Raymond Ng, Steve Lee, Gerry Oh, Michael J. N. Tan, Marcus John, Andre Tegner, Ji-Suk Kang, Jakob Hinrichsen, Melissa Kang Su Yi, Sarah Young, Ryoko Orihata, Erik van Vulpen, Renzo Scacco, Lydie Lamont, Ian McKee, Karen Low, Johann Tse, Ray Poletti, Andrea Newman, Sarah-Anne Fong, Lars Wiskum, Myungwoo Nam, Midori Matsuoka, Alan Tan, Tyan Yee Ho, and Jay Yaw.

Finally, I want to thank my editors Stephen Partridge, Josephine Taylor, and Tamsine O'Riordan, and their brilliant teams at Palgrave in London, Hong Kong, and New York. They have supported me and helped shape the book.

It should be noted that every effort has been made to trace all copyright holders, but if any have been inadvertently overlooked, the publisher will be pleased to make the necessary arrangements at the first opportunity.

Martin Roll
Singapore, January 2015
www.martinroll.com

chapter 1

Introduction

A journey of a thousand miles begins with a single step.
—Confucius

The face of business in Asia is changing faster than one can blink one's eyes. Asian companies that used to be back-end workhorses, manufacturing consumer goods cheaply for Western companies, are slowly realizing the benefits of branding. In China, a smartphone manufacturer established in 2011 was able to overtake Apple to become the nation's dominant mobile phone maker.[1] By nearly replicating Apple's processing power and design while improving distribution and manufacturing, some say the mobile industry's future will no longer be decided in Silicon Valley, but in the Beijing headquarters of Xiaomi. Even Apple co-founder Steve Wozniak has admitted Xiaomi is "good enough to break the American market."[2] However, Chinese mobile brands like Xiaomi will face bumpy roads ahead when they expand globally due to patent disputes, user concerns over cyber spying, poor brand recognition, strong branded competition, and other challenges.[3]

In a market where competition implies slashing prices on unbranded products, Asian businesses are slowly realizing the power of brand identity in capturing consumers and returning larger profits on their investments. Asian boardrooms are realizing that instead of wearing themselves down on razor-thin margins to compete with the next supplier, they could increase returns through brand investment and differentiation.

Starting with a ladies' footwear store in Singapore in 1996, brothers Charles and Keith Wong observed that while selling wholesale shoes provided a cost advantage, the lack of uniqueness meant limited growth. This made them realize the potential of creating a brand that consumers could identify with – leading to the creation of the Charles & Keith brand. Today, it is well-known among fashion-conscious shoppers for its distinctive designs and quick in-season turnaround that offers 20–30 new designs in stores every week. Charles & Keith has expanded its product range to include bags, belts, shades, tech accessories, and bracelets, evolving from a footwear brand to a lifestyle brand. The group has also created Pedro, a line of men's footwear and accessories.

With the sale of a 20 percent stake in the company to L Capital Asia in 2011 – a private equity group sponsored by the LVMH Group and other investors – the world is taking notice of Charles & Keith. With more than 500 stores across Asia, Eastern Europe, and the Middle East, Charles & Keith is looking to conquer China, the US, and Western Europe to become a global aspirational fashion brand by utilizing the expertise of L Capital Asia and their sponsors.[4]

Sometimes, successful branding means doing the opposite of what is fashionable. Japanese clothing chain Uniqlo has become Asia's biggest clothing retailer, thanks to its "Made for All" brand philosophy.[5] Often mistaken as a fast fashion brand, Uniqlo's strategy is to "totally ignore fashion" by not chasing trends.[6] Instead, they focus on basic, affordable items that transcend age, gender, and ethnicity so that every individual can create his unique style. Uniqlo now has more than 800 stores worldwide and an ambitious CEO, Tadashi Yanai, who intends to make Uniqlo the world's largest clothing retailer by 2020. The firm has learned much from its first failed attempt at expanding overseas. After opening too many stores too quickly in the UK in 2002, only eight remained open by 2006. Executives have admitted that they did not do a good enough job establishing a brand identity in new markets.[7] With seven stores in the US, Uniqlo's planned expansion of 1,000 locations in America will surely rely on their commitment to branding at the boardroom level.[8]

Most Asian firms, however, still view branding as advertising or logo design. If firms are to benefit from branding, they must recognize that it impacts the entire business – the structure, goals, attitude, and the very outlook of those in the boardroom. Managers will need to see branding not as an appendage to the ongoing business, but rather as an infusion that seeps through the very spirit of the organization, driving healthy return on investment (ROI). It will require a shift in focus and priority for every functional aspect of the organization.

Before branding can be implemented, it is important to understand its implications, its various shades and hues, its forms and practices, its purpose, and its advantages. It is indeed a paradigm shift that executives must undertake across Asian boardrooms. How this change in thinking can be analyzed, captured, and managed by Asian boardrooms and corporate management teams forms the core of this book.

Lack of Value Creation

Goldman Sachs has forecast that, by 2026, China will have overtaken the US economy in size to become the world's largest economy. The Indian economy would be larger than Japan's by 2028. China and India are indeed leading Asia's growth path, with implications for industries and companies all over the world.[9]

The changes in the Asian competitive environment are driven by several factors: the rapid development of China and India, increasing deregulation and trade liberalization, and the emergence of new demographic and social trends throughout the region. These changes involve entire value chains in manufacturing and services, issues related to efficiencies in operations and productivity gains, innovation and design, and a reduced focus on broad diversification – which has been the prevalent structure of Asian businesses, particularly within family businesses.

The Eroding Low-Cost Advantage

A large part of Asia's economic development can be attributed to low-cost advantages which enabled Asian companies to gain market share from other suppliers. In the past two decades, Asian countries have slowly but surely attracted many industries: light manufacturing in Guangdong, electrical equipment in Guangxi, and software development in Bangalore. But Western companies, by buying these Asian firms or aggressively outsourcing their operations, are already streamlining their cost structures. Low-cost alone no longer provides a significant advantage. The cut-throat competition in many industries, resulting in tremendous pressure on margins, has forced companies to look for additional measures for survival and growth. One example is mobile phones, where brand owners can reach gross margins up to double that of contract manufacturers.

Major companies based in Asia and expanding outside their home market believe innovation and brand building will be vital to flourishing overseas. Accenture asked senior executives what they believed the source of their competitive advantage would be in three years' time. From 2012 to 2013, low-cost R&D slid in importance by 16 percent while low operating costs were down by 34 percent. Replacing them was an increase in importance for selling high-value, quality, branded, innovative products and services.[10]

However, Asia is still one of the world's biggest providers of commodity products, a production hub housing 47 percent of the world's manufacturing.[11] Asian manufacturers mostly produce for other companies and the majority of these products are therefore non-branded. In other words, these are volume products without strong brand identities. Instead, the largest financial value is captured by the manufacturers' customers – the next player in the value chain – primarily driven by strong brand strategies and successfully planned and executed marketing programs.

The difference in the proportion of value captured between the Asian manufacturing price and the Western retail price serves as a good example. A branded sports shoe is produced in Asia at an estimated US$5, sold to the sports shoe brand for US$10, and the consumer buys it in the retail store for US$100 – in other words, a twenty-fold increase throughout the "product-to-brand" value chain. This leaves the Asian manufacturer with only a fraction of the substantial value that consumers are willing to pay for, in addition to the fact that the consumer never comes to know the name of the Asian manufacturer who originally made the sports shoe.

Figure 1.1 illustrates four scenarios of how a brand is integrated in the value chain. In certain cases, companies are vertically integrated and can own part of the channels, including retail outlets, the distributors, and/or the production facilities.

Since 2000, the number of distributors in the sports goods industry has declined more than 50 percent as many sports brands became distributors themselves. This is particularly the trend among larger brands. The sports shoe brand captures an estimated 40–95 percent of the entire financial value depending on its level of vertical integration.[12]

Successful global companies share certain common characteristics, including strong brand equity. Despite Asia's size and economic growth, it has not seen the emergence of many strong, international brands.

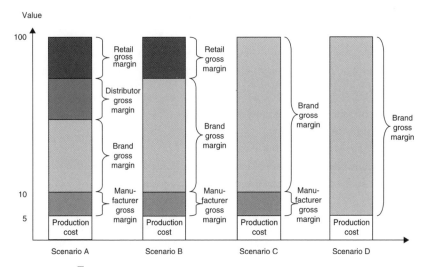

FIGURE 1.1 / Four scenarios for value creation through branding

Source: Martin Roll Company.

Few Global Brands Originating from Asia

In a 2014 Interbrand study measuring the financial value of worldwide brands, only 11 of the top 100 global brands originated in Asia.[13] These brands are the familiar technology and automobile giants from Japan and South Korea, such as Samsung, Toyota, Honda, Canon, and Hyundai, and a single Chinese brand Huawei (ranked 94th) appeared on the global list for the first time. A simple question arises: What about the rest of Asia?

Given the size and volume of Asian businesses today, it is evident that Asia could build many more prominent brands and capture more financial value through better price premiums and customer loyalty. Asia certainly has some of the world's largest companies. China is home to the world's three biggest public sector companies and five of the top 10 public sector companies in the world. With 674 members on the Forbes Global 2000 list of largest public companies coming from Asia, it is the most strongly represented region. Yet these companies lack the brand recognition and value which accompany most of America and Europe's largest companies.[14]

Branding can become an important driver of shareholder value for Asian companies in the future, as this book will illustrate.

Reasons for the Lack of Strong Asian Brands

There are many reasons why Asian companies have not developed many global brands until now. The appreciation of branding in Asian companies is primarily inhibited by the following five factors:

- Stage of economic development of societies
- Less focus on innovation
- Broad diversification of businesses
- Asian business structures
- Implications of intellectual property (IP) protection

Stage of Economic Development of Societies

Asian countries are at different stages of development. At one end of the spectrum are developed countries like Japan, South Korea, Singapore, Taiwan, and Hong Kong. At the other end are developing countries like Vietnam, Cambodia, and Indonesia. In between are countries like Malaysia, Thailand, China, and India, which are moving through rapid transitory phases. The development stages of these countries can influence business priorities, the degree of business sophistication, and where to fit into the value chain.

When countries and industries move from a low to a hi-tech environment, they are generally more inclined to supplement their low-cost advantage with a holistic value perspective. Very often they are forced to move up the value chain while losing their low-cost advantage in manufacturing to competitors with lower labor costs. Although the value perspective does not exclude seeking to drive costs down constantly, it aims primarily at creating additional perceived value for products and services. This is where brands often start to play their role as drivers of shareholder value through better price premiums and enhanced customer loyalty.

It is incorrect to assume that the economic stage of development and degree of branding are always correlated. In general, any company can decide to build brands. However, the economic development stage of a country and the level of sophistication of an industry can serve as important indicators to estimate whether branding gains wide appreciation and momentum.

Another important factor to consider while formulating a brand building strategy is the level of importance a consumer will place on a brand or a trademark name when buying a product. Successful companies with strong brands have created the need for a brand and the associated equity, when it previously did not exist.

THE INDONESIAN CONSUMER OPPORTUNITY

By 2030, 90 million Indonesians will join the consumer class and contribute an additional US$1 trillion in annual spending. Indonesia's consumer spending of 61 percent of GDP (2010) is already close to levels in developed economies. The urbanization of Indonesia's population will migrate from roughly 53 percent (2013) to 71 percent by 2030. It is estimated that categories like financial services, leisure, travel, and apparel will grow to satisfy the upwardly mobile, tech-savvy, individualistic urban consumers.

Indonesia comprises more than 17,500 islands with a complex, fragmented distribution infrastructure. Mom-and-Pop stores predominate in many categories, but channels are evolving and modern retailing is emerging rapidly. Brands need to manage multiple channels to cater to various consumer segments. At the same time, digital technology is influencing marketing in Indonesia, and is increasingly playing a significant role with the rise in numbers of consumers connected to the Internet (100 million by 2016) and on mobile devices (60 percent of Indonesians own a mobile phone).

Indonesian consumers generally attach strong importance to brands compared to other emerging markets. The important aspect is to build brand positions that resonate with local consumers rather than relying on country-of-origin. Indonesian consumers are not strongly aware of brand ownership and background, but are mostly concerned about what the brand offers them. Many Indonesians consider Nestlé's Kit Kat chocolate brand to be local, and the Japanese brand Honda used the Bahasa Indonesian words satu hati ("one heart") in a successful local advertising campaign.[15]

Finally, about 30 percent of the world's middle-class spending is contributed by Asians, up from 20 percent in 2000, according to the Brookings Institutions, a think-tank, which defines the middle-class as those earning US$10–100 daily.[16] Asia has therefore become a great cluster of consumer markets with increasing potential for global brands as well as emerging Asian brands.

Less Focus on Innovation

An anonymous survey of senior executives from some of China's largest state-owned enterprises shows that over half believed that China will be a bigger economic power than the US by 2025. However, only 13 percent believed that China would have overtaken the US on the technology frontier by then.[17]

Although innovation is difficult to measure, R&D spending can be an indication. On a national level, Asian economies have traditionally lagged behind the rest of the world on R&D spending as a ratio of GDP, with the exception of a few nations. Countries that spend the most on R&D are the US, China, Japan, Germany, South Korea, France, and the UK.[18]

In 2013, the following five countries filled the most patent applications in the world: the US (57,239), Japan (43,918), China (21,516), Germany (17,927), and South Korea (12,386).[19]

Asian countries are trying to take a lead in three areas likely to generate the next wave of innovation: biotechnology, nanotechnology, and information technology (IT). Asia spends as much as the US and Europe combined on nanotechnology. In addition, China, India, South Korea, and Taiwan have shifted from top-down, state-directed technology policies to more flexible, market-oriented approaches in order to foster innovation and entrepreneurship. China spent 1.98 percent of its GDP on R&D in 2012, almost tripling the levels it was spending in 1998.[20]

As low cost is ceasing to provide a competitive edge for Asian companies, differentiation driven by enhanced innovation capabilities will be paramount for future success. Innovation needs to become a top priority for Asian companies aspiring to build strong brands.

Although design is only a tiny part of a broader brand strategy, it can help to create visible differentiation for products and shape customer perceptions.

Sometimes, the right partnerships can boost a brand's ability to innovate. One of the easiest ways to build creative capital is through joint ventures, mergers, or acquisitions. Lenovo benefited from the purchase of IBM's personal computer business in 2005, instantly becoming the world's number 3 computer maker, while the longstanding relationship of Apple with Foxconn and other Chinese partners via the beloved iPhone is having a trickle-down effect.

Broad Diversification of Businesses

Another impediment to building brands in Asia in the past was the diversification of businesses spanning many industries with limited overlap and synergies. The prevalent mindset in Asia is based on trading rather than branding, and revenue generation, rather than profit. It is hard to create a relevant, clear, and differentiated brand strategy, and build a corporate brand that encompasses all areas, when a business has its hands dipped in every pie.

Conglomerates are far more prevalent in Asian markets than the rest of world. McKinsey's research finds that over the past decade, the largest conglomerates in China and India have continued to diversify rapidly, making an average of one new business entry every 18 months, while nearly half of these companies are not directly related to the parent companies' operations.[21]

Thailand's Charoen Pokphand (CP) Group is an example of an Asian company moving against the common diversification trend. Traditionally, it had interests in telecommunications, satellite, cable television, motorcycle manufacturing, petrochemicals, and brewing. Despite its diversified businesses, CP has continued to expand its integrated food business by controlling the entire supply chain. By transferring its agribusiness formula to other agricultural products and across countries, CP has also become one of the world's leading agribusiness groups. Its annual revenue in 2013 was US$41 billion.

The Korean beauty firm AmorePacific is one of the best examples of a former, diversified conglomerate that has found great success by focusing on only a single core business. Under the leadership of CEO Suh Kyung-Bae, AmorePacific sold off non-core assets such as a baseball team and an underwear maker in order to focus on becoming Asia's third largest cosmetics maker.[22]

Asian Business Structures

Another important reason for the lack of strong brands can be found in the prevalent business structures within Asia, which consist of many small and often family-owned businesses – with diversified business interests. It is much harder to overcome the barriers to brand building when resources are limited. In this case, the management perspective would favor short-term business wins against brand strategies, which require more resources and long-term perspectives. Despite younger generations taking over as leaders, it can still be a major barrier to convince older generations about the need for investing in intangibles as it runs against the business heritage and prevalent internal wisdom.

Family-controlled companies are typical for Asia, where many trace their origins to the 19th-century migration of mercantilist entrepreneurs from China. They account for about half of all publicly listed companies and 32 percent of total market capitalization across 10 Asian countries, according to Credit Suisse.[23]

Eu Yan Sang started as a provision shop in 1910 in northern Malaysia providing traditional Chinese herbs. Today, Eu Yan Sang has become an iconic, international brand in the Traditional Chinese Medicine (TCM) industry and the global fast-growing "health and wellness" sector. Richard Eu, former investment banker and fourth-generation family-owner of Eu Yan Sang, provided his perspective on family business and transition in Asia: "Every generation, you have got to think what you want to do with the family business. Is your business the right business for the future? Is it more important to preserve the family or more important to preserve the business? This is not just about the patriarch or the founder – it has got to include everybody."[24]

When Richard Eu took over in the 1990s, Eu Yan Sang was barely profitable with a few shops in Singapore and Malaysia. In 2000, Eu Yan Sang was publicly listed. In 2012, net profit was US$16.8 million, from sales of modern, high-margin products.[25] Its core markets are Singapore, Malaysia, and Hong Kong, where it enjoys significant market share.

Implications of IP Protection

The challenges of IP protection in Asia have been a major barrier against building brands. Many Asian companies have faced rampant counterfeiting and infringement of IP rights in their own backyards. Until and unless legislation and law enforcement get better in the region, it may be a hurdle that prevents a deeper appreciation and respect for intangible asset management in the Asian boardroom.

The World Customs Organization has estimated that 5–7 percent of global merchandise trade is due to counterfeits. In the US, China and Hong Kong are the primary sources of intercepted counterfeit products, representing 84 percent of seizures amounting to US$1.3 billion.[26] A staggering 75 percent of all fake goods seized worldwide from 2008 to 2010 were primarily from China, and fake goods account for approximately two percent of world trade.[27]

In one year, French luxury house LVMH spent more than US$16 million on investigations, busts, and legal fees against counterfeiting.[28]

One of the famous spots in Beijing used to be Xiushui or Silk Street. Ranking in the top three of Beijing's attractions, the narrow and crowded street would attract thousands of foreigners every year to buy cheap counterfeit versions of global luxury brand names like Louis Vuitton, Prada, and many others. It was eventually closed down by the Chinese authorities for renovation. While this seemed like a tough stance on the counterfeit industry, it could almost be considered a move to profit from it. Stall holders were given an option to take up a stall at the nearby Xiushui shopping centre where a trading corner of less than 5 square meters auctioned for as much as US$400,000.

Counterfeiting does not just involve products, but entire store concepts too. Famously in 2011, at least 22 fake Apple computer stores were found operating in parts of China.

A New Paradigm for the Asian Boardroom

Many of the ideas and recommendations contained in this book are driven by the Asian brand leadership model, illustrated in Table 1.1. The model illustrates the paradigm shift that Asian brands need to undertake in order to unleash their potential.

First, mindsets and practices need to change in Asian boardrooms. This book invites a complete shift in the way that Asian boardrooms think of branding: from a tactical view to a long-term, strategic perspective; from fragmented marketing activities to totally aligned branding activities; from a vision of branding as the sole responsibility of marketing managers to branding as the DNA and most essential function of the firm led by the boardroom.

Second, this new perspective must be grounded in in-depth understanding of consumer behavior patterns. Asia is not a homogeneous entity. More importantly, Asian countries are more and more traversed by cultural flows permeating the region: cinema, music, and fashion trends that at present extend beyond national borders to capture the imagination of millions. Branding and brands do not operate in a vacuum; they are closely linked to developments in society, to people and cultures.

Third, managers wanting to succeed in Asia need to abandon the oriental Asia of the past. Asian consumers are all vying for an Asian type of modernity that has nothing to do with colonial imagery.

Fourth, to create iconic brands, Asian managers will have to become trendsetters. The perspective developed in this book is that, in order to be successful, Asian brands need to capture the spirit of the region, and lead the way by creating that spirit.

TABLE 1.1   Asian Brand Leadership Model

Asian Brand Leadership – A new paradigm for the Asian Boardroom	Old paradigm	New paradigm
	Manufacturing-driven agenda	Branding-driven agenda
	Production	Design, innovation, and production
	Tactical advertising	Strategic branding and marketing
	Low cost/ low perceived value	Low cost/high perceived value
	Silos of activities	Collaboration
	Price as driver of sales	Value as driver of sales
Success factors for Asian boardrooms	OEM	Trademarks and IP (Intellectual Property)
	Short-term financial value	Long-term brand value
	Mid-level and separate marketing functions	Boardroom driven marketing functions
	Fragmented marketing activities	Totally aligned marketing programs
	Disparate product lines	Synergies between brands (brand architecture)
	Marketing through promotion	Branding through people
	A function drives the brand	An organization drives the brand
	Company-centric value creation	Co-creation of value
Consumer behavior	Collectivist	In-group/Out-group
	Regional homogenous	Scapes/Flows/Hybrids
Symbols	Oriental	New Asia
	Products and services	People and places
	Western celebrities	Hybrid + Asian celebrities
Culture	Following trends	Creating trends
	Japanese and Korean icons	Fragmented icons, Pan-Asian icons
	Silos of activities	Collaboration
Strategy drivers and measures	Sales perspective	Branding perspective
	Market share	Brand equity
	Awareness	Brand audit
	Tangible financial value on balance sheets	Tangible + intangible value on balance sheets
	Marketing as cost	Branding as strategic investment

Source: Martin Roll Company.

Finally, this shift can be achieved only if everybody in the company is convinced of the power of branding. This, in turn, can only happen through account-ability and systematic monitoring of branding investments and performance. Organizations that utilize data-driven decision-making are 5 percent more pro-ductive and 6 percent more profitable than their competitors.[29] This will make Asian brands truly great.

The Scope of the Book

This chapter has discussed the implications for a new Asian business landscape, where Asian companies can step up and capture more financial value through brands.

Chapter 2 looks at branding and how the discipline relates closely to business strategy. Branding can drive shareholder value. There are many managerial challenges, processes, and tasks needed to succeed with it, which are discussed further.

Chapter 3 is dedicated to Asian consumers and cultures and describes some of the transformations taking place in Asia. It provides a new way of looking at the region and covers issues like group versus individual orientation, roles, symbols, and family. The chapter looks at the transformation from a purely col-lectivist perception toward an in/out-group perspective, which can help us to understand Asian consumers better. It also discusses scapes, flows, and hybrids.

The quality perception of a brand can be derived from the perception of a given country. Chapter 4 discusses country branding and the country-of-origin effect, how it affects brands, and which measures companies should take to benefit most from a given country's image. This includes examples of how some Asian countries have branded themselves.

Strong brands are often driven and influenced by popular culture and multiple activities and trends in society. Celebrities and other public figures can act as potential endorsers for products and services and be an instrumental part of brand strategy. Chapter 5 discusses how to involve celebrities and other endorsers, and their ability to support Asian brand building.

Chapter 6 is dedicated to brand strategy. It provides frameworks for aligning the brand and an entire brand management model.

Chapters 7 and 8 illustrate case studies of successful as well as aspiring Asian brands. The two chapters illustrate different angles of building and managing brands in an Asian context through a selected portfolio of Asian brands. The multiple and diverse brand stories can inspire the Asian boardroom and serve as discussion points when crafting future brand strategies.

Chapter 9 is a step-by-step guide to brand building for Asian boardrooms, and discusses the processes and systems needed to successfully manage brands.

Finally, Chapter 10 provides a discussion of the challenges in the years to come for Asian boardrooms, what brand change agents will become, and how Asian brands can potentially challenge their Western counterparts.

The appendix provides a useful guideline to brand valuation based on the method used by Interbrand.

chapter 2

Branding – The Driver of a Successful Business Strategy

Today, businesses and consumers are placing increasing importance on brands. Brands give a sense of identity, stimulate the senses, and enrich life experiences. People have a need to affiliate and surround themselves with things they know well, trust, and aspire to be. From a customer viewpoint, a brand is a signal of quality and creates a bond of trust with the manufacturers behind it.

A strong brand is defined and characterized by the dimensions shown in Table 2.1.

There is a distinction between companies, products, and services of which customers might be aware, and *real brands* with strong brand equity. Strong brands are more than trademarks and trade names (logos that identify the products and services). Before delving into an analysis of branding, it is important to get the terminology right. "Branding" is a widely misused and misunderstood term, around which clusters everything even vaguely related to strategy, marketing, and communication. Branding is an investment that must be perceived as such and is required to deliver ROI, just like any other feasible business activity. It must appear on the left side of the balance sheet as an intangible asset and its value is subject to change.

Lifestyle over Technology

Asian consumers are known for being very technologically savvy. Mobile phone usage penetration and the number of text messages sent in Asia are

TABLE 2.1   The nine characteristics of a strong brand

1. A brand drives shareholder value

2. The brand is led by the boardroom and managed by brand marketers with an active buy-in from all stakeholders

3. The brand is a fully integrated part of the entire organization aligned around multiple touch points

4. The brand can be valued in financial terms and must reside on the asset side of the balance sheet

5. The brand can used as collateral for financial loans and can be bought and sold as an asset

6. Customers are willing to pay a substantial and consistent price premium for the brand versus a competing product and service

7. Customers associate themselves strongly with the brand, its attributes, values, and personality, and they fully buy into the concept, a response that is often characterized by a very emotional and intangible relationship (higher customer loyalty)

8. Customers are loyal to the brand and would actively seek it and buy it despite the availability of several other reasonable and often cheaper options (higher customer retention rate)

9. A brand is a trademark and marquee (logo, shape, color, etc.) that is fiercely and pro-actively protected by the company and its legal advisors

Source: Martin Roll Company.

just two examples. But consumers do not merely buy technology – they buy lifestyle and design and tap into a "brand culture."

Psychological research demonstrates that brands are durable because people are cognitive misers. Modern society is overloaded with information, and the average person receives far more information than they can possibly digest properly. Therefore, people seek to simplify the world by relying on a variety of heuristics to minimize the amount of searching and information processing needed to make reasonable decisions. Once people believe that a brand works for a certain purpose or reason, they are less likely to seek out new information that challenges that assumption. Sociological research also demonstrates why people are less likely to switch brands. Many elements – images, stories, and associations – are attached to a brand. As these elements are shared collectively by groups and networks of people, they form generally accepted conventions about brands. It is therefore relatively difficult for individuals to abandon these shared conventions and switch brands.[1]

As many cultures in Asia are collectivist in nature, the social context of brands plays an important role. Brands provide competitive advantages as they create strong bonds and loyalty with customers and create barriers for competition.

Today, a large part of Asia is still developing. Although Asia's rapid economic development will result in an increase in people's disposable income, the divide between the "haves" and the "have-nots" is still significant. This segment of society (the bottom of the pyramid) has traditionally aspired to own brands of international repute as symbols of social class and prestige. In the future, many from the bottom of the pyramid will be able to afford internationally known brands. Asian customers crave to get their hands on a Louis Vuitton bag, drive a Mercedes, run in their Nike shoes, wear their Giorgio Armani suit, and listen to music on their iPod from Apple. Luxury brands have started adopting specific tier-driven pricing strategies to tap into this ever-increasing level of disposable income of Asian consumers. In 2013, luxury brands like Burberry and Moët Hennessy started offering their product ranges in India at price points within direct affordable reach of the Indian middle class.[2]

Over time, however, the Asian consumer's taste for luxury brands has started maturing. A recent study indicated that the growth rate of the luxury goods market has slowed down from 7 per cent in 2012 to 2 per cent in 2013, but the Chinese remain the largest buyers of luxury goods worldwide.

The Importance of B2B Branding Strategies

In business-to-business (B2B) environments, branding also plays an important role. Most decision makers would feel comfortable choosing IBM computers (known for quality), buying networks from Cisco (security), acquiring consulting from McKinsey & Co (credibility), ordering shipping services from Maersk (precision), or leasing aircraft engines from Rolls-Royce (reliability).

In Asia, a large number of companies are in the upstream parts of business value chains (manufacturing) and B2B value chains. Many companies are seeking to build and sustain more value as global competition is intensifying, and business owners and C-suite executives are questioning the effectiveness of branding and brands. The management topic of branding is often met with a fair degree of skepticism among Asian executives operating in commodities, manufacturing, and other B2B industries.

According to brand consultancy Interbrand, many of the world's most valuable brands, including IBM, General Electric, Intel, Cisco, Oracle, SAP,

UPS, Caterpillar, Adobe, and Huawei, can be described as predominantly B2B-oriented.[3] A key characteristic of industrial brands is that their demand is derived from their own strategy for delivering value to their customers and other stakeholders.

The key reason that branding is so much more vital as a means of differentiation for B2B brands is that their profits are derived from a much smaller number of customers and stakeholders. The typical industrial firm probably has no more than a few hundred customers, with often fewer than ten accounting for more than 50 per cent of total sales.[4]

Industrial buyers act very differently from typical household consumers. B2B purchase values are significantly higher in value than normal consumer goods, purchase cycles are longer, and sourcing managers are mandated to consider multiple options for every purchase. Most B2B purchase decisions also need to pass through multiple stages of executive or boardroom approval.

Strong brands deliver financial results: According to Forrester Research, B2B companies with strong brands deliver 20 per cent higher financial returns than those with weaker brands.[5] Close relationships, credibility, and reliability are vital to building and sustaining brand equity for an industrial brand.

Relationship management: According to global management consultancy McKinsey, personal interactions with sales reps remain the most influential factor for B2B customers. Leading companies make extensive use of face-to-face contact and market research to stay in tune with their customer needs.[6] Customers want an ongoing relationship with a knowledgeable and reliable supplier.

Thought leadership: Thought leadership in the digital age has transformed the way brands build loyal followers, especially in the B2B arena. Customers need resources to turn to that help them solve problems and predict trends in their industry. Becoming a leading authority on a subject not only solidifies a relationship with existing customers, but aids in the conversion of new ones, hence building the prospect base. Effective thought leadership means adopting more of the characteristics of a newsroom and requires a shift most marketing departments are not designed for. Brands need to create effective publishing and content management strategies. Thought leadership – content well and timely delivered – combined with a strong social media presence, are vital elements in the B2B marketer's branding strategy.

Perceived Risk

One of the main underlying reasons for the above behavior pattern is the trust that customers develop in certain brands. This trust helps customers reduce the inherent risks involved in any purchase. Researchers refer to this concept as "perceived risks" and define it as "the consumer's perception of the uncertainty and adverse consequences of buying a product and service."[7] There are six dimensions of perceived risks: performance, financial, opportunity/time, safety, and social.[8] Table 2.2 illustrates the various perceived risks that customers face during a purchase phase.

Brands can reduce these perceived risks by authenticating the source of the goods and serving as a strong promise of the perceived value of the goods sold. Through this, customers are assured that the risk-to-reward ratio of purchasing a strong brand is higher than that of purchasing a similar unbranded good.

Asians are Brand Conscious

Asia-Pacific consumers are highly brand conscious and are among the world's most reluctant to try products from unfamiliar brands.[9] The Nielsen Global Survey of New Product Purchase Sentiment in 2013 revealed only 45 per cent of Asia-Pacific consumers will try an unknown product compared with 57 per cent of consumers in North America, and 56 per cent in Europe.

Compared to other countries, Asia-Pacific respondents also attach a higher degree of prestige to global brands versus local brands. According to the Nielsen Global Survey of New Product Purchase Sentiment in 2013, only 38 per cent of Asia Pacific consumers said they would prefer to purchase local brands when given a global option compared with 47 per cent in North America.[10]

TABLE 2.2 Potential perceived risks involved in a purchase

Performance:	Will the product or service perform to expectations?
Financial:	Is the product or service worth the price charged?
Opportunity/time:	Will there be associated opportunity costs if the product or service fails?
Safety:	Is the product or service safe to use? Does it pose a threat to health or the environment?
Social:	How will the product or service be perceived in a social context?
Psychological:	Does it fit the personality and values of the customer?

Note: Figure inspired by the six perceived risks dimensions developed by Cunningham (1967).

T W G T E A

The TWG Tea Company was founded by Moroccan-born Taha Bouqdib in Singapore in 2007. The 1837 date on its logo marks when the island became a trading post for teas, spices, and fine epicurean products. The brand is present in 14 countries including Japan, Korea, Hong Kong, China, and the UK. In Australia, TWG Tea works with retailers like David Jones, and in the US the brand has tea counters at Dean & DeLuca.

TWG Tea, which stands for The Wellbeing Group, is a luxury concept that incorporates an international distribution network to professionals, unique and original retail outlets, and exquisite tea rooms.[11]

TWG Tea is looking to expand further into the Middle East, including Qatar by 2015. About 40 per cent of sales come from five-star hotels, airlines, and fine dining restaurants, and TWG Tea positions itself alongside luxury brands targeting the same segments as Louis Vuitton and Prada.[12] The brand offers over 800 single estate fine harvest teas and exclusive blends, as well as tea patisseries and other tea-infused delicacies.[13]

According to research firm Euromonitor, tea remains an enjoyable, occasional diversion for high-income consumers in developed markets, driving demand for increased customization, as consumers look for the same kind of personalized variety associated with tea shops.

Branding Drives Shareholder Value

The primary objective of boardrooms is to build and sustain shareholder value, and deliver competitive returns to shareholders.[14] One way to achieve this is by building a brand with strong brand equity. "Brand equity" is the reputational asset that any successful business builds in the minds of customers and other stakeholders.[15] This is one of the main reasons why a company's market capitalization often exceeds its book value. The strength of brand equity can therefore be an indication of future financial performance. The concept of brand equity is further discussed in Chapter 6.

Right pricing can be an effective way to increase profits. A strong brand allows for higher premiums: For the average income statement of a Standard & Poor's (S&P) 1500 company, a *price increase* of 1 per cent, if volume remained stable, would generate an 8 per cent increase in operating profits; an impact almost 50 per cent greater than that of a 1 per cent *decrease* in variable *costs* like materials and direct labor, and more than three times greater than the impact of a 1 per cent *increase in volume*.[16]

Therefore, marketing strategies and activities must be equally aligned with business strategy to fulfil corporate objectives. For modern companies, the creation of value increasingly depends on the control of intangible assets such as brands, intellectual property, systems and data, human capital, and market relationships.[17]

Many Asian companies have traditionally focused on asset-intensive industries. In a McKinsey study, the most profitable Asian companies demonstrated focus on intangibles such as human capital, exploiting network effects, and creating synergies based on brands or reputation, rather than investing in tangible assets.[18]

In a 2014 article in *The Economist*, five megatrends are cited, which organizations with ambitions to become successful in Asia need to watch and adapt toward. These five major influencing factors now and in the future are:

1. Deteriorating diplomatic climate
2. Demographic differences across Asia and rising labor costs
3. Strong desire in Asian societies to move from quantity to quality
4. Potential disruptive nature of the internet
5. Intense global competition faced by Asian companies

The article cites that Asian organizations are better prepared for these challenges because they are more financially disciplined than other countries. This is where astute brand building by Asian brands will emerge as a strategic differentiator.

The article also mentions that the key barriers for growth of Asian businesses are sector mix, branding, innovation, and internationalization. Asia has too few global brands, and out of the 100 most valuable brands (ranked by Interbrand) only 10 are Asian. In emerging Asian markets, local brands are considered to be inferior in both value and quality, and foreign brands are perceived to be more superior and trustworthy, showing that Asian firms have insufficiently invested in building brands, because they lack pricing power.[19]

In other words, intangible assets like brands play a significant role in value creation and can become an important driver of shareholder value for many Asian companies today.

Brands and Market Capitalization

For many Western companies, a large part of their intangible assets is related to the value of their brands. An examination of the market capitalization of companies on Western stock exchanges demonstrates that a large proportion of a company's value is derived from powerful brands and the profit streams they provide. On the New York Stock Exchange and NASDAQ, intangible assets are known to account for 50–75 percent of the market capitalization of the listed companies, and the majority of this is accounted for by their brands.

The market-to-book ratio for Fortune 500 companies is approximately 2.5 to 3, which indicates that more than 70 per cent of their market values are comprised of intangible assets.

A study concluded that companies with high relative brand value and high relative corporate reputation ratings had significantly higher market-to-book ratios than companies with low relative brand value and low relative corporate reputation ratings. The results indicated that corporate reputation adds incremental explanatory value in explaining high book-to-market ratios.[20]

Brands' Contribution to Stock Market Performance

A study investigated the causal linkage between branding and shareholder value creation, using statistical tools and concepts from the finance discipline. It also examined whether the performance of companies with "strong" brands would outperform the overall market, and whether these returns remained after adjusting for risk.[21] The strong brand portfolio (a selection of 111 companies with strong brands) yielded an average monthly return of 1.98 per cent against 1.34 per cent for a benchmark portfolio (a large selection of companies from major US stock exchanges). The risk attached to a business is determined by the volatility and vulnerability of its cash flows compared to the market average.[22] Using beta as a measure of risk, the less volatile and vulnerable the cash flows, the lower the beta measure. The risk was 0.85 for the strong brand portfolio against 1.07 for the benchmark portfolio – the average market risk is 1.0. In summary, the strong brand portfolio outperformed the market with less market risk.

A study analyzed the performance of strong brand portfolios on different financials compared to the benchmark portfolio, as illustrated in Table 2.3. The strong brand portfolio outperformed on most financial ratios.

TABLE 2.3   Impact of brand performance on financial ratios

Financial ratios[*]			Results
Liquidity ratios	Measure a firm's ability to meet cash needs as they arise	Current ratio / Quick ratio	The strong brand portfolio outperformed both benchmark groups in liquidity
Activity ratios	Measure the liquidity of specific assets and the efficiency of managing assets		The strong brand portfolio outperformed the benchmark groups on only one indicator: the average collection period where they collected funds from their customers in approximately half the time
Leverage ratios	Measure the extent of a firm's financing with debt relative to equity and its ability to cover interest and other fixed charges	Debt-to-equity / Times interest earned	The strong brand was financed more by equity than debt. The debt-to-equity ratio for strong brand companies was 52.63 against 151.48 and 133.56 respectively for the two benchmark portfolios. There were significant differences between strong brands and the benchmark companies on the times interest earned ratio
Profitability ratios	Measure the overall performance of a firm and its efficiency in managing assets, liabilities and equity	Gross profit margin / Operating profit margin / Net profit margin / Return on equity	The strong brand portfolio outperformed on all aspects. They also demonstrated greater return on equity

Source: Adapted from Madden et al. (2002).
Note: "Brands matter: an empirical investigation of brand-building activities and the creation of shareholder value," Thomas J. Madden, Frank Fehle and Susan M. Fournier, Working Paper, 02-098, May 2, 2002.
[*] "Understanding Financial Statements," Lynn Fraser and Aileen Omniston, Fifth edition, Upper Saddle River, NJ, Prentice Hall.

Growing Significance of Intangible Assets

Today, corporations are not only trading factories, but also retail outlets, aircrafts, and other types of tangible assets; increasingly they are trading intangibles, of which most are related to brands, brand equity, and the financial value of those brands.

A recent example is the Chinese computer manufacturer Lenovo's acquisition of IBM's PC division, announced in December 2004, for US$1.25 billion.[23] Lenovo obviously bought tangible assets, high-quality product know-how, distribution networks, and a strong customer base. But a significant part of the deal is unquestionably related to the brand value. A fair estimate is that Lenovo paid US$488 million, or approximately 39 per cent of the acquisition price, for the right to use the globally recognized IBM Think brand on laptops for the next five years.

It is therefore important to understand what drives brand valuation and how brands can be managed in organizations as Asia enters a new era of consolidations, alliances, joint ventures, and mergers and acquisitions. Organizations and brands will change owners, and it is imperative to understand the strengths and values of brands in order to make fair value assessments of the intangible assets. Chapter 6 further discusses an approach to brand strategy, brand metrics, and brand valuation.

The Need for Brand-Driven Organizations in Asia

Long-term branding success will only occur through a planned and well-managed exercise where the corporate management team knows exactly what the complex drivers behind the brand are, how the drivers inter operate, how to achieve and leverage all elements of the brand equity, and how to evaluate the brand's performance. In other words, corporate management need to know how their brand contributes to shareholder value. Only then can branding become a relevant and trusted strategic discipline in the Asian boardroom along with other well-recognized functions like operations, logistics, finance, and human resources (HR).

Three essential pillars of a brand-driven organization are:

Innovation: A continuous cycle of innovation is essential to ensure a high degree of relevance and competitiveness for the organization's brands. This critical innovation cycle should ideally identify opportunities for innovation through a) new products, b) extending/expanding existing product lines, and c) cross-overs into adjacent segments or categories.

Culture: The organizational culture is a critical factor influencing the success of a brand-led operating and business model. An enabling culture should place strong emphasis on the development of skills, embracement of the organization's values, openness toward change, and the ability to repeatedly work out of one's comfort zone.

Leadership: In a brand-led organization, leadership at the board level should have a strong sense of purpose, a long-term strategic vision, and the right amount and quality of resources at their disposal to initiate and implement change (Figure 2.1).

Some Asian organizations have recognized this need and implemented a strategic plan in place to pursue brand equity. The Chinese telecommunications and network equipment brand Huawei is quickly establishing itself as a leading global player with 65 per cent of its revenues coming from outside China.[24]

A strong brand is characterized by a unique brand promise (the customer focus) and outstanding brand delivery (the organizational system and performance behind the promise). The brand promise and the brand delivery must be consistently balanced to achieve branding excellence (Figure 2.2).

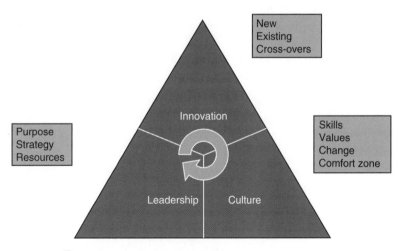

FIGURE 2.1　**Brand-driven organization model**

Source: Martin Roll Company.

Strong brands have 2 basic components	
A. Brand Promise ⬌	**B. Brand Delivery**
• Brand Essence	• Attributes, benefits and values
• Brand Identity	• Organisation and distribution
• Brand Position	• Brand Image
Characteristics:	
1. Brand Promise and Brand Delivery are equally balanced and leveraged	
2. Uniqueness and differentiation are key drivers	
3. Consistency across products, markets, organisations and cultures	
4. Strong brand management systems and processes in place	
5. Board and corporate management are deeply engaged and committed	

FIGURE 2.2 **Branding Excellence Model**

Source: Martin Roll Company.

Singapore Airlines is an example where the brand promise and brand delivery are well balanced. The brand promise of "A Great Way to Fly," with its emphasis on service and technology excellence, has long served the airline well and been consistently communicated since the airline was founded. What sets Singapore Airlines apart from its competitors is the dedication of the corporate management to ensuring delivery of the promise throughout the entire organization. The airline runs a highly structured and comprehensive training scheme, has standard operating procedures (SOPs), numerous guidelines, benchmarking schemes, and detailed performance evaluations on every thinkable function and aspect of the organization.

This illustrates how branding is not just the communication of a distinct promise, but the promise throughout the entire delivery. Branding has to be real and infused throughout the business. Although advertising is often one of the most visible parts of an organization and its offerings, it plays a relatively small part in the entire brand building process. The processes to manage the brand promise and delivery are covered in Chapter 6.

The modern brand-driven organization is characterized by three distinct aspects, which set it apart from less brand-focused organizations:

• The right boardroom *mind-set* toward and *beliefs* about branding
• The right *skill sets* to build and manage brands
• Allocation of the right *organizational and financial resources* to achieve the various business objectives and build sustainable brand equity.

At first glance, these three elements seem obvious and fairly easy to achieve, but in reality they are more complicated to execute. They require orchestrated and detailed efforts in all parts of the organization. as well as a long-term perspective that can also survive short-term downturns in the overall economy, industry, and among customer segments. The following section examines these three characteristics.

Right Boardroom Mind-Set Toward and Beliefs about Branding

Unlike their Western counterparts many Asian business leaders still have strong reservations about investing in intangible assets like brands. It is not uncommon for branding to be perceived as and referred to as "marketing communication (advertising)," a "cost on the marketing budget" on the profit and loss statement, and a "discipline residing in and managed by the often lower level marketing department" in Asian corporate structures. These perceptions are barriers for building more successful and international Asian brands.

It has been clearly demonstrated in this chapter that a significant amount of shareholder value is created by and tied up in brands. Therefore, as Asian boardrooms are primarily responsible for driving shareholder value and earning positive returns to investors, they must be equally involved in measuring, managing, and directing brands and their strategies.

Branding Is a Comprehensive Process

When everyone in an organization serves the customers and creates customer value, then everyone is doing marketing, regardless of function or department.[25] The comprehensive task of aligning and managing customer touch points cannot be left to or even controlled successfully by marketing departments alone. All customer touch points have to be aligned and optimized around the brand. As Professor David Aaker has illustrated in *Aaker on Branding – 20 Principles That Drive Success*, profound brand management is based on a holistic, company-wide effort driven by continuous supervision from top-management.[26]

This calls for a more cross-functional orientation of marketing in the Asian organization as well as dedicated boardroom attention to ensure that it happens. Hence branding is not a one-off session run by a separate marketing function by mid-level marketing managers, but a truly integrated part of the boardroom strategy along the lines of finance, operations, HR, and legal issues.

This will require a major shift in how the Asian boardroom and corporate management team are structured and operated.

CEOs as Primary Brand Ambassadors

Asian business leaders can benefit tremendously by representing and leading their brands by example, both internally and externally. Although this does not imply being overly exposed in public and becoming personal media stories themselves, most Asian business leaders prefer to stay private and rarely appear in public media unless absolutely necessary. Asian business leaders can help to build their brands by appearing more outside the boardroom, and acting as the primary spokespeople of the brand vision and identity, internally and externally. This can add tremendously to the success and cost-effectiveness of the brand.

The success of the UK-based Virgin Group, led by its legendary founder and CEO Sir Richard Branson, is indisputable. Branson has been successful mostly because of his ability to attract media attention for the company's widespread activities and worldwide marketing launches. This strategy, along with his charisma and talent for being in the limelight at the right time, have helped to build the Virgin brand into a global success, comprising music, airlines, mobile communications, and many other businesses. The strategy has also been cost-effective as it has decreased spending on marketing communications.[27] Asian CEOs need to learn from the charismatic Sir Richard Branson to push their organizations into a path of growth. In Asia, where business leaders are recognized and respected for their contributions, having them in the forefront of the organization's marketing and brand strategies will definitely be helpful.

Zhang Ruimin, founder and CEO of the Chinese company Haier, is an example of an Asian business leader following the same strategy. He is regularly featured in the international business press, which has contributed tremendously to the growth and recognition of Haier outside China. One benefit is that communication costs are a fraction of what they would have been for a mass communication advertising driven strategy. In 2011, Haier was honored with the Inspired Leadership Award, which recognizes global business leaders who combine outstanding business performance with values and behaviors that sustain the human and natural environments in which their organizations operate.[28]

What the CEO does and says can truly influence the success of a company in a very positive way. From an investment perspective, a large part of a company's market value is attributed to its reputation, and the CEO plays a key role in shaping that reputation. A significant number of consumers say that their perceptions of CEOs affect their opinions of company reputations. While a new crop of prominent Asian CEOs are starting to take over, including Alibaba's Jack Ma, more are needed to change the perception of Asian companies in the global competitive landscape.

A mind-set change is inevitably needed in Asian boardrooms if more companies wish to succeed in building strong brands. Branding is not a luxury. It is a necessity for Asian companies who aspire to compete successfully in the future, capture better gross margins, and enhance customer loyalty.

UNIQLO: THE JAPANESE FASHION POWER BRAND

Japanese clothing brand Uniqlo (a wholly-owned subsidiary of Fast Retailing Co. Limited) provides high-quality private-label casual wear at low prices. Parent company Fast Retailing's market capitalization is over US$38 billion[29] and it employs more than 23,000 people globally.[30] As of August 2014, Uniqlo had 1,486 stores around the world, and it is the biggest apparel chain in Asia[31] with 1,438 stores.[32] For the year ending August 2014, Fast Retailing had revenues of US$11.7 billion and a profit of US$670 million.[33] The company's home market, Japan, contributed 60 per cent to its revenue,[34] with one in four Japanese said to own a Uniqlo down jacket.[35]

With profits declining due to margin erosion over the years and an impairment charge on J Brand premium denim clothing,[36] Uniqlo is looking at its international operations to sustain its profitability. Its visionary CEO Tadashi Yanai thinks big and the company aspires to become the world's largest clothing retailer by 2020 with an annual revenue of US$50 billion.[37] If Uniqlo achieves this ambitious target, it will dethrone Inditex (Zara's parent company) as the leader in global apparel.

In November 2014, Tadashi Yanai was number 11 on the list of the best-performing CEOs in the world compiled by the *Harvard Business Review*. Since 2002, he has provided an 862 per cent shareholders' return, and the market capitalization of Uniqlo has increased US$39 billion.[38]

Uniqlo's brand message encapsulates a clear vision: "Uniqlo is a modern Japanese company that inspires the world to dress casual."[39] The corporate strategy that has worked for Uniqlo so far is to "totally ignore fashion," instead of chasing fast-fashion trends like its competitors.[40] The brand philosophy "Made for All" – positions its clothing to transcend age, gender, ethnicity and all other ways to define people.[41] Contrary to its name, Uniqlo's clothes are simple, essential yet universal, enabling the wearers to blend them with their individualistic style.

This design-driven clothing brand offers unique functional performance owing to in-house fabric and design innovation. The company distinguishes itself from its price-driven competitors by branding its signature innovations with names like HeatTech, Lifewear, and AIRism.[42] Uniqlo provides a superlative physical shopping experience by managing its stores impeccably, inculcating a positive employee culture through in-store technology like video tutorials that describe product attributes.

However, it has not been all plain sailing for Uniqlo. Its biggest dilemma is probably brand differentiation as it tries to be "everything to everyone" – a known brand strategy mistake.[43] Notable differences between global customer groups are being overlooked and Western consumers often complain about the clothes' size and fit to body shape.[44] The brand's footprint and awareness are relatively low outside of Asia, something the company is tackling through advertising and marketing.[45]

Uniqlo's merger talks with J Crew Group broke down in March 2014. The deal would have given Uniqlo access to 400 stores in the US. It also faces stigma for producing clothes in poor countries, conjuring images of exploitation of low-wage workers, although the company signed a European retailer's safety pact in 2013.[46]

Finally, Uniqlo is still two-thirds the size of its global peers – Swedish fashion retailer H&M, American brand Gap, and Spanish Inditex, who have been long dominant in basic wear and are determined to stay ahead.[47] But Uniqlo is on track to challenge the global players in the fashion retail industry.

Skill Sets

Marketing functions and marketing as a discipline have come under increasing pressure to demonstrate financial results. Marketers have traditionally been perceived as implementers of tactics, linked strongly to the classic four Ps (product, place, price, and promotion). This has helped to cement the internal perception of marketing as an expense rather than an investment that drives shareholder value. With increasing market fragmentation, product commoditization, strong competition, shorter product life cycles, and powerful distribution channels, among other factors, the role of marketing has never been more important than it is today.[48] To solve this paradox, the role and scope of marketing has to change within the Asian organization. Two important changes need to take place.

The first is the *role* of marketing. As marketing increasingly takes place along the entire value chain, it is not the responsibility of the marketing function alone. An example is the hotel industry, where many functions within the organization deliver customer value, from doormen, front staff, and check-in personnel to back-end functions like accounting, purchasing, and training. This requires a more cross-functional orientation of marketing, with a solid understanding of all the elements in the value chain, including skills within engineering, purchasing, manufacturing, logistics, and finance.

This changing role requires the Asian marketer to focus heavily on multi-functional teamwork throughout the organization and on the integration of marketing in all processes. These might require an upgrade of skill sets and ongoing training of the marketing personnel.[49] Marketing must be seen as an important driver of strategy and what has been described as a "transformational marketing effort" throughout the entire organization.[50]

David Packard, the co-founder of Hewlett-Packard, once famously remarked, "marketing is too important to be left to marketing people." Similarly, boardrooms must take charge of the organization's brand strategy and be fully involved in its design, rollout, and implementation. When two-thirds of brand managers say that their brands do not influence corporate decisions at the highest level, it implies that two-thirds of companies are not strategically following through on their promise.[51]

The second change required is the *outcome* of marketing. Traditionally, marketers have focused on measures tailored to activities in marketing, like advertising and promotion. For marketing to become integrated into the boardroom agenda, the key issue is to focus on demonstrating the financial consequences of marketing expenditures. The default language of companies is based on accounting and finance, so the challenge is to translate marketing outcomes into financial measures.[52]

The Chief Marketing Officer (CMO) is the strategic link between the boardroom and the marketing department of an organization. The CMO is responsible for two very critical, and sometimes contradictory, functions. He or she is responsible for ensuring that branding gets a voice and has a representation in the boardroom, and is also responsible for implementing board-level branding decisions. In sum, he or she is responsible for ensuring consistency and interconnectedness between strategic and tactical branding decisions (Table 2.4).

CMOs and Chief Financial Officers (CFOs) are focused on vastly different measures of performance. While the CMO typically focuses on top line growth measures such as loyalty, resonance, and engagement, CFOs focus mostly on the bottom line. Yet both functions are pivotal to creating and sustaining shareholder value. The problem is that one typically has more power and influence on strategy than the other, and, consequently, cost-cutting measures often trump longer-term, less tangible branding efforts. There is good news, however: three quarters of CMOs and CFOs believe in the importance of aligning with each other.

CMOs generally have to work harder to justify their places on boards, a consequence primarily of legacy mind-sets. CFOs are considered pragmatic while CMOs have to prove that they are not only marketers but also individuals with strong commercial acumen and the ability to deliver growth. The most

TABLE 2.4 Ten CMO leadership principles

1. Elevate the marketing function (CMO).
2. Think like a leader – act like a challenger.
3. Be bold! Differentiate! Be aspirational.
4. Involve all stakeholders.
5. Balance brand promise with brand delivery = touch points.
6. Innovation – The strategic theme towards 2020.
7. Glocalize: Be culturally knowledgeable and sensitive.
8. Unique organizational culture – live the brand.
9. Measure and benchmark brand performance.
10. Avoid arrogance and complacency – raise the bar and be your own change agent.

Source: Martin Roll Company.

effective companies have found ways to identify key performance indicators (KPIs) that matter to both CMOs and CFOs. Bringing deeper analytics in to branding strategies has also allowed many marketing functions to become more cost-effective by improving targeting, effectiveness, and efficiency – ideas any CFO can get behind.

Apart from the cross-functional orientation, the key skillset required is a brand toolbox. This comprises three components: brand audit, brand strategy, and brand marketing plan. Furthermore, it requires insights and knowledge about the society and cultures the brand will be part of as it heavily influences decisions around the brand. A strong brand arises from the synergy between what the corporation aspires to become (the brand vision) and how well its aspirations (the actions taken by the company) resonate with target customers who are strongly influenced by the surrounding society and its norms, beliefs, cultures, and many other intricacies. Brand building is therefore strongly related to how well the corporation understands consumers, markets, and upcoming trends, and how effectively it responds to them.

The success of these efforts can be measured and managed through brand metrics and brand equity, which are KPIs for the boardroom and corporate management team. A framework for brand management and metrics is presented in Chapter 6.

Resources

A carefully planned brand strategy driven by the Asian boardroom will only be successful if the entire organization is empowered around the brand vision and the brand strategy, and adequate financial resources are allocated.

The human resource aspect is an often-overlooked issue at the boardroom level when it comes to branding. Most often, branding is an isolated activity in a mid-management level marketing department that is only vaguely related to other aspects throughout the organization. The entire organization is crucial to bringing the brand to life; marketing cannot carry this out alone. The entire organization must be fully aware of the brand objectives, the brand marketing plan, and its execution.

The above again proves the correlation between employees and brands. The more employees are trained and involved in delivering the brand promise, the more efficient and competitive the brand strategy will become. The boardroom must ensure the entire organization delivers on the brand and stays true to it.

Brand management is a dynamic, continuous process that needs consistent investment of time and money. The boardroom must ensure that brand management is allocated a specific budget, as it is much more than mere marketing communications. Due to the intangible nature of a brand, results may not accrue immediately, as it takes time and reinforcement to build customer loyalty.

Many companies increasingly complain that financial markets focus on short-term results and give little credit for long-term value creation strategies. These claims are contradicted by empirical evidence.

The quarter-by-quarter nature of financial market reporting has resulted in boards becoming more short-term oriented in their decision making. This short-term focus is increasingly reflected in organizations' urgency to meet quarterly targets above anything else and the increasingly shortening tenure of CEOs in publicly traded companies. Since 1999, the average tenure of CEOs in the US has dropped from 10 to eight years, with 40 per cent lasting less than two years. In Asia Pacific, the average CEO tenure is even lower at four years. In 2013, the CEOs of S&P 500 organizations switched jobs at the fastest pace since 2008, but the average CEO tenure grew to 9.7 years, reversing a decade-long decline.[53]

A McKinsey study has shown that expectations of future performance are the main driver of shareholder returns. Across industries and stock exchanges, up to 80 per cent of a company's market value can be explained only by cash flow expectations beyond the next three years.[54] These expectations are driven by growth judgments and long-term profitability. An examination of leading consumer product company stock prices illustrates that future growth accounts for more than half of the stocks' total value.[55]

A study of S&P 500 companies illustrates that average total returns to shareholders were up to 10 percentage points better among companies that balanced short- and long-term performance compared to less balanced peers.[56] The best performers also survived longer in the market, had their CEOs remain in office three years longer, and achieved significantly less volatile stock prices.

In an address by Dominic Barton, Global Managing Director of McKinsey, it was claimed that boards play a critical role in shifting an organization to a long-term mind-set. 46 per cent of executives named their board as a significant source of increased pressure to demonstrate short-term performance over the past five years.[57] In a McKinsey article co-authored by Barton, four practical steps were recommended for organizations serious about focusing capital on the long term: [58]

TABLE 2.5   The boardroom audit

Mindsets and beliefs:
Does the boardroom believe in branding? Why? Why not?
Does the boardroom believe that branding drives ROI?
What are the opportunities and challenges moving forward with a brand strategy?
Does the boardroom have a shared brand vision for the entire corporation? Will the overall brand management be led by the boardroom?
Skills:
Has the boardroom conducted a strategic brand audit comprising the relevant brand portfolio (incl. the corporate brand) to assess strengths and weaknesses?
Has the boardroom decided on a comprehensive and long-term brand strategy linked closely to the overall business strategy?
Has the boardroom developed a company-wide brand marketing plan?
Resources:
Has the boardroom ensured a strong company culture around the brand?
Has the entire organization been given training and guidelines on how to live the brand?
Will the brand strategy and its implementation be supported with adequate financial resources?
Does the company have a human capital strategy and the necessary recruiting procedures to ensure recruitment of competent talent?

Source: Martin Roll Company.

1. Invest after defining long-term objectives and risk appetite
2. Unlock value through engagement and active ownership
3. Demand long-term metrics to inform decisions
4. Structure institutional governance to support a long-term approach.

Therefore, corporate management must align short- and long-term objectives and expected outcomes of branding, and be committed to supporting them accordingly with well-balanced strategies and time horizons.

Table 2.5 illustrates how the boardroom can carry out an internal audit of the level of the three crucial cornerstones of branding and the implications for the corporation.

Human Resource Strategies for a Brand-Driven Organization

A brand is created out of thousands of experiences with products, services, and systems created by people. Therefore, employees are the driving force of strategy and should be the core element in business design. The C-suite vision is useless without culture, rewards, process, strategy, and structure that effectively support employees.

Despite the importance of employees, few companies pay enough attention to their workforce compared to capital investments or production. CEOs often pay lip service when they refer to people as their company's most important asset and simply allow culture to happen by chance. If CEOs and CMOs are serious about building an iconic brand, HR must become a gate-keeper and cultivator of culture by aligning all responsibilities with the brand proposition – the recruitment processes, training and leadership development, compensation systems, and analytics and measurement. None of these strategies exist in a vacuum – they are all deeply interconnected. The recruitment stage, for example, should consider culture and retention systems should aim to create an organization that attracts great people.

HR must break free from their traditionally reactive roles as compliance officers and become proactive drivers of brand value – even a source of competitive innovation. HR executives must begin to think like the CMO and infuse branding into their process, as covered in Chapter 6.

chapter 3

Transforming How We Understand Asian Cultures and Consumers

Asia is not going to be civilized after the methods of the West.
There is too much Asia, and she is too old.

—Rudyard Kipling, 1891

Introduction

This chapter looks at connections between countries and people across Asia, as a way to understand the region and how it is building a new form of modernity. As explained in Chapter 2, Asian brands will increasingly have to move beyond functional benefits to appeal to Asian consumers. The first step is to understand Asian consumer culture. It is important for companies to realize that Asia is (see Table 3.1):

- A mosaic of cultures rather than a homogeneous region
- An urban form of modernity rather than an exotic continent
- A region of countries connected by history, cultural heritage, religious affiliations, migration, and the pattern of rural vs. urban divide
- A region where Asian music and images are gaining prominence every day, rather than being invaded by Western popular culture.

Finally, developing successful brands in Asia requires that companies understand the Asian consumer psychology by:

- Nuancing the view that all Asian cultures are collectivist by looking at the different forms of in-group affiliations in Asia

TABLE 3.1   **Blueprint to changing the way we think of Asia**

Transforming the way we view Asian culture	
From	**To**
Homogeneous region	Mosaic of cultures
Exotic Asia	Modern urban Asia
Separate countries	Connected countries
Invaded by American images	Prominence of Asian images and music
Transforming the way we view Asian psychology	
Collectivist cultures	Different types of in-group affiliations
Conformist cultures	Being different but in the same way

Source: Martin Roll Company.

- Looking at specific forms of conformity existing in Asia where consumers try to be different but similar to other people around them, using an individualist type of conformity.

From a Homogeneous Region to a Mosaic of Cultures

It is obvious that Asia is far from being a homogeneous entity. For example, the member states of the Association of Southeast Asian Nations (ASEAN) – Brunei, Cambodia, Indonesia, Laos, Malaysia, Myanmar, the Philippines, Singapore, Thailand, and Vietnam – collectively constitute the seventh largest economy in the world, but have many differences.[1]

Cultural differences greatly impact the success or failure of a brand. As brands enter different cultures, they must carefully tread the standardization-customization continuum wherein they not only retain the inherent brand identity, but also adopt the brand elements (images, advertising, channels, and others) that appeal to the local tastes and preference of customers.

De Beers quickly realized this when conducting research in Asian markets. In South Korea, jewelry purchases happen around weddings. In Thailand, the desire for adornment motivates jewelry purchases. In China, De Beers' usual positioning of diamonds as a symbol of everlasting love did not resonate with young couples' desire for success and their belief that marriage was "the graveyard of love."[2] Shying away from a purely romantic proposition, De Beers eventually positioned diamonds as symbols of harmonious and successful futures for Chinese couples.

South Korea is a strategic market for global luxury brands as the country is viewed as the fashion and luxury leader in Asia. Trends originating in Korea spread across the region due to the growing popularity of Korean TV dramas, music, and digital content. Success in Asia requires a strong foothold in Seoul (where almost half of South Korea's population reside) to identify potential trends. Luxury sales at South Korea's airports' duty-free shops also remain strong due to large numbers of Asian visitors, especially Chinese travelers, who are big spenders on luxury products. Chanel, Gucci, Louis Vuitton, and other global luxury brands have used product placements in Korean TV dramas to broaden their appeal.[3]

McDonald's is a successful case of how cultural differences across the region can indigenize a global brand. A myriad of local adaptations and perceptions of McDonald's can be found in Asia. To align with Japanese perceptions of what a meal should be, McDonald's Japan created rice-based dishes and teriyaki burgers. Some of the unique menu items include "The Gratin Korokke Burger," "The Salsa Burger," "The Tamago Double Mac," and "The Teri Tama Burger."[4] In Korea, McDonald's caters to busy women by providing a delivery service that delivers 24/7.[5] In Taiwan, McDonald's is a hangout where students do their homework. In Hong Kong, McDonald's is where kids have lavish birthday parties with trendy fruitcakes that establish their status. It is also a youth haven where teenagers hang out until late in the evening to avoid the tensions of cramped households. In China, McDonald's has been able to establish *renqing* (goodwill, concern) with customers by building positive personal feelings between staff and customers. In the late 90s, McDonald's staff regularly asked children to record their names, addresses, and birthdates on a list called the Book of Little Honorary Guests. The restaurants capitalized on the attention that Chinese families devote to their children, who are affectionately known as Little Emperors.

With a presence in more than 100 countries, McDonald's has created a wide range of menu adaptations to please global tastebuds. These adaptations include the whole shrimp Ebi Burger in Japan, deep-fried brie triangles in Italy, and green tea McFlurry and Seaweed Shaker Fries in most Asian markets. Constantly innovating, McDonald's is not afraid to stray from its tried-and-tested American formula, thereby maintaining relevance overseas by acknowledging unique local tastes.

D : F U S E   S C A N D I N A V I A

D:FUSE Scandinavia is a Guangzhou-based company established in 2006 by two Scandinavian entrepreneurs and former McKinsey consultants. Their aim was to build a fashion shoe brand based on a mixed Chinese and Scandinavian heritage. The brand operates close to 250 shops in China, mostly in department stores (November 2014). The plan is to slowly take the brand outside China over the coming years.[6] D:FUSE is interesting as it is based on a cross-cultural team, a brand identity that is Scandinavian despite being Chinese-based. Brands today can emerge from all cultures, locations, values, and beliefs to build unique, differentiated brand equity.

From Exotic Asia to Modern Urban Asia

Geishas, samurais, jonques, pagodas, and lush jungles: these are images of Asia that still resonate with many Westerners. These exotic images still fill many advertising campaigns striving to sell Asia to the West. For many Westerners, Asia is still an unsolved mystery. Seeing only the exotic and traditional side of Asia would be misleading. Of course, many Asian brands have actively reinforced traditional Asian values: hotel brands such as Banyan Tree and Shangri-La have all emphasized hospitality, as have airlines like Thai Airways and Singapore Airlines. British India's clothes evoke images of colonial times in India, while fashion brand Shanghai Tang surfs on the pre-Communist era of the 1920s.

S H A N G R I - L A — B R I N G I N G   A S I A N   H O S P I T A L I T Y   T O   T H E   W O R L D [7]

The Shangri-La brand began in 1971 with its first hotel in Singapore. With over 80 hotels and resorts throughout Asia Pacific, North America, the Middle East, and Europe, the Hong Kong-based Shangri-La group has over 37,500 rooms and over 40,000 employees.

Inspired by the legendary land and mythical earthly paradise featured in James Hilton's 1933 novel, *Lost Horizon* – which evoked a safe haven from a disquieting and alienating world – the name Shangri-La encapsulates the serenity and service for which the hotels and resorts are renowned worldwide. James Hilton described Shangri-La as a lamasery that lived by the same values that Shangri-La Hotels and Resorts espouse: humility, respect, courtesy, helpfulness, selflessness, and, above all, sincerity.

The cultural insight

In 2009, Shangri-La faced a brand and category challenge that encapsulated luxury hotel growth globally. Rooms outstripped supply, and the financial crisis had made its impact on demand. The luxury category dropped 14 per cent globally.

Shangri-La was determined to grow globally, so it started analyzing and gaining in-depth insights on its main customer group: premium frequent business travellers. It found that business travellers dislike the misery of always departing and arriving alone, constantly missing birthdays, weddings, and other important social gatherings.

Most communications in the luxury industry highlight the brand's hardware (interiors, rooms, reception, restaurants, etc.) but Shangri-La found that it often bored business travellers. Instead, admiration and brand loyalty would be won through the heart and more emotional appeals.

A big part of Shangri-La is its culture: The brand believes its guests should be treated not as kings but as kin, as human beings who make the world a better place. Offering hospitality from the heart, not the rule book, thus took center-stage. The heart and humanity in every interaction constantly brought people back.

The big brand idea

Shangri-La, together with global ad agency Ogilvy, developed a new communication platform that broke category norms and won global awards. It needed to bypass the sophisticated business traveller's cynicism, to awaken and force them to reassess their choices. The advertising spoke to the heart with metaphors of kindness – stories of ultimate hospitality offered to stranded humans.

The TV commercial shows an exhausted traveller, wandering alone in snowy wilderness. He collapses, not expecting to rise again. But the wolves that have been tracking him warm him with the heat of their bodies. The line, "There is no greater act of hospitality than to embrace a stranger as one's own. Shangri-La. It's in our nature," encapsulated the idea.

Shangri-La advertisement

Source: Courtesy of Shangri-La Hotels & Resorts.

The brand results

Shangri-La used the new communication platform to inspire, instruct, and guide the behavior of all employees. Staff training was aligned around a brand manifesto printed in a pocket book to ensure they delivered an exceptional culture of warm hospitality. Shangri-La's employees indeed felt pride in their brand and were motivated to deliver: an internal employee opinion survey showed that 91 per cent of employees had a favorable opinion of the company brand and their employer.[8]

Overall results of the new communication platform:

- Guests and prospects appreciated the campaign, and positive feelings for the brand ran over 90 per cent among those who saw the campaign and TV-commercials
- In China (the brand's heartland) and in the US, the campaign achieved much higher recognition than industry norms
- The TV-commercial went viral on YouTube and Youku
- Social media mentions, sharing, and number of searches on Google expanded.

Images of an exotic Asia, like the ones published in Tiger Beer's advertisement in the UK, would probably not appeal to most Asians.[9] Shanghai Tang, while popular with a portion of the Hong Kong middle class, does not fare well with most Chinese, to whom the idea of buying a watch with Mao pictured on it seemed absurd. Similarly, British India would probably not appeal to Indians. Both brands are, unsurprisingly, much more popular with Westerners.

Focusing on a traditional or exotic Asia is missing half the picture. A new form of modernity that is true to its Asian roots, but imbued with images of a new and optimistic Asia, is emerging.

Asian consumers are all vying for an Asian type of modernity that has nothing to do with colonial imagery, and global brand managers need to adapt to this new perspective while not completely abandoning the idea of an oriental Asia of the past. The trick is to balance legacy and vintage with modernity and contemporary edge.

Founded by Sir David Tang in 1994, Hong Kong-based fashion retail brand Shanghai Tang has built a strong franchise on its modern interpretation of Chinese culture. The fundamental design concept of Shanghai Tang is inspired by traditional Han Chinese clothing combined with 21st-century modernity. Shanghai Tang is recognized for using bright colors in its design, retail store design, and packaging. David Tang sold the brand to the luxury group Richemont in 1998 and opened a new 325sq meter home and lifestyle emporium, Tang Tang Tang Tang, in Hong Kong in 2013. Located inside a legendary building from 1888, it targets China's younger generations on the basis of a philosophy of resonating with Chinese ideas.[10]

SK-II — PREMIUM ASIAN APPEAL

Many people believe that SK-II is a Japanese beauty brand, when it is in fact owned by Procter & Gamble (P&G). Developed in 1980 by Max Factor and acquired by P&G in 1991, SK-II was not introduced into the US market until 2004 when 11 Saks Fifth Avenue department stores started to sell the products.[11]

Widely popular in Asia and regarded as a premium brand, the brand's heritage is Japanese, with a deep maroon color scheme – seen as more sedate than a typical American cosmetics brand. Additionally, SK-II products have multiple skin benefits including hydration, anti-aging, spot care, and skin tone involvement, which all bring it under the Asian concept of flawless beauty.

When SK-II was launched, whitening skincare was nothing new, as Japanese brands Shiseido, Kanebo, and Kose had similar products. But P&G was the first to use popular Asian celebrities to promote the brand, such as the actress Kaori Momoi in Japan.[12]

SK-II became popular in South Korea when word of mouth spread the "high quality" perception of the brand. It quickly became a status symbol. South Koreans are very status-driven compared to other Asian cultures, and regard only French and Japanese cosmetics brands as high quality and must-haves. Interestingly, there are many South Korean mid-market cosmetics brands which are popular in Southeast Asia, but not at home.

Adding to the brand experience, SK-II products have usage instructions in Japanese but with local language translations for specific markets. This maintains the brand's Japanese origin. Freebies and testers are not distributed in public, which helps maintain the value of the brand.

From Separate Countries to Connected Ones

The proliferation of images, music, and the movement of people across Asia create all sorts of connections between Asians that did not necessarily exist before. This increasing number of interconnections between Asian countries creates opportunities for marketers to launch pan-Asian initiatives for their products and services.

Although Asia is home to so many different cultures, religions, and levels of societal wellbeing, people in ASEAN countries feel a strong cultural connection and proudly identify themselves as being "Southeast Asian." The majority of Indonesians, for example, say countries as far away as the Philippines and Thailand are culturally similar to them and share many key values such as "respect for tradition," "warmth of the people," "family orientation," "respect for the aged," and "love of religion."[13] This illustrates the beauty and complexity of cultures in Asia. Despite the high heterogeneity level across the region, brand marketers can find common connections which they can integrate into their brand building strategies.

Arjun Appadurai,[14] a well-known commentator on globalization, argues that nation-states are becoming more and more irrelevant in an era of flowing images, people, and finances. It is not so much the physical geography of their current location that is important, but the geography that they construct and hold onto in their minds. The country and culture – images, sounds, practices, languages – which people bring with them when they migrate connect people living in different parts of the world and create a much stronger impact than mere physical geography. Pakistanis listening to mosque-recorded prayers while driving to work in Sydney, and Chinese carrying their rice cookers when traveling all testify to this point. People move around and carry their homes with them in their hearts and minds, accessing them more easily through various forms of media – email, satellite television, downloadable music, and DVDs of ethnic movies. As people move around more, the relevance of the nation as a definer of identity is slowly fading away. With the help of this burst of media, people construct their versions of home, culture, and, therefore, their identities through their imagination. Brands too can play the same role.

To make sense of globalization, Appadurai has structured his theory of globalization and modernization on "scapes." These are the imaginary landscapes that we create in our minds which we build our identities. These are shifting sands, nebulous worlds that change into and take on new shapes and forms, new accents, and colors as the imaginers move around, and are subject to influence from various sources and, in turn, are agents of influence on other people.

A good example is the growing popularity of Bollywood. A commercial for Motorola in India, made by Ogilvy & Mather India, featured a teenager on a local train who, when he plugs his headphones into his new Motorola MP3 mobile phone, is transported onto the top of a rural train in a Bollywoodesque singing and dancing extravaganza. The ad recreates a famous scene from a Bollywood song ("Chamma Chamma" from Raj Kumar Santoshi's *China Gate*) – a hit several years ago which was picked up by Baz Luhrmann for the soundtrack of his film *Moulin Rouge*. Motorola remixed the original song into a clubby version for the ad, which was a big hit. Motorola later released it as a single, which got plenty of airtime in nightclubs in India. Motorola executives liked the ad so much that they also released it throughout Southeast Asia. What was originally made in India went around the globe, back to India, and then spread through Southeast Asia.[15] What goes around comes around, but with a new accent, shape, and color.

There is no longer a definable center that pulls people toward it and orders their world, even as they move around. What is important is its dynamism, the idea that cultural influence does not necessarily come from the US or Europe. What Appadurai suggests is a decentralization of the world: the world not according to the Western world but according to wherever people choose to imagine themselves. This is of particular interest to understanding and creating brands in Asia.

Understand Asian Differences and Similarities

Global brands targeting Asia should not only strive to understand the nuanced differences between countries they are targeting, but also their similarities when building brands. According to Singapore's Nanyang Technological University Institute of Asian Consumer Insight (ACI), consumers share many traditional values, and can be grouped into four major consumer segments based on the emotional needs they share.[16]

Consumers categorized as having "Mainstream Asian Values" are the largest of the four consumer segments, making up 39 per cent of the Asian population. Coming mainly from China, Hong Kong, Singapore, Korea, and Malaysia, they rank near the "Asian average" in terms of behavioral attitudes and emotional needs. "Inner-Directed Traditionalists" highly value religion and tradition, are thriftier and less materialistic, and constitute more than half the consumers in Indonesia, Thailand, and the Philippines. "Outer-Directed Strivers" tend to have lower education and incomes, but value work success. This group, who care most about work success, materialism, celebrities, and so on, comprise 59 per cent of India's population and 25 per cent of China's. "Survivor Oriented" consumers tend to be older and less financially optimistic, and this group of consumers mostly comes from Japan and South Korea, reflecting their older populations.

Given the global availability of local TV channels, countries in Asia are now even more connected to each other. This is the new Asian mediascape. Koreans, Japanese, or Taiwanese are often watching the same TV soap operas, such as the hit *My Love from the Star*, or listening to the same music. Cultural similarities between different East Asian countries have boosted sales of TV programs, CDs, and movies. Most TV shows are conservative and steeped in Confucian values, revolving around the issues arising in extended families and love stories.

THE KOREAN WAVE

Korean pop culture "Hallyu" – embracing fashion, music, and film – has rapidly become an export success for the country. Korea's positive national image today is owed to its K-pop, television dramas, and movies that spurred the Korean Wave during the 1990s. "Hallyu," which loosely means "flow of Korea," was a phrase coined in 2001 by Chinese journalists to describe the explosive popularity of Korean pop culture in fashion, music, and film across Asia.[17] In recent years, the Korea Culture and Information Service (KCIS), a state-run PR agency, has been working extensively on a promotional strategy for Hallyu that reflects varying preferences across regions.[18]

This phenomenon is not unprecedented. In the 1950s as much of Europe and Asia slowly recovered from World War II, Hollywood cinema and American TVs shows became the major source of syndicated television programming worldwide, leading to the widespread preference for American lifestyles in many countries.

Hallyu first spread to Japan, and later to Southeast Asia and several countries worldwide where it continues to have a strong impact. In 2000, a 50-year ban on the exchange of popular culture between Korea and Japan was partly lifted, which improved the surge of Korean popular culture among the Japanese.[19] South Korea's broadcast authorities have been sending delegations to several countries to promote their TV programs and cultural content.

Korea's cultural exports have been pushed heavily by the Korean governments' well-funded Ministry of Culture, which runs the cultural content office with a US$500 million budget and a US$1 billion investment fund to nurture it. The Korean Ministry of Culture, Sports, and Tourism (MCST) is also continually increasing the budget.[20] According to a ministry official, the country wants to more than double its collective cultural industry exports to US$10 billion in 2019.[21] The Korean government is raising funds of US$200 million to build Hallyu World, a multi-complex theme park, in Ilsan, a town northwest of Seoul, to open in 2016.[22]

Korean popular culture has had an impact on the global fashion industry as an increasing number of Korean celebrities are included in the social fiber of fashion.[23] New York has had its appearances of K-Pop girl groups like Girls' Generation, Hyuna from 4Minute, and CL from 2NE1. The singer G-Dragon dresses in an influential way that gets noticed as Korean celebrities are known for mixing styles and genres in clothing.

Korean popular culture exports well and TV series including *My Love From The Star*, and music from Psy, boy bands like EXO, and girl bands like Girl's Day, are putting Korea on the global scene.[24]

Korea's income from merchandise, film, television programs exports, and tourism was US$1.87 billion in 2004 or 0.2 per cent of national GDP, according to the Korean International Trade Association.[25] In 2012, Korea was a net exporter of creative content with US$4.6 billion in exports versus imports of US$1.7 billion. The second largest net exports after games were for music and broadcast content, with gross exports of approximately US$235 million each.[26]

The Korean Wave has a direct impact in encouraging foreign direct investment (FDI) and the tourism industry in Korea. Korea attracted US$16.2 billion in FDI in 2012, the highest ever. Over half of the FDI was invested into the service industry including the tourism sector.[27]

A study across 196 countries from 1995–2012 illustrated that once the Korean Wave reaches a new country, Korean imports rise immediately. A one per cent increase in exports of Korean cultural content increases Korean consumer good exports by 0.083 per cent, and a 0.019 per cent increase in tourism the following year.[28] The visual content from the Korean Wave is very effective in promoting Korea and consumption of Korean goods.

More than 12 million tourists visited Korea in 2013 with 9.8 million from Asia. The growing number of tourists provided travel revenues of US$9.7 billion in 2012, a three-fold increase since 2007.

Korea had 968,000 tourists in 2004, of which 67 per cent visited the country due to Hallyu.[29]

Although Japanese brands are still world-class, Korean companies have become arguably the best brand builders in Asia recently, including brands like Samsung, Hyundai, AmorePacific, CJ Corporation and also their subsidiary O-Shopping, which is now the second-largest TV shopping brand in the world. The success of Korean companies can be attributed to their acknowledgment of and vision toward the issue of branding being "the issue of survival."[30]

For Chinese-originated brands, in lieu of a similar pop-culture phenomenon it may take another ten years of great design and quality for overall perceptions of the country to shift. Until then, the country of origin effect of China is still moderate to neutral compared to South Korea's, thanks to the Korean Wave.

Some anthropologists describe this phenomenon as "close distance."[31] Close distance is a type of relationship with films or other cultural products where audiences are both drawn to the unfamiliar and comforted by the familiar, close but at a distance. This is evident from the popularity of hybrid singers, actors, and models. On Asian silver screens, one of the stars is Takeshi Kaneshiro. Half-Taiwanese and half-Japanese, he is a big star in both countries and easily crosses the border between Chinese and Japanese movies. Hybrid models and actors are the perfect illustration of close distance: people who look familiar but alien enough to become aspirational. This logic also applies to music in Asia, with its mix of Asian and outside influences.

From American Images to Prominence of Asian Images and Music

Asian countries are increasingly recognizing the importance of cultural industries. For example, in 1999, South Korea's government decided that cultural industries could boost the economy, and deregulated them.[32] It has invested heavily in broadband technology and considers the gaming industry a national economic priority. The industry is a huge business in South Korea with revenues of US$9.7 billion in 2012.[33]

Asian managers can draw three lessons from the music and media landscape in the region.

First, rather than seeing the region as a homogenized product of Western popular cultural influence, it is important to think of Asia as increasingly traversed by diverse flows of culture coming from different cultural centers: Tokyo, Taipei, Hong Kong, Seoul, and so on.

Second, the modernity Asians have created is different from that in the West, due to a resurgence of nationalism in Asia in the past ten years. This alternative form of modernity is showcased in the toned-down lyrics of Korean pop songs or in the themes of popular TV shows across Asia where stories of family tensions are most popular. Most countries in Asia are adopting new technologies but retaining their identity at the same time. There has been a resurgence of nationalism in Asia, which suggests that, rather than becoming like the West, Asian countries are developing their own forms of modernity. Consequently, Asian managers should be careful when analyzing Asian consumer trends. Extrapolating from the experience of consumers in Europe and North America to predict Asian consumer behavior is dangerous. The failure of many multinationals in Asia shows how models developed in the West are not easily adaptable to the Asian context.

L'Oréal, along with other brands from Europe and the US, has also been forced to tailor its celebrity endorsement strategy in Asia. Asian consumers used to be willing to pay a premium just because a cosmetics brand was Western. If the makeup was good enough for Hollywood actresses, it was good enough for them. But that mind-set started to change. Asian brands like Japan's Shiseido and Korea's AmorePacific naturally have a better understanding of Asian complexions than Western companies. Today, L'Oréal, Estée Lauder, and Lancôme all use Asian models on the posters and ads they place around the region. Revlon of the US, the only brand that has persisted with the Hollywood approach, withdrew from China at the end of 2013.[34]

The third lesson is managers need to think beyond Asia as a collection of states. Because of globalization, it is important to recognize the new forms of connection between people. The British sociologist Anthony Giddens defines globalization as "the intensification of worldwide social relations which link distant localities in such a way that local happenings are shaped by events occurring many miles away and vice versa."[35] Despite the heterogeneity in religious and ethnic affiliations within Asian countries, people are connected across countries in ways that have powerful economic implications.

Opportunities in Subcultures

The Chinese Diaspora in Asia

Ethnic commonality is clearly facilitating the growth of economic relations between the People's Republic of China and Hong Kong, Taiwan, Singapore, and overseas Chinese communities. In his influential book, Murray Weidenbaum[36] predicted that the Chinese-based portion of the Asian economy will rapidly gain importance:

> This strategic area contains substantial amounts of technology and manufacturing capability (Taiwan), outstanding entrepreneurial, marketing and services acumen (Hong Kong), a fine communications network (Singapore), a tremendous pool of financial capital (all three), and very large endowments of land, resources and labour (mainland China) … this influential network – often based on extensions of the traditional clans – has been described as the backbone of the East Asian economy.

The Chinese diaspora has tremendous economic weight in the Southeast Asian region.[37] The cultural similarities amongst ethnic Chinese, such as their adherence to Confucian values and cultural heritage, provide avenues for Asian brand managers wanting to develop products or services. Brands that can leverage a Chinese heritage, or even better, a platform of Chinese cosmopolitanism in this situation, are at an advantage. The image of the cosmopolitan Chinese who has succeeded abroad has a lot of currency in the Chinese diaspora. There is the concept of a "bamboo network," which conceptualizes the connections between businesses run by ethnic Chinese individuals in Southeast Asia (Malaysia, Indonesia, Thailand, Vietnam, the Philippines, and Singapore) and the overseas Chinese community.

The Muslim Scape in Asia

Approximately two-thirds of the world's Muslim population live in Asia. The four largest Muslim countries are Indonesia, with 205 million Muslims, Pakistan with 178, Bangladesh with 147 million, and India with 138 million. This significant chunk of the world population has a distinct set of beliefs and needs that have largely been ignored by mass-marketing efforts. The total size of the halal food and Islamic lifestyle products market worldwide is estimated at US$1.62 trillion, expected to grow to 2.47 trillion dollars by 2018.[38]

The first consideration is banking and financial services. Consider the dilemma that Muslim consumers face: Koran teachings prevent Muslims from any dealings involving interest payments. Consequently, instead of the usual loans, Islamic banks structure profit-sharing agreements for their loans and other products, which usually generate interest. Deposit accounts operate like trusts, with funds invested on the depositor's behalf and a share of the profits replacing interest payments.

Understanding the intricacies of Islamic banking is especially important for Asian managers in the financial services sector. Islamic banking is a promising avenue to research and do business in. The assets managed by Islamic financial institutions were approximately US$230 billion worldwide in 2004. By 2013, this number exceeded US$1 trillion. Islamic finance products are now available in about 75 countries, which include non-banking products, such as insurance, micro-lending, and Islamic mutual funds.[39] It is becoming increasingly common for Islamic and Western financial institutions to form joint ventures to provide services that meet the needs of Islamic investors. Big local banks and foreign banks such as HSBC and Citibank are aggressively targeting Muslim consumers in different Asian markets like Malaysia and Indonesia. Almost all financial institutions in Malaysia have opened separate Islamic departments.

After banking, the second business sector where Muslim beliefs have a large impact is food. Beliefs in the Koran significantly impact food marketing, with all food products having to be halal. Muslims use two main terms to categorize food: haram and halal. In Arabic, *halal* means permitted, while *haram* means forbidden. Halal is an important part of Islamic life. The restrictions of halal are similar to kosher requirements: no pork, no blood, the name of Allah must be pronounced at the moment of slaughter, and intoxicants of any kind are forbidden.

The success of soft drinks targeting the Muslim population in Europe, such as Mecca Cola,[40] shows that there are interesting opportunities in targeting overseas Muslim populations. Global brands targeting Asia must have halal products as a priority in their portfolio, especially for packaged food manufacturers and other restaurant chains. In Asia, astute companies have launched technological products targeting Muslim populations. Korean company LG Electronics was lauded for launching a cell phone featuring a compass which allows consumers to find the direction to pray,[41] and numerous apps have been developed to offer information on Muslim prayer times.

Paying attention to the distinctiveness of Muslim consumer behavior is likely to become even more important in future years. According to United Nations (UN) projections, Pakistan's population will be about 434 million by 2050, making it the third largest country in the world after China and India.[42] The immense majority of this population will undoubtedly be Muslim. Understanding the needs and preferences of Muslims in Asia remains essential.

Professional, Empowered Women in Asia

The independent, single woman is becoming a powerful force in Asia thanks to greater financial freedom, education, and the preference to marry and have children much later in life. Asia will soon account for four of the top ten nations with the most one-person households, and brands are noting this next wave of growth.[43] The Boston Consulting Group estimates that by 2020 the female economy in China and India alone will account for US$5 trillion annually.[44]

As a newly-empowered segment in many countries, purchasing behavior among women reflect a desire to be trendsetters. Brands such as Nike, Adidas, and Lululemon are noticing that women are trying running, yoga, cross fit, golf, racquet sports, and team sports in droves and demand fashionable yet functional attire and accessories. Besides the gender-stereotyped product categories like cosmetics or fashion, financial products, automobiles, and homes are also reporting more female purchasers. Female consumers are also more likely to shop online than male consumers.[45]

In Korea, professional women who marry late are called the "gold misses"[46] while in China, they are called the "shengnu" or "holy goddesses." However, there are some stigmas attached to this trend. Chinese women, if not married by age 27, are considered unwanted and can feel trapped by their careers and societal pressures toward family life. Indeed, the Chinese term "shengnu" has a double-meaning of "leftover ladies." Brands will have to be sensitive and supportive in their communications.

Female consumers in Asia-Pacific are increasingly controlling the purse strings in household spending. While men were generally more likely to take charge in the area of savings and investments, MasterCard found that women in half of the 16 countries across Asia-Pacific control domestic finances – specifically in Indonesia, the Philippines, Myanmar, South Korea, and Vietnam. Men also tend to make decisions on big ticket items in the majority of markets, except in South Korea, Indonesia, and Vietnam. By comparison, the countries least likely to see female involvement in the household finances were Bangladesh, Singapore, Malaysia, and Thailand.[47]

The role of Asian men is also changing. According to JWT Asia-Pacific, Asian men today are significantly more likely than their fathers to be engaged in the running of households. In Singapore, China, and Malaysia, 81 per cent of men thought their parenting styles differed greatly from their fathers'. Most were assuming a greater role looking after children, helping with chores and focusing on work–life balance.[48] According to some experts, the implication for brands could mean "dialling down the testosterone factor" in their messaging while emphasizing different aspects (such as durability or efficiency) when selling diapers or other items typically purchased by mothers.[49]

Rural and Low-Income Consumers in Asia

An important segment that marketers cannot ignore in Asia is the bottom of the pyramid and those consumers living in rural areas. According to McKinsey, the standard deviation in average incomes among ASEAN countries is more than seven times that of EU member states.[50] Extreme poverty in the region continues to decline rapidly, with the proportion of the population earning just enough for basic needs predicted to fall over the coming years.

The Boston Consulting Group estimates the per capita disposable income of China's total urban population to grow 60 per cent between 2010 and 2020.[51]

The challenges marketers face in addressing these consumers are numerous due to the fragmented nature of the rural market and low margins.

First, rural consumers have less purchasing power. In China, the income gap between urban and rural residents, which is around 5 to 1, greatly restricts rural people's consumption of products. There is a significant difference in the way wages are earned. A majority of the rural working population are paid daily instead of weekly or monthly. This means that they will generally spend their daily wage on necessities such as food, and have little left to spend on personal care items and other relatively luxurious items.

This has driven companies like Unilever to sell sachets in rural China and India, instead of the normal sizes of detergent and shampoo. The company is increasingly relying on Asian rural markets to drive its sustained growth. Hindustan Lever, Unilever's Indian subsidiary, is now a major force in the Unilever network of subsidiaries, with many strategies emerging from India. For example, it used its Indian managers' expertise in rural markets to develop the Chinese shampoo and soap market.

Another example is Coca-Cola, which began to sell 200-milliliter bottles of Coke in India in 2003 to increase demand among consumers who cannot afford bigger portions.[52] Vodafone India has slowly extended the scope of its rural community-driven marketing effort called Project Samriddhi in India. It empowers rural women by giving them employment opportunities as saleswomen for Vodafone prepaid recharges and e-top-ups. Honda Motorcycles and Scooters (HMSI) is setting up a "rural vertical" to compete effectively with Hero MotoCorp, which has an established rural distribution network.

According to Nielsen, the FMCG market in rural India will cross US$100 billion by 2025, representing a massive opportunity for organizations to tap into. Estimates of India's rural purchasing power are indicative of significant increases in the future. A McKinsey Global Institute report indicates that annual real rural income growth per Indian rural household will increase from 2.8 per cent over the past two decades to 3.6 per cent over the next two decades.[53]

A second element of difference between rural and urban consumers is density. The number of villages in China and India is extremely high, pushing companies to develop extensive distribution networks. According to McKinsey, Unilever deploys massive resources in India to cover 1.5 million stores in tens of thousands of villages. Many salespeople carry a handheld device so that they can book replenishment orders anywhere, any time, and sync data with distributors. In Indonesia, Coca-Cola sells 40 per cent of its volume directly to local retailers. The lion's share of Coke's remaining Indonesian volume is sold to wholesalers with fewer than five employees and less than US$100,000 in annual revenues, which distribute Coke products to smaller retailers. To improve in-store execution, the company deploys additional support, including supplying them with free coolers and dispensers and providing sales effectiveness training for merchants.[54]

Companies that know how to address the needs of rural and low-income customers are ready to compete in Asia. In the Chinese market, SAB (South African Breweries) adopted a different strategy from its competitors Heineken and Budweiser and started its expansion in China with the northern hinterland, gradually expanding into other markets. This allowed the company to build capacity slowly, without having to face tough competition from the foreign breweries who were ready to slash prices in Shanghai or Beijing. SAB started its Chinese expansion by establishing a beachhead, then slowly increasing its presence in ever-expanding circles until it firmly controlled the region. In 2004, SAB was the second largest beer maker in China, while facing increasing competition from other international players and local Chinese brewers. This was no small achievement at that time: demand for beer in China increased by more than 40 per cent between 1997 and 2002, compared to just 4 per cent in the US during the same period.[55] Today, China accounts for about one-quarter of the world's beer sales by volume.[56] In 2013, SAB increased its exposure to the China market by buying seven breweries in a deal worth US$864 million. In 2013, China accounted for around 25 per cent of SAB's total beer volumes around the world but only 2 per cent in earnings, due to the competitive environment in China.[57]

In the Indian market, the detergent maker Nirma adopted a similar strategy of developing a base in the hinterland and rural areas before attacking the big metropolises. Karsanbhai Patel, Nirma's founder, knew chemicals well enough to develop an effective, low-priced detergent of good quality but did so starting in his home state of Gujarat before launching in other regions.[58] He started by selling to his neighbors for a small profit and built his consumer base slowly. Due to the importance of a strong distribution network, Nirma began surfacing all over Gujarat, in small shops in the remotest villages. After enjoying leading market share in the detergents market and tackling the multinationals head-on, Nirma has lost its edge in the detergents category in India. Much of this has been blamed on Karsanbhai Patel's retirement from the company. In 2010, Nirma's market share in detergents was a low 10 per cent and it lost first place to a brand called Wheel, specifically designed and launched by Hindustan Unilever to challenge Nirma.[55]

Another example of a company with rural expertise is the Indian company Asian Paints. With almost 50 per cent of the market for house paints in India despite the presence of major foreign multinationals, the company has succeeded by developing an extensive distribution network in the rural market. Its products are priced low and have been successful in other developing countries, like Nepal and Fiji. Asian Paints has developed an expertise in dealing with low-income, often illiterate consumers who only buy small quantities of paint that they later dilute to save money. The company has developed two brands, Utsav and Tractor, which are tailored specifically to the needs of this market.[59] With 52–53 per cent market share, Asian Paints remains the undisputed leader in India, with a significant gap between it and its next largest competitors, global giants Berger Paints and Akzo Nobel.[60]

Companies like Asian Paints, Nirma, Unilever, and Coca-Cola have understood that the key to succeeding in markets like China and India is a good understanding of the rural consumer and a vast distribution network.

Even luxury brands are finding ways of reaching new middle-class consumers as poverty rates decline. By creating lower-priced fighter brands under the broader luxury umbrella brand, products become attainable to a new, emerging customer segment, allowing brands to expand to new territories without damaging overall brand equity.

While Asian countries are diverse and need to be understood in their own context, there are similarities across the region. Companies like Unilever, Asian Paints, and HSBC have captured these in the development of brands that address segments with similar needs in different countries. As Asian companies venture into new markets and try to appeal to consumers from other Asian countries, an understanding of these similarities as well as the specificities of Asian consumer psychology remains essential.

Transforming How We View Asian Consumer Psychology

The Western conception of a person as a bounded, unique, more or less integrated, motivational and cognitive universe, a dynamic centre of awareness, emotions, judgment and action, organized in a distinctive whole is, however incorrigible it may seem, a rather peculiar idea, within the context of world's cultures. Clifford Geertz[61]

Most of the consumer behavior models that are used in Asian boardrooms today were developed in some Western countries; however, what is "normal" in Western contexts doesn't necessarily hold true across cultures. Studies have found that psychologists and sociologists routinely base their conclusions on test subjects who represent only a minority of the world's population: those in WEIRD (Western, Industrialized, Rich, and Democratic) societies.[62] Citizens of the West are in fact more likely to be outliers when compared to the behaviors and attitudes of other cultures.

Most marketing and management theories rely on a Western perspective of the individual as an independent, autonomous identity, a maker of free decisions based on purely personal desires and affiliations, living life in accordance with Maslow's hierarchy: food, shelter, and clothing are the most basic needs, followed by haute cuisine, decoration, and fashion.

Marketing textbooks still use this model to show how consumers move from the satisfaction of basic needs to higher order goals such as self-actualization. This model, however, fails to consider cultural differences. The widespread practice of dowry in India, although illegal, highlights the plight of parents who are forced to save money to buy enough jewelry for their daughters'

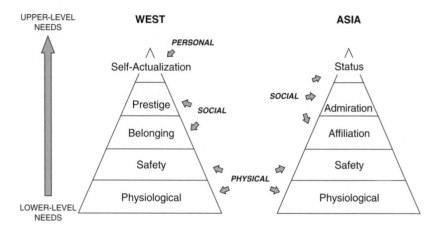

FIGURE 3.1 / **Maslow's hierarchy of needs and the Asian equivalent**

Source: Hellmut Schütte with Deanna Ciarlante, *Consumer Behaviour in Asia*, Macmillan Business – now Palgrave Macmillan, 1998, p. 93, figure 4.2.

weddings. In some emerging countries, people may deprive themselves of food to buy a refrigerator to enhance their social class.[63] Clearly, the hierarchy of priorities is different in an Asian context, where interpersonal relationships and social interactions are more valued than self-actualization needs. Figure 3.1 shows that the Western need for self-actualization is replaced in the Asian context by social needs of status, admiration, and affiliation. Autonomy and independence are less important or at least have different connotations than they do in the West.

Hofstede's well-known model of national cultural difference is more culturally attuned than Maslow's hierarchy of needs. The four dimensions of cultural difference – the level of power distance within the country, the extent of masculinity, the predominance of individualism or collectivism, and the level of uncertainty avoidance that societies engage in – have shaped marketers' thinking for many decades.[64] Figure 3.2 illustrates the conceptual differences between Asia and Western countries on two of Hofstede's dimensions.

These dimensions make up the social psyche of the individual. A country that seeks to avoid uncertainty will have rules of behavior and strict structures for thought that ensure that individuals do not face uncertainty. A highly masculine country is one where men's and women's roles are divided distinctly by gender, the masculine side being more assertive, and the feminine side being more caring and modest. In feminine countries, both men and women will share the same values of modesty and caring. A culture that is individualistic

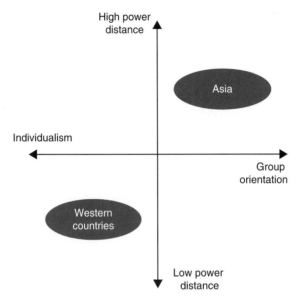

FIGURE 3.2 Power distance versus individualism/group orientation

Source: Adapted from Hofstede, G. *Culture's Consequences: International Differences in Work related Values*, Beverly Hills: Sage, 1980.

expects individuals to be independent and look after only their own immediate family. Ties between individuals are looser, compared to a collectivist culture where individuals are part of a group from birth, which protects them in return for unquestioning loyalty. There is greater conformity to the needs and goals of the group. Social psychologists label this as in-group vs. out-group behavior. Those who form part of this in-group are viewed favorably; those who do not form part of it are regarded as outsiders.

Although the concept of in-groups and out-groups exists universally, when combined with collectivist cultures, the in-group becomes exceptionally strong. Group membership is salient and individuals belong to a number of in-groups, usually family, school, company, and country.

The Importance of In-Groups in Asian Cultures

Asian cultures have a different conception of individuality, placing more emphasis on how individuals are connected to others around them: attending to others, fitting in, and living in harmony. Many non-Western cultures do not value a strict separation of the self from the family unit and the community, while in the West individuals generally define themselves through certain individual talents, abilities, and personality traits.

In many Asian cultures, people believe in the fundamental connectedness or interdependence of individuals within the same in-group. These differences are captured in Figure 3.3. In most Western cultures, people have an independent self where the individual is the primary locus of consciousness. In contrast, in cultures where the interdependent self dominates, it is better to think of the self as connected to others, as always within the context of others. This concept is evident in Japan with the importance of *Ie*, often translated as family or household. *Ie*, researchers have argued, is fundamental to understanding various social organizations in Japanese society, from kinship to the company. *Ie* refers to a family institution, a recruitment strategy for household succession, and a group enterprise.[65]

The differences between Western and Asian cultures are not black and white, though. It would be too simplistic to label all Asian cultures collectivist and all Western ones individualist. After all, the number of associations, church groups, and other types of social engagement is extremely high in the US.

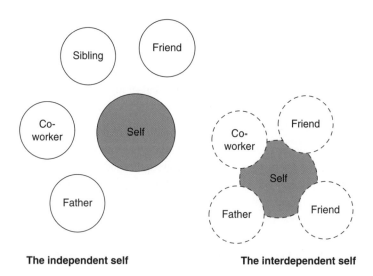

The independent self   **The interdependent self**

FIGURE 3.3 Independent versus interdependent self

Source: Adapted from H. Markus and S. Kitayama, "Culture and the Self: Implications for Cognition, Emotion and Motivation," *Psychological Review*, 1998, pp. 224–53.

With the recent advent of economic liberalization, many Asians have also embraced individualist pursuits. Despite these counter-examples, it can still be argued that the Western concept of the self is different from that in most Asian cultures: an independent versus an interdependent self.

Consider Louis Vuitton, which for many years has been one of the most successful luxury brands in Asia. The brand balances the individualistic and collectivistic consumption patterns perfectly. Louis Vuitton offers a wide range of different products providing multiple choices and has also built very strong brand equity across Asian luxury consumers through intense, premium retail presence and marketing efforts, providing an effective platform for consumption decisions on a group level.

Within Asia, vast differences exist in the way the interdependent self is expressed. There is a tendency across the region to engage in socially engaging behavior, but this varies greatly. For example, the Japanese view of the self is evident in everyday episodes where Japanese emphasize the notion of "losing face," acting on the basis of others' expectations and needs, blurring the distinction between self and others.

In contrast, Indians' in-group is limited to their family and their ethnic community. With 18 official languages, regional differences, religious feuds, and extreme social class disparities, the ability of Indians to empathize with others becomes limited at best. Instead, in India the interdependent self means enduring loyalty and a sense of belonging to a community defined by caste, language, geographic origin, and social class. What constitutes the Indian in-group is different from the Japanese or Chinese in-group. It is important for marketers to realize the importance of the in-group for consumers who will seek advice, think of products, and evaluate products within an in-group.

Being Different Like Everybody Else

The importance of the in-group does not mean total social conformity though. Professor Dae Ryun Chang has described the "We-Me" concept, which illustrates how collectivistic and individualistic tendencies of South Korean consumers can co-exist in broader Asia. The Korean word "Jae-Ban Tae-Ban" means "Half-Me" and "Half-We." The need to be part of a group in Korea is very strong. In cosmetics, for example, demands for brands may be similar (the "We" part), but people may set themselves apart from others using a slightly different style of point makeup. Many young Korean women may ask for an acceptable brand like Chanel lipstick, but then use a different shade of red that is to their personal liking.[66]

Luxury brands in Asia show that consumers are trying to differentiate themselves from other members of society through iconic brands such as Chanel, Louis Vuitton, and Gucci.[67] In 2013, 30 per cent of the total turnover of French luxury giant LVMH was concentrated in Asia,[68] which was the only geographic region to grow its share of revenue in 2013.[69]

The popularity of luxury brands depends largely upon the perceived scarcity of these goods. Accordingly, people assign more value to options, including products, when they are less available. Marketers have long used some of these scarcity tactics, such as advertising "limited number available" or "deadline." This principle works because people typically value things that are difficult to obtain and also because we can't stand to lose any freedoms. According to psychological reactance theory, the more we freedoms we lose (such as the opportunity or the ability to buy a luxury item), the more we want to retain these freedoms.[70]

The scarcity principle can also explain the Asian madness for collectable items. Consider the cases of limited editions of toys: in Taiwan, after McDonald's started selling Hello Kitty dolls, customers, having stood in lines for hours, started to get into fights. One McDonald's restaurant was ordered to close because of the chaos. Another toy fanatic threatened McDonald's staff at knifepoint when they ran out of Hello Kitty toys.[71] Some disappointed customers suffered nervous breakdowns after failing to obtain the prized dolls. A Hong Kong security guard was arrested by police after stealing 21 McDonald's Snoopy collectable figurines from office desks.[72] The scarcity principle holds even more for these items because not only are they newly scarce but also there is a sociological component to the principle: we desire scarce products more when we compete with others for them.

But while the scarcity principle helps to explain the type of behavior mentioned above, it does not, on its own, explain the manic fascination for luxury brands in Asia. Japanese teenagers, for example, could hardly see Louis Vuitton bags or Gucci sunglasses as scarce items. The penetration of such items reaches more than 90 per cent of some Japanese.[73] There are distinct forces in Asian societies that lead Asians to adopt icons projecting their social status. One of these forces is the concept of *mien tsu* or "face." The amount of *mien tsu* stands for a kind of prestige and is a function of social status. Thus, an individual is forced to consume commodities that measure up to his social class, as not doing so would mean a loss of face. Even though traditional Chinese values have changed rapidly over the past 20 years in the process of the country's modernization, many studies show that some of the traditional values, such as face, still exist and influence social orientations. Researchers have also provided evidence that Chinese conform to strong pressures to behave like members of their social class.[74]

Another force leading to the purchase of status symbols is the level of what Hofstede has called "power distance." Hofstede defines power distance as the extent to which less powerful members of society accept power being distributed unequally. Cultures with high power distance believe that the more powerful people must be deferred to and not argued with, especially in public. Likewise, low power distance cultures believe in more equality. China, for example, has a significantly higher power distance level of 80 compared to 60 for the other Southeast Asian countries, and a world average of 55. This reflects a high level of power and wealth inequality within the society. It is not necessarily forced upon people, but rather accepted by the society as their cultural heritage. Luxury brands are purchased to show dominant status and distance to other consumers. Worm argues: "In China, personalized relationships combined with greater power distance tend to result in greater emphasis on status and status symbols than in Scandinavian countries where status symbols are viewed as suspicious and negative by other employees."[75] Some of the key differences between low and high power distance countries appear in Table 3.2.

TABLE 3.2 Differences between low and high power distance countries

Low power distance	High power distance
Privileges and status symbols frowned upon	Privileges and status symbols expected
Teachers expect initiatives from students in class	Teachers are expected to take all initiatives in class
Inequalities between people should be minimized	Inequalities between people are expected and desired
Parents and children treat each other as equals	Children respect parents and parents expect obedience
Ireland, Scandinavia, Austria, Israel	Malaysia, China, India, The Philippines

Source: Adapted from Geert Hofstede, *Cultures and Organizations: Software of the Mind*. Maidenhead: McGraw-Hill, 1991.

The driving force behind luxury sales worldwide today is Asia. Driven by the new-affluent consumers from booming economies, Asian luxury spending grew more than 20 per cent in 2013.

The global spotlight, however, is on Chinese luxury consumers. In 2013 alone, Chinese consumers accounted for 27 per cent of all global luxury purchases. The world's third-largest consumer of luxury goods, China will become number one by the end of 2015, according to Goldman Sachs.

The Hurun Report, a luxury magazine that publishes China's annual rich list, reports that China has 63,500 super rich individuals, defined as those who have assets worth US$16 million or more. A Bain & Company study estimated the total value of luxury goods sold in China to be US$21 billion.[76] The 2013 Julius Baer Wealth Report states that affluent Chinese customers consider buying luxury brands an integral part of their lives, and not an occasional treat.

Recent disappointing results from LVMH, Gucci, and Prada are indications that global luxury brands, after chasing long periods of rapid growth, have failed to understand the Chinese consumer. In stark contrast to the West, Chinese luxury consumers have quickly developed a stronger sensibility and understanding of the luxury market. They have started spending more in the luxury capitals of New York, London, and Paris, attracted by lower taxes, the latest product lines, and better service. These trends strongly indicate that there is still huge untapped demand for luxury goods in China, but luxury brands need to adopt a more knowledgeable, customized, and sensitive strategy to cater to the needs and aspirations of the Chinese consumer.

Who are Chinese luxury consumers?

Self-expression has fuelled China's luxury boom after 50 years of little means and limited ability to differentiate from friends and neighbors. Very wealthy Chinese households are powerful drivers of growth, while the middle class, consisting of households with incomes between US$8,000 and US$40,000, have become the fast rising consumer segment worthy of attention. These population segments, mostly located in second-tier cities, spend large amounts of their income on luxury, using their purchases as symbols to display their social and financial status.

Even though middle-class consumers spend less in total than their wealthier counterparts, their numbers are significant enough to make a strong impact on total luxury spending. In 2009, the Chinese middle class consisted of 13 million households and accounted for 12 per cent of the Chinese luxury goods market. This number is expected to mushroom to around US$76 million by 2015.

An interesting characteristic of Chinese luxury consumers is that they are younger than their European and American counterparts: 45 per cent of Chinese luxury consumers are under the age of 35; 14 and 25 years younger than their European and American counterparts, respectively. In the next three to five years, Chinese consumers between the ages of 25 and 30 will become the domi-nant group in luxury consumption.

Women have become an increasingly important demographic in the Chinese luxury goods market, which has traditionally been dominated by males between 35 and 45 years old. Chinese women are beginning to catch up with men in numbers in the workplace, and thus are gaining more financial independence and social status. Consequently, their purchasing power has increased, and they are buying more luxury goods to reward themselves for hard work and personal accomplishments. With 25 per cent of Chinese women earning more than their male partners, they now account for three-fifths of the luxury goods consumer segment.

With domestic growth rates falling from double to single dig-its due to a slowing economy, government efforts to mitigate ostentatious displays of wealth, and increased purchases abroad, luxury goods companies need to make adjustments to their exist-ing business models to meet the needs of the evolving Chinese market. China's wealthy spent 15 per cent less in 2013 on luxury items, and 25 per cent less on gift-giving. Despite slowing growth, the country is still expected to rebound, with the nation's share of global luxury spending continuing to soar to more than one-third by the end of 2015.

Logo fatigue

While Chinese luxury consumers have historically preferred outwardly visible and status-driven products, demand is beginning to evolve as consumers are increasingly turning to niche and unbranded high-end products.

"Logo fatigue" has set in among China's consumers and there is a noticeable shift in demand from luxury products flaunting logos to more understated and stylish products, leaving well-known brands like Louis Vuitton and Gucci struggling to keep up with prior yearly growth rates. This phenomenon is most apparent in tier one cities, such as Beijing, Shanghai, and Shenzhen, where consumers have been buying luxury for a few years and are becoming knowledgeable about fashion and curious about what is perceived as stylish.

In a 2012 McKinsey report, the share of respondents agreeing or strongly agreeing that "showing off luxury goods is in bad taste'" was 51 per cent – the same as Japan, and a big jump from the 37 per cent who said so in 2010. According to the study, customers are no longer interested in "me-too buys" – that is, choosing a brand if everyone has it. Instead, they are searching for items that speak to the individualism of the buyer with greater focus on materials, craftsmanship heritage, durability, and tastefulness. This trend has been described as "stealth wealth,"[77] with the super-rich no longer wanting to appear ostentatious.

There will still be strong demand for well-known, logo-emblazoned products, however, as they clearly help display newfound status in the Chinese social hierarchy. But China has definitely entered phase two of its luxury transformation as the market splinters across income levels and social classes.

Maturing toward customer service

When foreign brands first came to China, market strategies were to create awareness as quickly and widely as possible, but now brands are switching focus from opening stores to improving customer service.[78] 92 per cent of Chinese consumers were not satisfied by brands' services in their home country.[79]

As the luxury market enters phase two of its growth story, stores are ramping up their in-store service and special treatment of their best customers, focusing on custom-made items (e.g. Louis Vuitton's flagship Shanghai outlet). For a steep price, Johnnie Walker now offers the company's master blender to fly in and brew a special batch of Johnnie Walker precisely matched to a customer's taste. Other brands are following the route of Macau casino operators, flying customers on all-expenses-paid trips from the mainland to Hong Kong to buy their goods. Swiss luxury watch brand, Piaget, stages two such trips each year for 50 VIP customers.

Conclusion

Chinese luxury consumers are constantly growing and evolving. More than ever, it is essential for luxury companies to stop viewing Chinese consumers as homogeneous, but instead structure their business models according to the differences within various regions, social classes, and income levels. Luxury companies need to find a middle ground in the tailoring of product portfolios that meet the needs of different groups while maintaining consistent quality and service.

Conclusion

This chapter has mapped some of the most important forces, flows, and dimensions of Asian culture that can influence how Asian consumers think and behave. There is an important caveat to this analysis, though, and it has to do with the dynamism of the region. Societies in Asia are moving fast and the dimensions described above are not set in stone. Asian countries are increasingly connected to other countries within and beyond Asia. These connections only enhance and increase the rapidity of the Asian evolution. What remains, though, are these connections between these different countries. The examples discussed in this section testify to the rich cultural exchanges between

Asian countries. To become astute marketers and understand Asian consumers, the corporate management of companies will first have to look within Asia.

Companies striving to build successful brands in Asia should understand the unique mosaic of cultures that is Asia. As discussed, Asia represents a blend of modernity and traditionalism. This is a doubled-edged sword for companies seeking to develop brands in Asia. On the one hand, this presents a huge set of opportunities with diverse customer segments, latent rural demand, and an immense potential to weave exciting new stories. But on the other, it compels companies to fine a balance between the different perspectives to become local and regional at the same time. Fine-tuning products and services to satisfy local tastes and preferences while also appealing to a pan-Asian identity by leveraging the common underlying cultural underpinnings will be one of the possible ways ahead for companies in Asia.

Δ

Asian Country Branding

The past few decades have seen many Asian countries embrace market capitalism and open their economies to foreign participation and influence. With a considerable increase in the number of global companies setting up shops in Asia and exotic locales, unique cultures, and sun-kissed beaches, tourism has become a booming industry in Asia. The active promotion of high-quality, affordable healthcare and a renewed focus on developing a world-class education system have developed health and edu-tourism.

As many Asian countries are able to boast one or more of the above attractions, the need to differentiate and brand themselves to attract capital and people is rapidly gaining importance.

Countries can create distinct identities. As the number of tourist arrivals and business travelers continues to increase in the world,[1] countries must increase their share of the pie by building strong top-of-mind awareness. Destination recall should be instant when a holiday or the next company-wide conference is planned. Branding is the answer.

Although countries brand themselves to persuade tourists (and their dollars) away from others, it is important to create a positive image and gain instant cachet for local products, when exported. Selling Italian shoes and German engineering is much easier than selling Australian shoes and Czech engineering. Branding can also serve a purpose in the global marketplace through attracting investments and skilled workers.

Internally, governments can use their new brand identity to channel development and boost public morale. For many decades, due to Asia's relatively lower social and economic development levels, Asian products and services did not enjoy a positive country-of-origin effect. Now, with new branded identities, they can fight entrenched beliefs not only in their home countries but outside as well.

According to Futurebrand research, whose annual Country Brand Index (CBI) ranks countries on the strength and power of their nation's brand, the country in which a brand is based, designed, and manufactured all rank higher than traditional drivers of choice like price, availability, and style.[2]

Asian brands, especially Chinese, are often a source of negative association. In Futurebrand's 2014 "Made In" study, China ranks ninth, signifying a change in how the country is perceived as a country of origin. China is slowly evolving from being a low-cost manufacturing base to a global source of manufacturing and development for high-skill industries (e.g. technology, electronics and fashion).[3] The Made-in-China brand is increasingly getting recognition in industries where high-quality manufacturing is the underpinning of product and brand success.

Excluding Japan, South Korea, and Taiwan, Western consumers find it difficult to associate Asian countries with a competitive advantage other than low-cost and low-quality.

But there are positive examples too. Consumers value South Korea as one of the most important beauty trendsetters not only in Asia, but also the world. South Korea has now surpassed Japan as the model for Asian beauty. As home-grown cosmetic brands like AmorePacific expand overseas, they will owe much of their positive brand equity to this country of origin effect. Samsung had a similar positive impact on the nation brand equity of Korea due to their rapid, global rise as a brand, influencing global stakeholders' perception of Korea.

Overall, country branding can be divided into three main categories by purpose:

• Export branding
• Generic country branding
• Internal country branding.

The benefits of each branding activity are listed in Table 4.1. While branding is beneficial, it offers different types of challenges.

TABLE 4.1   Benefits of branding places

Country branding activities	Benefits
Export branding	Positive halo effect on products
	Increased ability to export
Generic country branding	Ability to attract tourists and skilled workers
	Increased ability to attract investments
	Ability to reduce incentives for investors
	Increased cost-pressure on competition
	Resilience to financial crisis
	Ability to sustain higher prices
Internal country branding	Ability to retain skilled workers
	Increased productivity from better morale

Source: Martin Roll Company.

Export Branding

International marketers have long realized that stressing country of origin can help sales: German cars, French wines, and Asian hotels all stress their country of origin to leverage positive associations with these places. "Made in" Germany, France, or Japan helps to improve a brand's equity, especially for low-profile companies. In these cases, country of origin acts as a proxy for judging product quality. A country's intangible assets are quality dimensions that a country has gradually acquired through the export of goods and services.

A product's country of origin acts like a heuristic or rule of thumb for consumers. Psychologists emphasize that most people are "cognitive misers," relying on mental shortcuts to make decisions. Princeton researcher Daniel Kahneman's research on these shortcuts won him the Nobel Prize in 1996. A study found that the framing of information greatly influences how we perceive it. In one study, people had to decide hypothetically what procedure to take to cure a disease. Unsurprisingly, most preferred a procedure that "saved" 80 percent of people to one that "killed" 20 percent.[4]

Consumers will rely on product origin when they are unable to detect its true quality before purchase. For example, consumers typically infer the quality of a Japanese car from the "halo effect"[5] of Japan's association with high-quality, reliable products. Country image, in this case, is used as an "extrinsic cue," a piece of information that is distinct from the product characteristics but tells the consumer something about the product.

Paying attention to country-of-origin labels is particularly important for brand managers whose brands are in the initial development stages. For relatively unknown brands, consumers are more likely to rely on country of origin. In contrast, for high-awareness and loyalty brands, the country of origin plays a minor role.

In a Harvard Business School survey on global brands,[6] researchers found that most people dissociated American brands from the actions of the American government. About 88 percent selected well-known global brands rather than local alternatives when asked which products they would like to buy. For them, buying global brands showed a connection to a global society. They did not regard big US brands as being identified with America itself. Only 12 percent did not want to buy such brands.

However, understanding where a brand originates is not always simple. Today, a product can be designed in Country A, manufactured in Country B, assembled in Country C, by a brand based in Country D with strong cultural ties to Country E using resources sourced from dozens of other countries. So which origin component is most important or influential to consumers?

According to global brand agency Futurebrand, a brand's nationality – that is, where it is perceived to be from – is more important to consumers than place of design, but less important than place of manufacturing. For brands, this means that they can borrow associations from various places as much as they wish, but the name on the "Made In" label matters most in the end. When it comes to a decision between two brands, the most authentic in terms of production, not just image, is preferred by the majority of consumers.

Brands must, however, be careful of the extent to which they control where their products are manufactured. The "Italian luxury" image was damaged in 2012 when it was revealed that the Italian government endorsed sweatshop working conditions so that luxury brands could maximize profitability while still claiming authenticity. Consequently, the prestige of "Made in Italy" became the subject of skepticism – a huge misstep in the ultra-competitive high-fashion world. Think of how this potential crisis could affect Italian-based luxury brands Prada, Giorgio Armani, Ermenegildo Zegna, and so on.

Asian managers should pay particular attention to country associations. In an academic study, researchers examined people living in a collectivist country (Japan) compared to those in an individualistic country (the US) – collectivists favor home country products more than individualists do, because their group affiliations are stronger.[7]

One of the challenges of this kind of branding is to note historical and cultural sensitivity. It is crucial to remember the history of relations between different Asian countries when planning a branding campaign. In a study about Chinese perceptions of Japanese products, Jill Klein and her colleagues from INSEAD business school found strong animosity toward Japanese brands.[8] The authors developed the "foreign animosity model" to capture the likelihood of consumers boycotting products from different countries. As Japanese brands try to expand in their former colonies such as Taiwan, South Korea, and China, sentiments of animosity are likely to be rampant, especially among older generations. In fact, until the late 1990s, Japanese television programs were banned in South Korea.[9] In China, war memories still resonate strongly and impact how Japanese managers manage their brands.

The Toyota campaign in China serves as a good example of a campaign that went wrong because managers did not pay enough attention to this history. In 2003, Chinese consumers complained en masse about a series of magazine ads released by Japanese car maker Toyota, saying that Toyota had insulted their country. One of the ads featured a Toyota vehicle towing a truck, which looked like a Chinese military vehicle, through a Tibetan landscape. The other ad showed two stone lions, traditional Chinese symbols of authority, bowing in front of a Toyota truck. The copy read: "You cannot but respect the Prado." Chinese journalists commented that the pictures implied the superiority of Japanese products over Chinese ones. Confronted by these attacks, Toyota had to recall the ads and issue a public apology to Chinese customers for hurting their sentiments. While Toyota remains popular because of product quality, the company will have to improve its sensitivity to the history of relations between both countries.[10] After this debacle, Toyota has slowly strengthened its position in the Chinese market, with sales expected to cross 1.1 million units in 2014.

Government's Role in Country Branding

As discussed earlier, branding a country is far more complex than branding a product or a service. A strong country brand creates a strong channel for countries to attract foreign investment. Malaysia and Singapore serve as examples where the governments have envisioned branding as a crucial factor in the countries' future.

Given the tremendous advantages for countries and businesses from positive brand image, Asian countries traditionally enduring the brunt of a low-cost, low-quality image can benefit from building strong country brands.

HOW NATIONS CAN SUCCESSFULLY OVERCOME ORIGIN CHALLENGES

Emphasize and diversify sources of competitive advantage: The first aspect begins with understanding what a nation does well compared to its neighbors, and harnessing those advantages. As a small nation with few natural resources, Switzerland was the first country in the world to establish a national brand board, closely supervising "Made in Switzerland" and other national imagery. Beginning with chocolate and expanding to other high-value segments including watches, fashion, and private banking, Switzerland currently ranks higher than France and Italy as the pre-eminent country of origin for luxury.[11]

Industry branding must be a multidisciplinary effort. Research shows a country's reputation is stronger when it excels in multiple categories. Similarly, focusing on only a few industries while others languish can bring down the overall national image. Therefore, countries should strive to improve poorly-performing categories. The US is the best example of diversified strength – achieving a top 5 ranking in all six major categories (F&B, personal care, automotive, electronics, fashion, and luxury), thus making American brands the most likely ones that consumers would buy overall.[12]

Improve English language skills: In the largest ranking of English skills by country, Education First's English Proficiency Index has shown a direct correlation between English language skills and economic performance. Whether measured by gross national income, average salaries, GDP, or quality of life metrics such as the Human Development Index (a combination of education, life expectancy, literacy, and standards of living), a nation can expedite development and expand opportunities by improving language skills of their most valuable resource – human capital. According to McKinsey, this is a major reason why the Philippines has overtaken India – the once dominant player – as a hub for call service centers. Cultivating a globally-ready workforce can give home country brands a stronger platform for global growth.

Improve health and safety regulations: Consumers are more conscious of brands' social and environmental behaviors. The backlash against fashion brands exploiting hazardous conditions in Bangladeshi garment factories is one prime example. "Made in China" has also suffered greatly from incidents such as flammable children's clothing and contaminated baby formula, which creates doubt about the nation's commitment to safety and craftsmanship. These have prompted governments to demand more stringent labeling of products crossing their borders. Packaged food in Europe must now indicate all countries involved in production – not just the final or most important stage.

Improve intellectual property rights: The lack of stringent regulation and enforcement of intellectual property rights has been a major challenge for brands from emerging countries. A thriving counterfeit market in their own backyard creates a hurdle if competitors can easily copy technology, undercut profits, and dilute their brand. Unless legislation and enforcement improve in regions that face rampant IP infringement, knockoff economies will contribute to the global perception that emerging market brands are not incentivized to offer anything new or different.

Be conscious of foreign policy's impact on flagship brands: How corporations are perceived overseas has much to do with government behavior in the political arena. The plight of Huawei in the United States speaks for itself. Although Huawei's products and solutions are deployed in more than 140 countries, serving more than one third of the world's population, the Shenzhen-based company has been branded a security threat by the US government thanks to the military background of Huawei's CEO and R&D ties with the Chinese military. The fact that China is regularly accused of hacking institutions such as the *Wall Street Journal* and Google does not help. To shake lingering suspicions, Huawei has started a charm offensive but faces seemingly insurmountable resistance in what could be the world's largest market for their services.

Source: Martin Roll Company.

Generic Country Branding

With generic country branding, an important challenge is to find a single, all-encompassing message that differentiates the country from its competitors. Many countries have tried this in the past ten years, with varying levels of success. Figure 4.1 documents the different country branding initiatives in Asia. "Inclusiveness" refers to the ability of country branding campaigns to be comprehensive – whether these campaigns are able to capture the diversity of the country within their scope. "Differentiation" refers to the ability of campaigns to project a unique positioning and value proposition to stand apart from other campaigns.

The difficulty of finding one unifying message is because countries are, by their nature, diverse, with activities that are far more difficult to summarize than those of a company. Countries have diverse populations who are audiences and stakeholders for the generic country branding campaigns. For Malaysia, this could have been a big challenge, given its ethnic diversity. But the country turned an apparent difficulty into strength, developing one of the most successful Asian branding campaigns.

Level of Inclusiveness

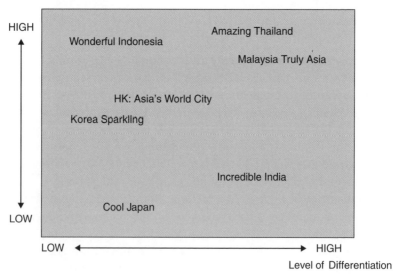

FIGURE 4.1 Country branding initiatives

Malaysia, Truly Asia

In 1997, the Malaysian government launched the Malaysia, Truly Asia campaign to counter the crippling effects of the Asian financial crisis on its economy.

Although a former British colony, Malaysia was not as big a tourist destination as other neighboring countries like Thailand and Singapore. The Malaysian government had the challenge of establishing a position in tourists' minds who knew nothing about Malaysia.

The brand team found a unique and differentiated positioning by projecting Malaysia as a place to sample diverse Asian cultures – Chinese, Indian, Malay, and those of other nationalities – in a safe, modern environment where customers enjoy great value for money. It also offered multiculturalism with cosmopolitanism, concentrating on the region's diversity in food and culture. It projected Malaysia as a safe destination for tourists who feared the vastness and incomprehensibility of Asia – its cultural practices, cuisines, and languages. Malaysia could become a great destination for those who wanted a safe taste of Asia.

A resounding success, the campaign continues to successfully embed Malaysia in the public consciousness as a destination of choice. Backed by vast amounts of money spent on tourism development, the country sees 25 million tourists annually[13] compared to 13 million annually prior to 2004,[14] and has the goal of attracting 36 million international tourists a year by 2020.[15] The 10th most visited country in the world, Malaysia is well-equipped to provide niche tourism – health and medical tourism, ecotourism, edu-tourism, Formula 1 events, international golf tournaments, extreme sport and adventure tourism, and culture and lifestyle tourism.[16]

Over time, the country is also being promoted as a great shopping destination. Tourists from the Middle East, wary of Europe and America, are traveling to Malaysia during their summer months – May to August. Although hot, Malaysia is cooler than many places in the Middle East.

Although the campaign has enjoyed success so far, difficulties are inevitable with time. Because of its heavy association with "Asia," the brand will take a beating if world events cause "Asia" to take on a negative connotation. Another challenge may be to stress qualities other than its diversity, because if ethnic tensions were to arise in Malaysia, its positioning of "Truly Asia" could risk becoming a grotesque joke.

Amazing Thailand

Another successful generic country branding campaign, "Amazing Thailand," was also created just after the economic crisis of 1997. It was able cleverly to bring together diverse aspects of a country under one word: amazing.

The Thai government launched the campaign in 1998. Together with ad agency Leo Burnett, hotels, tour guides, restaurants, and souvenir associations, they came up with the Amazing Thailand idea after two months of brainstorming, cashing in on all things Thailand had to offer – historic and cultural sites, fabulous cuisine, beautiful beaches, and very friendly people.

The Thai government allocated US$37.9 million in 1998–1999 for the promotion of Brand Thailand. Although this caused uproar at the time because Thailand was facing an economic downturn due to the Asian financial crisis, the effects were extraordinary – tourist arrivals went up from US$7 million to US$10 million in the next five years. Amazing Thailand's focus was on increasing tourist influx by promoting shopping, food, beaches, and traditional massages.

The campaign tagline was successful because of its blanket nature – it was able to capture all "amazing" aspects of Thailand. If the royal palaces and beaches were amazing, so were the traffic, and the spicy food. If Thai hospitality was amazing, so were the shockingly low prices. The slogan was able to create a discrete identity for Thailand by infusing every part of it with amazement for tourists. It was broad enough to capture the many aspects of life, be it leisure, culinary indulgence, or historical sites, yet memorable enough to stand out for what it was selling: amazement.

With time, the tourism board has changed its positioning of Thailand, as the brand has established itself worldwide. Once it had carved a market for itself and made its presence felt, the government started developing a more mature brand. In 2003, the government launched the Unseen Thailand campaign, which was expanded to cover not only culture, food, world heritage sites, and boutique hotels, but also golfing, adventure, diving, and wedding packages. Thailand was also being promoted as the ideal destination to shoot films. The brand was reaching maturity. In an analogy with human maturity, one could say it went from a gawping backpacking tourist to a young urban professional looking for "something different."

The Thai positioning of 2004 was Happiness on Earth. Wanting to shed the earlier ambiguous connotation of amazing, the government wants to equate holidays, which people associate with happiness, with Thailand. The new stress is on the outstanding spa facilities, golf courses, and river cruises that Thailand has to offer. These new offers position Thailand as a luxury brand, aimed at the rich professional desiring an indulgent holiday. Thailand has come a long way from the gawping backpacker it once was, and in 2014 launched a new campaign titled "Amazing Thailand: It begins with the People," intended to deepen the emotional value and human experience of immersing one's self within the culture of the Kingdom of Thailand.[17]

In 2015, the Tourism Authority of Thailand will launch its "2015 Discover Thainess" campaign. Thailand had more than 26 million visitors in 2014 and projects close to 30 million visitors in 2015.[18]

India Shining to Incredible India

Over December 2003 and January 2004, Indians were bombarded with the government's advertising campaign called India Shining. It aired 9,472 times on all leading television channels, with 392 print ad appearances during the first two weeks of January. This massive media attack was due to the party in power having a great run during its four-year term, and preparing for early elections. Its win came at the very height of its popularity.[19]

In October 2003, the government briefed several advertising firms on what it wanted to project through the ads. Of all the slogans created, one in particular seemed to hit the mark: India Shining. It was time to remind people of the fabulous four years of economic growth, prosperity, and stability for everyone: urban and rural, old and young. The campaign was unique – the first time a political party in India had used corporate branding strategies to project itself to the people.

But the ads would not work if they were seen to be an overt political campaign. Therefore there was never any mention of the party. They were "government" advertisements.[20] The campaign was followed up with almost half a million phone calls made every day to the Indian public with a pre-recorded message by the prime minister, leader of the ruling party, highlighting the achievements of his party. Discussion and debate followed in all the leading media about the content.

The content of the advertisements tried to create a "feel-good" factor for the viewer. One example showed a young girl getting dressed for school. The punchline said: "I am going to study further. Lower interest rates on education loans."

Similarly, other ads sent messages like: despite low interest rates in the country, senior citizens were benefiting from higher interest rates on their investments through the "Dada Dadi" bonds; people were able to start their own businesses because of a US$2.3 billion fund created to promote small-scale industries; the state of the Indian economy was improving because of increasing foreign exchange reserves due to increased exports. The mood everywhere was soaring. India was truly shining.

All indicators pointed to a win for the party in power, the NDA (National Democratic Alliance) in the May 2004 elections. But to everyone's surprise, it lost to the opposition, the Congress Party. Media watchers could not fathom how their opinion and exit polls could have been so wrong. But while the NDA was getting viewers to feel good, the Congress Party had launched its own ad campaign. The advertising was in black and white only, in Hindi, and targeted the lower middle class and the rural market. It used the claims made by the NDA, reversed the imagery and used the slogan *Aamadmikokyamila?* – What did the common man gain? The Congress Party focused on all things the common man had not been a part of in the new, rising, and shining India. There were still problems of infrastructure, water, electricity, and unemployment. The chasm between the rich and the poor had never looked wider. The NDA government's policies had benefited the rich and had allowed the middle class to rise while rural citizens and the lower middle class struggled harder to bridge the gap.[21]

There were many reasons for the failure of the NDA brand, but it was mainly the gap between promise and delivery. Some media pundits said that there was nothing wrong with the campaign; it was the core product that was not strong. Others said that the brand was not forward-looking; it did not promise anything. What were the viewers getting in exchange for their votes? The campaign was also created in English, a language foreign to the masses of India. The slogan India Shining and the byline Feel Good have no straightforward equivalents in the regional languages,[22] hence alienating the largest voter bank. The use of technology to connect with the public posed another problem. It was damaging to the prime minister's image to be perceived as the equivalent of a telemarketer.[23] However, the most important reason why the critical mass of people did not connect with the advertisement was because it did not portray their experience of the past few years.[24] Seeing the ad made the masses compare their situation with the beneficiaries, which caused them to perceive the advertising as arrogant and callous.

So although the NDA had tried to take advantage of slick, emotional advertising techniques, the brand failed to take off because of the stark difference between their projection and reality. Also, to brand a country means having a unified communication – projecting the values of the brand in a cohesive message. This is difficult because there are a number of realities that need to be merged and streamlined. Inevitably, some will be missed. It was the NDA's downfall to have picked the smallest group – the urban middle class – as its key audience. It ignored the realities of those who had fallen by the wayside, something the Congress Party was quick to pick up on.

But history repeats itself with forceful impact. In 2014, the Bharatiya Janata Party (BJP), which was leading the NDA coalition, inflicted a crushing defeat on the Congress Party by winning the general elections by a record margin. This was the heaviest defeat for the Congress Party in its long history. The elected Prime Minister, Mr. Narendra Modi, immediately embarked on a tour of the US to address the sizeable Indian diaspora residing there. He delivered a speech to nearly 19,000 Non-Resident Indians (NRIs) at Madison Square Gardens, New York in September 2014. The theme of his speech centered on asking them to join him in the development of the nation. For one, the new Prime Minister of India is using the tools made available by social media to the fullest, with an active Twitter feed and an up-to-date LinkedIn profile.

The India Shining campaign evolved into the "Incredible India" campaign in 2002. The primary objective was and continues to be the promotion of tourism in India to a global audience. More recently, the Government of India has started inviting bids from organizations who would be interested in developing and maintaining the "Incredible India" website. The intention is to make it a one-stop destination allowing the seamless booking of hotels, trains, flights, and tours. Additionally, mobile solutions and digital integration and analytics are also key focus areas for the website.[25]

The "Incredible India" campaign has been endorsed by leading Bollywood superstars like Aamir Khan, who brings in a huge amount of credibility to marketing campaigns because of the sheer popularity and following of Bollywood in the country.

Cool Japan – Learning and Lessons for Nation Branding

The Cool Japan initiative is at the heart of Japan's nation branding exercise aiming to tie together "culture and industry" and "Japan and the world."[26] The concept of "Cool Japan" originated in 2002 as an expression of Japan's emergent status as a cultural superpower.[27] After the Great East Japan earthquake in 2011, the "Cool Japan" tagline was adopted as a brand to create a new Japan, to recover from the earthquake and restore the shine of brand Japan.[28]

The goals of the Cool Japan initiative are to promote the nation's creative industries like anime (animation), manga (comics), fashion, food, art, traditional crafts, tourism, and music. This "soft power" strategy hopes to encourage global entry for Japan's small and medium enterprises (SMEs), attract foreign companies to leverage Japan's creative industries, and entice international travelers to visit its shores. The Ministry of Economy, Trade, and Industry (METI) is responsible for this initiative. The global cultural industry is expected to grow by 40 percent and will be valued at US$9 trillion by 2020. Japan is aiming for a larger share of this market – between US$80 and 110 million – by leveraging the Cool Japan program.[29]

The program is part of Prime Minister Shinzo Abe's economic policies (dubbed "Abenomics") that focus on fiscal stimulus, monetary easing, and structural reforms.[30] His government will allocate US$1 billion to Cool Japan over the next two decades.[31] The Cool Japan Fund was launched in November 2013 to manage the initiative's investments[32] and has funded several events supporting traditional crafts, fashion shows, and heavy investments in overseas promotions.

One key inspiration for the campaign is the success of South Korea. Today, South Korean artists (like Psy) dominate the Asian music charts, South Korean television and movies are top sellers, and the country's goods like Samsung phones or Hyundai cars enjoy global success. Above all, the image of South Korea's culture to the world is modern, young, and fun.[33, 34]

The Cool Japan initiative has received mixed reviews since its implementation. Critics say that the failure to distinguish, brand, and engage the overseas audience and market may mean "Cool Japan is over."[35] Another criticism is that it is not doing enough to advance business interests, and structural inefficiencies are cited involving multiple Government agencies (METI, the Ministry of Foreign Affairs, and the Ministry of Agriculture, Forestry, and Fisheries).[36] Some experts question the need for taxpayers to pump money into private companies that are worthy and viable.[37] The initiative has suffered setbacks like the "Uncool" Cool Japan homemade video that went viral for the wrong reasons.[38] Famous Japanese artists, like Takashi Murakami, have also distanced themselves from the program.[39]

Marketing the phrase "Cool Japan" may be the source of the problem as identified by a participant – "to call yourself cool is by definition uncool and it defies Japanese modesty."[40] Although the benefits from nation branding exercises have longer gestation periods than conventional product branding, it may be wise to rethink "Cool Japan" due to the dissonance in its public perception.

Future Opportunities

As the brand image for Asian countries is refined for tourism, other economic agendas need to be branded too. After selling beaches, cuisine, and ancient temples, it is time to stress other financially advantageous qualities that can be developed into long-term, stable brand attributes. Two areas of opportunity seem especially promising and critical for Asia: education and healthcare.

Branding Places for Education

The market for education in Asia is booming and, given population growth estimates, the market is likely to be even more pronounced in the next few years, especially in the postgraduate sector where institutes are competing for large cohorts of Asian MBAs.

Between 1998 and 2003, the number of applicants to the GMAT, the qualifying entrance test for MBA schools, almost tripled in India and China.[41] Unsurprisingly, many American and European schools started seeing Asia as the only area of real potential growth. In contrast to the booming Asian market, the market for MBA students in the US is pretty sluggish, with an overall decrease of applicants in recent years.

This sluggishness is also reflected in a reversal in the number of GMAT applicants from India and China who are sending their scores to US universities. In 2012, in spite of a 19 percent increase in GMAT test takers from India, there was a decline of 11 percent (61 percent to 54 percent) in the proportion who sent their test scores to US universities. This increasing level of disinterest among Indian and Chinese applicants to send their scores to US universities is also due to the higher probability of them getting rejected. Analysis indicates that the primary reason for rejection is because US MBA school officials are finding an over-representation of applicants from both countries in the application pool. Coupled with the increasing attractiveness and availability of world-class MBA programs in Asia and Europe (India, Singapore, France, the United Kingdom), Indian and Chinese students are increasingly turning their attention to universities in these parts of the world.[42]

Many business schools in Europe, North America, and Australia are already benefiting from this boom in the Asian education market. For Asian countries to compete in this educational market there needs to be a concerted effort from governments, businesses, and universities to brand countries as places for education. One of the pitfalls of country branding in Asia is that it focuses on the exotic, at the expense of other brand dimensions like excellence, especially as it relates to knowledge development.

Many Asian countries have a strong tradition of promoting knowledge. Sima Qian, grand historian of the emperor and author of the first full history of China, emphasized the importance of knowledge in Chinese society:

> *A gentleman is eager and tireless in learning and makes unremitting efforts to improve himself. He always tries to extend the knowledge he has earned further, to expand it greater, to exalt it higher, and to explore it deeper.*[43]

However, countries like India and China are rarely associated with great education, but with low literacy levels. In the past five years, however, Asian engineering and business schools have gained credibility. Indian institutes of management and technology have been shown to be the most selective in the world, accepting only a small proportion of thousands of applicants. They also have the highest test level scores, although this must be seen in the context of the high number of applications received by these institutions every year.

INSEAD — THE BUSINESS SCHOOL FOR THE WORLD

INSEAD is one of the world's largest top-tier graduate business schools, with two comprehensive and fully connected campuses in Asia (Singapore) and Europe (France). The business school provides a unique, diverse learning experience. Participants interact with the faculty and fellow students in an unparalleled multicultural environment, gaining essential insights into international business practice. INSEAD's growing community of more than 49,000 diverse alumni living and working in over 171 countries worldwide creates lifelong opportunities for professional development and networking. This global and multicultural perspective sets INSEAD apart in the field of international management education and research.[44]

However, Indian and Chinese schools have not gained the global reputation of institutions like INSEAD because they have failed to attract high-quality faculty or students from other countries. As trade between countries within Asia intensifies, more cultural and educational exchanges will be necessary to boost a better understanding of cultural and trade practices. In addition, attracting students from other parts of the world will increase the reputation of these institutions, by building a global image. The global orientation of a brand has already been shown to increase product evaluations.[45] This halo effect holds true for educational institutions too – which is where INSEAD has found a unique differentiation against the competition, as it has always embraced cultural diversity and global perspectives.

Branding Places for Medical Tourism

Another great opportunity for country branding is health tourism and medical treatment. Medical tourism is defined as a country's efforts to brand itself as a destination for healthcare services and facilities. With the European and North American population aging, the rise of medical treatment in these countries, and a decrease in social security reimbursements, more people are targeting Asia for medical services. Add that to a lack of top-notch hospitals in the Middle East and Africa, and Asia is well poised to become a center for medical treatment and health tourism.[46] While this market has been dominated by European and North American facilities for a long time, Asian countries are now quickly catching up.

Although the demand for medical tourism is fundamentally driven by cost and quality considerations, the choice of destination depends on many factors, including proximity, brand value, and the range of available healthcare services. The Asian medical tourism industry has been growing at a double-digit rate for the past few years.[47]

An Asian country that is moving aggressively in this area is Thailand. It has become the number one Asian destination for medical tourists. In 2002, the number of foreign patients seeking treatment in Thailand grew by 13 percent,[48] totaling more than 600,000 foreigners visiting private hospitals. In 2003, the number of foreign patients had grown to 1 million[49] – a trend that has continued up to 2013.[50] As news gets around that Thailand provides superior healthcare and medical services at very affordable rates, the destination is attracting an ever-increasing number of visiting patients.

Another rising star in that sector is India. India has already attracted many software companies looking for low-cost development and staying for quality. The same phenomenon is happening in the healthcare industry, despite the fact that the country has fewer doctors for every 100,000 people compared with America. India is increasingly taking advantage of a lower cost structure and excellent doctors to treat foreign patients. The Associated Chambers of Commerce and Industry of India (ASSOCHAM) predicts that the medical tourism sector in India will double in size to US$1.69 billion by 2015 from US$728 million in 2011. It also predicts that by 2015, 3.2 million medical tourists will visit India, a significant increase from the 850,000 who visited in 2011.[51]

This is not surprising given the difference in costs with other countries. At Aravind Eye Hospital,[52] a leading facility specializing in the treatment of cataracts, the cost per operation is less than US$50, compared to around US$3,000 in the US. In the Narayana Health chain of hospitals in India, opened and run by heart surgeon Devi Shetty, a coronary bypass surgery can be conducted for US$1,583, which would cost US$106,385 in Ohio's Cleveland Clinic.[53] Cosmetic surgery costs three to four times less in India than in the West. Quality is ensured because of the high-level training that Indian doctors receive, as well as the number of operations they perform. While the business of healthcare services has long remained essentially domestic, this is rapidly changing and becoming more global.

Conclusion

Countries, like brands, exert a considerable influence on the products or services that originate from them. A strong country brand both attracts tourists and enhances a country's attractiveness to foreign investment. Most importantly, the strong country brand equity extends to the product and services emerging from it. Given Asia's historic perception around low cost, this assumes special significance. Asian countries and their governments must realize the criticality of branding their countries and extend full involvement and support for branding initiatives. Moreover, governments should take initiatives to ensure the buy-in of all internal and external stakeholders.

A strong nation brand is an advantage for competing on a global stage if companies have what it takes. For example, the country brand of South Korea is ranked 20th overall by Futurebrand.[54] It has achieved top 10 as a country to buy manufactured goods from because of brands like Samsung, Hyundai, LG, and Kia. This is partly driven by the dedicated efforts of the Korean companies to innovate and globalize, and the rapid rise and admiration for Korean popular culture across Asia.

Regardless of country brand strength, each country has much more independent work to do to change how the world perceives them. In these cases, government still plays a major role in creating favorable conditions for these conglomerates to build capabilities that make them global brands. Building a strong nation brand is a public–private partnership.

5

Celebrity Branding in Asia

It is only shallow people who do not judge by appearances.
—Oscar Wilde

For a long time, companies have used well-known public figures, movie stars and sports personalities to endorse their brands, as it is widely believed that these celebrities help to build or reposition brands by extending personality, character, and popularity to the brands they endorse. This chapter looks into this brand-building tool that is fast gaining currency with leading Asian corporations.

Brand endorsement has been covered widely in branding literature. It can be simply defined as a persuasive communication strategy in which companies use a spokesperson to represent their products and services. This can be paid, valued in kind, or unpaid. The main aim of product endorsement is to persuade consumers to buy a particular product/service, to shape perceptions toward it, and position it more as a lifestyle product or service rather than solely on its application merits. It is also intended to shape or change perceptions of a particular brand, increase its popularity and consumer mind share, strengthen brand recall, and highlight differentiation and uniqueness.

Comprehensive research suggests that celebrity testimonials do increase communications recall. Through extensive work, researchers have concluded that endorsement by celebrities has a positive effect on the overall brand communication and perception. Although no study has proved quantitatively any direct relationship between celebrity endorsement and an increase in sales, corporations worldwide resort to celebrity endorsements to create a positive effect for their brands.[1]

Brands are increasingly turning to Korean celebrities and drama for product placement. Korean pop star Hyuna filmed a music video for the Toyota Corolla. A lipstick made by French fashion group YSL sold out in January 2014 when it was revealed to be worn by Jun Ji-Hyun, South Korea's top actress and *My Love From The Star*'s female lead actor, who became famous after she appeared in the 2001 blockbuster movie *My Sassy Girl*. She has also popularized clothing from Chanel and Prada, as well as local Korean brands Shemiss and Seoul-listed Handsome.[2]

In 2014, a pair of US$625 Jimmy Choo shoes began mysteriously selling out in stores around the world after Jun Ji-Hyun wore them in an episode of *My Love from the Star*.[3] Similarly, SK-II had a reported 50 per cent sales increase in South Korea when P&G switched endorser from Shim Hae-Jin to the famous movie actress Chang Jin-Young in 2004.[4]

The impact of celebrity endorsements on sales revenues continues to be a highly debated and researched area. Although there are tangible short-term impacts, organizations often view celebrity endorsements from medium to long-term perspectives. This strategy involves lending the celebrity's character to the brand, building the brand through celebrity testimonials, enhancing brand equity by associating it with the celebrity's personality, and sometimes, more simplistically, increasing brand visibility through association with the celebrity.

The concept of celebrity endorsements and their effect on brand building is derived from seminal research conducted in psychology and sociology. The basic premise is quite simple. With so many products in the marketplace, it is impossible for any consumer to process all the information and evaluate its credibility. Hence, consumers seek to simplify things by depending on cues or easy rules of thumb. These cues can be either intrinsic or extrinsic and can be communicated through any medium, but they help customers sift through the massive amount of information to make an informed judgment or develop perceptions about products.

With ever-increasing numbers of advertisements and newer ways of communications, even these cues have become abundant. Thus, a brand endorsed by a celebrity seems to establish a connection with customers, as many relate to or aspire to emulate their personalities. A strong brand will not only provide basic functional benefits, but also an identity, a personality to relate to and express beliefs and attitudes. At another level, celebrity endorsement also helps the brand achieve wider awareness and better recall. Having said that, to maximize return on brand endorsement, companies must strive for a good match between the brand and the endorser.

One of the classic examples of a successful and effective celebrity endorsement is that of Michael Jordan endorsing Nike. Jordan, with his immense popularity, served as a role model for millions of kids around the world who aspired to become basketball stars. Thus, when Michael Jordan went on court wearing Nike shoes, sporting the slogan "Just Do It," it sent a clear signal to his fans and aspiring basketball players about the importance of wearing Nike if they wanted to emulate him. This relationship continues even now, long after Michael has retired from the sport. These sponsorships are proof that a celebrity's longevity and relevance in promoting or endorsing a brand can continue long after he or she has retired from the life or activity.

Another example is India's Amitabh Bachchan, almost a legend in the Bollywood film industry, who at the age of 72 continues to endorse popular Indian brands like Maggi (Nestlé) and Complan (Heinz).[5]

Companies can use celebrities in four different roles, namely as a testimonial, an endorser, an actor, or a spokesperson. In a testimonial, the celebrity endorses the brand based on his or her personal experience with it. As an endorser, the celebrity vouches for the brand by explicitly associating with it. As an actor, the celebrity becomes part of the brand story with an implicit endorsement. As a spokesperson, the celebrity is the official spokesperson for the brand, whereby he or she is explicitly identified with it and is authorized to express the position of the sponsor.[6]

Endorsements

Endorsements can broadly be classified into four categories:

- Endorsements by ordinary people
- Endorsements by experts in their respective fields
- Endorsements by celebrities
- Mixed endorsements.

In deciding the endorsement type based on product type, the focus is usually on how motivated or involved consumers are in processing or searching for information about the product. Although high or low involvement is relative, products can be classified into these two categories. For example, a less expensive consumer goods like shampoo or soap could be categorized as low-involvement, whereas an expensive digital camera, which requires an in-depth purchase evaluation, could be categorized as high-involvement.

In deciding the type of endorsement based on product benefits, these can be separated into functional benefits/values or social benefits/values.

Functional benefits/values relate to consumers at a cognitive or logical level, where the product's features help consumers to perform a certain function. A simple example would be of a shampoo that cleans hair.

Social benefits/values involve consumers emotionally. Besides providing consumers with a stronger bond toward the product/brand, it also helps them to project an image or strengthen self-esteem. Nowadays, marketers for products like shampoos try very hard to differentiate their value proposition, but they are hardly concerned about cleansing hair (a functional benefit). Whether it is to make hair silkier and smoother or to give more volume, the proposition basically concerns making consumers feel good about their hair; therefore, it is about themselves and improving their self-esteem.

By diligently analyzing product benefits and consumer involvement, companies can better decide on a particular endorsement type. The celebrity benefit involvement model in Figure 5.1 combines these two dimensions and provides useful guidelines for Asian companies in using endorsements as a viable channel for brand communications. This model provides useful guidelines to help companies decide on the nature of endorsements to be employed. Depending on the quadrants in which the products lie, companies can make an informed judgment for their celebrity communication strategy.

Endorsement by Ordinary People

The bottom left quadrant consists of products that provide functional benefits with low involvement. For these products, normal consumers can be used as endorsers. For shampoo and detergent advertisements, it is common to see actual users being interviewed for their opinion and experience of using a particular product. Research shows that using an ordinary consumer as a product endorser for low involvement products has two advantages.[7]

As the endorser belongs to the same community as other consumers, he or she is presumed to possess a similar lifestyle and is therefore in a better position to comment on product suitability for that user community.

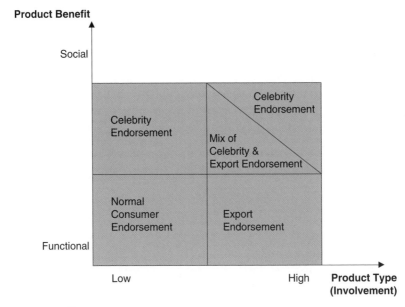

FIGURE 5.1 Celebrity benefit involvement model

Source: Martin Roll company.

Secondly, the endorser is perceived to speak the truth as he or she belongs to the user community and is presumably more believable than other paid endorsers. Despite this, many companies have used celebrity endorsements in low involvement categories to increase awareness levels and persuade customers to buy certain brands over others.

Endorsement by an Expert

The bottom right quadrant represents products that provide functional benefits with high involvement. For such products, expert endorsement would be a fitting match. An expert is someone who is seen to possess expertise related to the product class marketed and is able to give expert advice. Few would argue about the effectiveness of the Indian dental association's endorsement on Oral B's claims. The reason is simple. Customers tend to believe in the knowledge of the dental association. By the same token, a well-known appliance expert can be effective in endorsing refrigeration equipment, as would be a well-respected health practitioner for health-related products. Expert endorsement is more feasible for high-function and high-physical-value products. Such products are likely to be of high involvement, where the diligent consideration of information and evaluation of the product's true merit are essential.[8]

Celebrity Endorsement

The top left quadrant represents products that provide social benefits without high involvement. As social benefits include emotional and self-esteem benefits, having a celebrity endorse these product categories would provide consumers with a strong personality and a persona to emulate. A celebrity can be defined as an individual who is well known by others and for whom most people have well-developed, trait-based impressions.[9]

A celebrity can also be someone publicly known for his or her accomplishments in his or her respective field, be it the movies, sport, music, or politics.

> The Korean cosmetics brand ETUDE used to be perceived as a lower-end brand. Then actress Song Hye-Gyo, who is famous across Asia because of the popular TV series *Endless Love* started to endorse it, and the brand caught great recognition, enabling the company to charge better price premiums.[10]

Sometimes, however, the celebrity endorses a product or product class that has no direct association with his/her accomplishments or achievements. Some of the better known examples are Tiger Woods endorsing Accenture and Tag Heuer, the Bollywood star Amitabh Bachchan endorsing Cadbury chocolates in India, and Yao Ming endorsing McDonald's globally.

Despite this mismatch, companies still continue with such endorsements as these celebrities help to pass on their charisma and personality to the products they endorse.

Since 2010, the trend of hiring celebrities not only as brand endorsers but as creative directors has skyrocketed. Compared to a typical endorsement, the role of creative director seems to provide brands with a more integrated celebrity partnership – not just using their name and face, but ideas too. This role requires much more time commitment from celebrities: Intel's Director of Creative Innovation, Will.i.am from the Black Eyed Peas, was responsible for presenting some of Intel's newest products at the International Consumer Electronics Show in 2012.

However, these partnerships are often criticized, especially when pursued by struggling companies. Many celebrities do not have strong business acumen, yet still cost a lot of money. Alicia Keys' stint as global creative director for BlackBerry lasted only one year before BlackBerry admitted defeat in the consumer device market in 2014 after its failed launch of the BlackBerry 10.[11]

MANDARIN ORIENTAL – AN ICONIC ASIAN LUXURY HOTEL BRAND

Only a few Asian corporations have successfully built and sustained global brands with Asian roots. Mandarin Oriental is one of them – it has built a world-class luxury hotel brand based on its oriental heritage and service reputation.

Mandarin Oriental is one of the leading global luxury hotel groups and operates or has under development 45 luxury hotels in different countries across the globe. With close to 11,000 rooms in 25 countries, it is one of the most iconic and well-managed Asian hospitality brands.

Mandarin Oriental has been running a consistent and long-term global advertising campaign based on top-notch celebrities endorsing the brand. Before any brand signs on a celebrity, they should consider three main aspects, discussed further in Chapter 5: celebrity attractiveness, celebrity credibility, and meaning transfer between the celebrity and brand.

Although these three major principles must be adhered to by any successful brand, it might be difficult to find celebrities that satisfy all three conditions. Depending on brand nature and the kind of product used, companies can selectively emphasize one factor over the other.

Mandarin Oriental has been very successful in carefully selecting and utilizing top-notch celebrities to build and sustain their global brand.

Mandarin Oriental's multi-million dollar global print advertising campaign, launched in 2000, continues to attract "fans" globally. The campaign simply and elegantly connects the Group's well-recognized symbol – the fan – with international celebrities who regularly stay at the hotels and are true fans of the Group.

In 2006, Mary McCartney was appointed as the official photographer of the Group's award-winning international advertising campaign, replacing the late Patrick Lichfield, world-famous photographer and British Royal. McCartney has established a strong reputation for portrait photography and advertising campaigns for international luxury brands.

Each fan is in a location of their choice that, for them, best represents the feeling of wellbeing. In appreciation, Mandarin Oriental makes a donation to each celebrity's individual choice of charity.

Mandarin Oriental recently welcomed two new personalities as fans – the award-winning US actor and director Morgan Freeman and the newest fan actress Lucy Liu, making a total of 28 celebrities endorsing their brand. Other recent additions include Lin Chiling, the Taiwanese model and actress, Italian actress Caterina Murino, Italian opera singer Cecilia Bartoli, and British collage artist Sir Peter Blake.

Mandarin Oriental advertisement with actress Lucy Liu

Source: Courtesy of Mandarin Oriental.

Mandarin Oriental logo

They join Mandarin Oriental's existing fans: Karen Mok, Kevin Spacey, Christian Louboutin, Sophie Marceau, Hélène Grimaud, Sa Ding Ding, IM Pei, Michelle Yeoh, Jane Seymour, Kenzo Takada, Jerry Hall, Vanessa Mae, Vivienne Tam, Barry Humphries, Frederick Forsyth, Darcey Bussell, Bryan Ferry, Liam Neeson, Helen Mirren, Maggie Cheung, Sigourney Weaver, and Sir David Tang.

Mixed Endorsement

The top right quadrant represents products that provide social benefits, with high involvement. High-end products like a premium luxury car, the latest mobile phone, or a high-end consumer electronic item are examples for this quadrant. This category of goods not only involves a lot of customer deliberation with regard to its functionality, technology, and design but also gives immense opportunity for customers to flaunt their personality and convey their beliefs. This product nature necessitates the combination of different types of endorsers. Celebrities are used to bolster customers' self-esteem and image needs, and experts are used to convey the functional credibility of the products. But in certain categories like sports goods, the celebrity sports stars double up as experts as they use the products on a regular basis.

WESTERN CELEBRITIES IN JAPAN

Japan has had a long affair with Hollywood celebrities who have endorsed many Japanese products and services. There seems to be no limit to the fees charged by film stars and other foreign celebrities for work in Japan. However, sports stars are catching up enormously in Japan and attracting more attention as brand endorsers. Football player David Beckham and his wife reportedly earned a fee of US$3.6 million from the cosmetics chain Tokyo Beauty Center on a three-day stopover in Japan – the highest fee ever paid to a foreign celebrity in Japan. According to Forbes, David Beckham earned US$37 million in brand endorsements in 2012, out of his total US$46 million in earnings.[12]

The Japanese tend to idolize Western figures when it comes to improving their image and self-esteem. These Western celebrities have to be A-list, as illustrated by David Beckham. Otherwise, Japanese companies tend to use national figures who customers can easily identify with, rather than Western figures of less than A-list status.

Using celebrity endorsements as a communication strategy has, on many occasions, been effective in influencing consumer attitudes and generating positive purchase behavior for products with high social and emotional values, involving elements such as good taste, self-image, and others' opinions.

Celebrity endorsements have been gaining higher levels of acceptance as an important tool to build brands by creating positive associations and building unique personalities.[13] Effective celebrity branding efforts focus on utilizing celebrity figures that can help to communicate a brand's unique value proposition, strengthen its identity, and provide it with a desirable personality.[14]

Celebrity Endorsers in Asia

Popularity is a key reason to use Asian celebrities. Besides being well known by Asian countries and communities, there is great similarity with the target audience. Generally, customers show a higher level of understanding and trust with familiar and relatable things. Therefore, things like similarity in ethnic background and cultural closeness can be important.

Compared to Western companies, Asian companies have not yet reaped the full benefits of celebrity endorsements. Few cases can match the phenomenal success that Nike achieved and continues to achieve with Michael Jordan. Two main reasons exist for the lack of such successful Asian celebrity endorsement stories. Firstly, the Asian trading mind-set and the way of doing business have prevented businesses from investing in building brands. Brand management as a corporate mantra is still catching up in Asian companies. Secondly, the number of A-list celebrities commanding a wide popularity and fan base is smaller in Asia than in the Western world. This has slowed the adoption of this channel of brand communications in Asia. But, as discussed in Chapter 3, the flow of pop culture across Asia will probably facilitate a generation of future South Korean pop celebrities in Japan.

SOUTH KOREAN POP CULTURE IN JAPAN

There has been a movement in Japan in recent years to look toward Asian celebrity figures. An example is South Korean TV star Bae Yong-Joon, star of the immensely popular South Korean television drama Winter Sonata, who became an A-list celebrity in Japan – much to the surprise of South Koreans. A South Korean celebrity in Japan would have been impossible to imagine a few years ago. When Bae, nicknamed Yonsama, arrived in Tokyo to open an exhibition in April 2005, he was met by 3,500 screaming Japanese female fans at the airport.[15]

Winter Sonata aired in 2002 and was shot primarily at the Nami Island in South Korea. Close to 800 fans turned up every day during the shoot and in 2005, Korean Air saw a passenger level increase of 20–30 percent between Japan and South Korea. The frenzy around the drama contributed an estimated US$1 billion to the South Korean economy.[16] Bae contributed significantly to the burgeoning popularity of South Korean pop culture across Asia, especially in Japan, where he featured in a Sony digital camera campaign in 2004.[17] The then Japanese Prime Minister Junichiro Koizumi even referred to Bae at an international conference on The Future of Asia in June 2004, noting the increased sense of unity in the entire Asian region.[18] Bae is lovingly called Yonsama by his Japanese fans. In 2013, he won a grand prize at a Hallyu awards ceremony hosted by the Japanese media industry.[19]

Celebrity Endorsement Models

For any celebrity endorsement to be effective, it has to full certain basic prerequisites. When a company hires a spokesperson, whether a common consumer, expert, or celebrity, the endorser has to be attractive, have a positive image in society, and be perceived as someone having the necessary knowledge. Based on these three requirements, researchers in this field have developed three main endorsement models. The descriptions of these three models provide companies with a strong basis for formulating and implementing celebrity endorsement strategies.

Source Attractiveness Model

This model states that an attractive endorser will have a positive impact on the endorsement. The endorser should be attractive to the target audience in certain aspects like physique, intellectual skills, athletic capabilities, and lifestyle. Research has proven that an attractive endorser can enhance brand memorability.[20] However, the success of a celebrity campaign depends on the "core capabilities" of the celebrity. If the celebrity is unsuccessful in his or her respective field, the campaign may not be successful, despite the celebrity's attractiveness. But companies need to be diligent in applying this principle in practice. Although the endorser's attractiveness could be a major factor in enhancing brand awareness, this is truer in low involvement product classes. As the product or features themselves are not powerful enough to capture consumers' attention, the attractive celebrities would do that. Moreover, these products do not demand long deliberation on the customer's part. Therefore the external cue of a celebrity can enhance customer perceptions. For higher involvement products, consumers would usually be more concerned about the authentication of the claims presented in the advertisements and endorsements than the endorser's attractiveness.

A case in point is the Cadbury brand in India, which suffered a major setback when worms were found in Cadbury's chocolates.[21] To counter this negative impact on the brand, the company hired Amitabh Bachchan, considered a demigod in India, to advertise the chocolates. The charisma and stature of Bachchan in the Indian mind-set were so powerful that the endorsement not only flipped brand perceptions, but also helped to the company sell more than it had previously. Although chocolate is a medium-involvement category, the attractiveness of Bachchan worked extremely well with the masses. Cadbury was able to turn around the negative perception that had developed for its brand. In addition to being a celebrity endorsement success, it was also a successful PR coup by Cadbury at that critical juncture.

Burberry, the UK fashion retailer, launched a Christmas campaign in December 2014. The campaign caused a stir as it featured 12-year old Romeo Beckham, son of fashion designer Victoria Beckham, and her husband, retired football player David Beckham. Romeo Beckham was reported to have earned US$70,000 for the campaign.[22]

Global demographic shifts mean that the baby boomer generation is becoming older. They have long been influential, driving trends in fashion, retail, and consumerism since the 1960s. They still aspire to look good and do not consider age a barrier. Global brands are beginning to tailor their appeal to older customers, and turn to more mature models. Marc Jacob's beauty line chose Jessica Lange (age 65) as its first celebrity face. L'Oréal has turned to actress Helen Mirren (age 69). Fashion retailer J Crew featured Lauren Hutton.[23] NARS Cosmetics (a Shiseido-owned cosmetics and skin care company founded by François Nars, make-up artist and photographer) chose Charlotte Rampling.

Source Credibility Model

This model emphasizes that the effectiveness of an advertisement's intended message to its target audience is also based on the deliverer's or endorser's level of perceived expertise and trustworthiness. A trustworthy celebrity is perceived to be honest and believable. Often, the credibility factor can be influenced to a great extent by the likeability and ethnic origin of the endorser. This theory helps to explain the special appreciation of Asian celebrities for endorsing Asian brands, as mentioned earlier.

Meaning Transfer Model

This model states that for the endorsement to be effective, a celebrity endorser should also possess a set of traits compatible with those of the brand endorsed. This helps customers to build a positive association toward the product being endorsed.[24]

As a marketing communication tool, the celebrity endorsement enhances this process by using an endorser, who has acquired a set of attributes after years of being in the public eye, to speak for the brand and transfer some of his or her attributes to the brand. These attributes can be status, class, gender, age, personality, or lifestyle. Simultaneously, the celebrity plays the role of a "super consumer" who has been to the place where the target audience is going. By borrowing symbolic meanings from its endorser, the brand can create strong positive images in the minds of its target audience.

As companies fight it out to sign deals with the biggest and most popular movie stars, sports icons, pop singers, and so on, it is evident that celebrity endorsement comes at a huge price. As there are not many Yao Mings or Shah Rukh Khans, it is important that companies are systematic when hiring celebrities for endorsements. Although some celebrities can easily pull off endorsing anything from soap to a luxury car because of their immense popularity, companies must examine the suitability and credibility of celebrities to their company's offerings.

Celebrity Brand Impact Model

Based on the three main endorsement models discussed, the celebrity brand impact model shown in Figure 5.2 is a framework for measuring the awareness and impact levels on the brand from celebrity endorsements.

This model measures the degree of meaning transfer between the brand and the celebrity, and the attractiveness (and credibility) of the celebrity. The result of the framework is evaluated under two parameters: brand awareness and brand impact. Brand awareness refers to customers' knowledge about the brand as a result of many past actions, interactions, and experiences with it. Brand impact is the level of positive spill-over of endorser equity onto the brand being endorsed.

Figure 5.2 provides guidelines for companies to decide on celebrity endorsements.

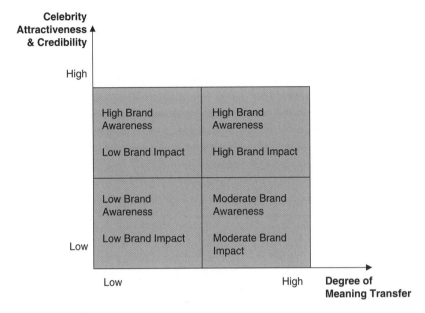

FIGURE 5.2 Celebrity brand impact model

Source: Martin Roll Company.

Challenges in Celebrity Branding

Despite the advantages of using a celebrity for brand endorsements, companies do face certain challenges.

Cost of Celebrity Endorsement

Celebrity endorsements can be extremely expensive. Companies can seek to use their resources judiciously by adopting innovative ways of using celebrities. Timing can also be crucial and signing an emerging star could prove prudent. Roger Federer earns more than US$40 million annually from long-term sponsor deals with Nike, Rolex, and Credit Suisse.[25]

A case in point is Yanjing beer's deal with the Houston Rockets (an NBA team) and its access to Yao Ming. Yanjing beer is China's third biggest beer by sales.[26] The beer is produced in China and distributed in the US exclusive through Harbrew Imports. In 2002, Harbrew Imports signed a US$6 million deal with the Houston Rockets for their endorsement of Yanjing beer for six years. This was before the Houston Rockets selected Yao Ming, who went on to become one of the biggest Asian sports star in the world until retirement.

Risks Involved with Negative Publicity

Brand managers should also be aware of and be prepared to deal with the risks involved in using celebrities for endorsements. Celebrities can deliver a low return on endorsements because of low compatibility with the brand or low levels of meaning transfer. Their image can be tarnished due to unforeseeable negative events. Clear and recent examples of endorsement failures for Nike include Lance Armstrong and Oscar Pistorius. Their symbolic meaning may also be weakened because of overexposure or poor management of images through multiple product endorsements.

Founder's Dilemma

Certain brands bear the name of their founders, and the brand's and founder's identities become entrenched in one other. In such a scenario, the brand could suffer from the demise of the founder or any negative publicity that the founder attracts. One example is the world-famous luxury brand Chanel. The company experienced a long period of inability to revive its brand in the 1970s, because the brand had until then always been hidden behind Coco Chanel, its founder, who passed away in 1971.[27] Today, Chanel is a well-recognized brand, with a lot of vintage value and a strong heritage.

Overexposure of the Celebrity

Studies have shown that the number of endorsements a celebrity engages in and the frequency of celebrity exposure are negatively associated with celebrity credibility. This can extend to the formation of unfavorable brand attitudes and a reduction in purchase intention.[28] In addition, celebrity endorsement is used intensively in today's marketplace, causing overcrowding in the market and increased consumer exposure to such promotional strategies. Celebrity endorsement might lose its advantage if companies are not careful about the relative match between the brand and the celebrity. Marketers will therefore have a tougher job to overcome the increasing skepticism toward celebrity branding in consumers' minds.

YAO MING: THE CHINESE BASKETBALL STAR

Yao Ming, the former three-time NBA all-star and Houston Rockets center, was an unstoppable force wherever he appeared, whether it was on court where he helped improve the Rockets' game rating dramatically, or in the business world where he was a spokesman for global brands like Pepsi, McDonald's, Walt Disney, Apple, Visa, and Coca-Cola.[29]

In 2005, Yao Ming signed an endorsement deal with GARMIN, a GPS (global positioning system) manufacturer in the US.[30] Traditionally, GPS had been used by specialists in yachting, aviation, trekking, and so on, but with Yao Ming maneuvering in the back streets of Houston and Texas, the company wanted to drive home the message that GPS had indeed hit the mainstream and could be used by everybody to make their lives simpler.

The basketball star had a team of professionals to manage the marketing of the Yao brand. Team Yao consisted of a veteran NBA agent, a University of Chicago professor, and Yao's agent, a Chinese entrepreneur who was also Yao's relative among others. Team Yao commissioned eight Chicago business school students to develop a 500-page formal marketing plan. Team Yao screened each endorsement deal to ensure an ideal collaboration between Yao and the brand by carefully following the plan to avoid overexposure of Yao.[31]

Yao's prominence as a brand endorser was driven by his popularity in both Western and Asian societies. Although there have been other Chinese basketball players drafted into the NBA, no others have been voted a three-time NBA all-star.

Although he started slowly, Yao surprised people with his performance on the court. Yao's international success served as a role model for his fellow Chinese and generated a lot of pride. He symbolized a new generation of Chinese who are capable of competing in one of the toughest sports, which requires big, tall, powerful men – not the typical image of Asian males.[32]

In 2011, Yao had to retire from professional basketball due to a series of foot and ankle injuries. He still remains one of China's most widely respected and best-known athletes.[33]

Celebrities in India

According to estimates, Bollywood sold 3.6 billion tickets compared to Hollywood's 2.6 billion.[34] This fact gives enormous power to the big and mighty Bollywood stars as they chart new territories beyond Indian soil. Amitabh Bachchan, a demigod in India, and Shah Rukh Khan (or King Khan as he is fondly called) are the new power centers. The new sought-after female actresses who have become huge celebrities include Katrina Kaif, Priyanka Chopra, and Deepika Padukone. They have tremendous public power and influence. With a strong list of achievements in their respective fields, these personalities are companies' new weapons in branding and marketing their offerings.

Moreover, these Bollywood personalities have such a huge fan base that it has become the norm for them to endorse a wide portfolio of products and brands. The spectrum spans fast moving consumer goods, consumer electronics, cars, cosmetics, and leisure destinations.

Another category of celebrities in India is cricket players, especially those who play for Team India. Cricket can be considered a religion that unites the diverse landscape of India. Its popularity is so enormous that literally the entire country shuts down when India plays against its neighbor Pakistan – such is the power of cricket in the Indian mind-set. Realizing this power and the loyalty that cricketers command, companies have used them as spokespersons for their companies' offerings since the early 1970s. Even here, the portfolio of products that cricketers endorse is very wide and often the endorsers have nothing to do with the products they endorse. But given the tremendous awareness and recall that these endorsers generate, companies appear to be willing to play along.

The huge population in India and the Indian diaspora in almost every other country in the world also enhances the reach and power of these Indian celebrities. Indian movies typically depict extended families that are attached to their roots and an Indian youth who is struggling to find the right balance between traditional values and the allure of westernization, themes which cut across many developing countries.

Conclusion

This chapter has discussed celebrity endorsements as an effective possible channel of communication and branding for Asian companies. The frameworks presented serve as useful guidelines for companies in making crucial decisions about celebrity endorsement strategies. The following box presents a brief 10-step framework.

10 STEPS TO SUCCESSFUL CELEBRITY ENDORSEMENTS

1. **Consistency and long-term commitment:** As with branding, companies should try to maintain consistency between the endorser and the brand, to establish a strong personality and identity. More importantly, companies should view celebrity endorsements as long-term strategic decisions rather than short-term tactical decisions that may be changed on a frequent basis.

2. **Three prerequisites to selecting celebrities:** Before signing on celebrities to endorse their brands, companies need to ensure that they meet three basic prerequisites, namely endorser attractiveness, positivity of image in society, and perception of having necessary knowledge (although it might be difficult for a celebrity to meet all three prerequisites).

3. **Celebrity–brand match:** In line with the earlier model, companies should ensure a match between the brand and the endorser so that endorsements are able to strongly influence the consumers' thought processes and create a positive brand perception. They should enhance consumers' perception about their lifestyle and elevate them emotionally.

4. **Constant monitoring:** Companies should monitor the behavior, conduct, and public image of the endorser continuously to minimize any potential negative publicity. One of the most effective ways to do this is to ensure that celebrity endorsement contracts are effectively drafted to keep in mind any such negative events. These contracts should guide companies and celebrities alike about their overall conduct in relation to the brand.

5. **Selecting unique endorsers:** Companies should try to bring on board celebrities who do not endorse competitors' products or other different products, so that there is a clear transfer of personality and identity between the endorser and the brand.

6. **Timing:** As celebrities command a high price tag, companies should be on the constant lookout for emerging celebrities who show some promise and potential and sign them on in their formative years if possible to ensure a win–win situation.

7. **Brand over endorser:** When celebrities are used to endorse brands, one obvious outcome may be the potential overshadowing of the brand by the celebrity. Companies should ensure that this does not happen by formulating advertising collaterals and other communications. Moreover, the brand scope and policy should dictate the kind of celebrity to be hired and vice versa.

8. **Celebrity endorsement is just a channel:** Companies must realize that having a celebrity endorsing a brand is not a goal in itself; rather it is one part of the communication mix that falls under the broader category of sponsorship marketing. Therefore companies should back up celebrity endorsements with several communications activities to obtain greater effect for the brand.

9. **Celebrity ROI:** Even though it is challenging to measure the effects of celebrity endorsements on companies' brands, companies should have a system combining quantitative and qualitative measures to measure the overall effect of celebrity endorsements on their brands.

10. **Trademark and legal contracts:** Companies should ensure that they hire the celebrities on proper legal terms so that they do not endorse competitors' products in the same product category, thereby creating confusion in the minds of the consumers. Comprehensive legal contracts must govern all aspects of the endorsement deal in order to avoid any disputes.

Source: Martin Roll Company.

6

Asian Brand Strategy

We are not in the business of selling handbags. We are in the business of selling dreams.
—Robert Polet, former CEO of Gucci Group[1]

Brand building takes time. The successful path can take many avenues depending on product, service, category, market, company heritage and many other factors. At one end of the brand-building spectrum lies the physical product or service with its tangible descriptors, and at the other end lie the intangible descriptors, with associations and perceptions linked to the brand's values and personalities. Where should the boardroom start the process, and what is the right direction?

It is the boardroom's responsibility to facilitate and manage this process, set the direction of the brand(s), and ensure availability of adequate resources.

Aligning the Brand

It is crucial to establish a common brand vocabulary within the corporate management team and the entire organization to ensure a common discussion and communication. Two essential brand vocabularies that organizations must understand are brand identity and brand image:

- **Brand identity:** the company's strategic intention for the brand, its uniqueness, meaning, and values, and how the brand aims to be positioned in the marketplace. It projects how the boardroom wants the brand to be perceived by customers and other stakeholders, and is the strategic charter for the brand, closely linked to overall business strategy. Brand identity is a long-term strategic concept closely linked to the organization's goals and objectives.

- **Brand image:** the picture of the brand in consumers' and stakeholders' minds. It refers to how customers and stakeholders decode all the signals provided by a given product, brand, company, or even country. Brand image is a result of many external factors, including marketing communications. It can be influenced by multiple factors, including targets, markets, communications, marketing objectives, and so on.

The boardroom's primary task is to develop and manage a sustainable brand identity, and ensure a balanced alignment between the brand identity and brand image.

The marketplace is dynamic and changes constantly. The competitive environment and its direction should thus be taken into consideration regularly to ensure that the intentions described in the brand identity are well-suited to readily compete in the marketplace. Companies must ensure that identity, image, and market space serve a common purpose (Figure 6.1).

The brand identity does not change often. However, the way it is communicated might change regularly, within the limits and boundaries described in the brand identity.

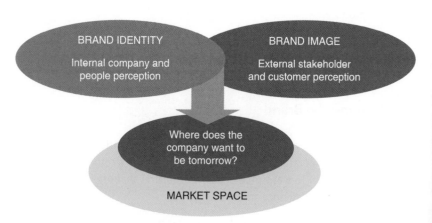

FIGURE 6.1 Brand alignment model

Source: Martin Roll Company.

Brand Management Model

The brand management model describes a six-step model for building, managing, and evaluating strong brands (Figure 6.2). It helps Asian boardrooms focus their processes and efforts in the right direction. In building strong brands, companies need to follow six important tasks:

- **Brand audit** (profound understanding based on data, experience and other insights)
- **Brand identity** (the brand's strategic charter)
- **Brand strategy** (intended direction linked to corporate strategy)
- **Brand implementation** (messages and channels of communication)
- **Brand equity** and **brand valuation** within a brand management-driven boardroom (systematic and organization-wide framework)

Brand Audit

The brand audit is the first essential step in the brand-building process. It is a comprehensive process that involves four major phases: company analysis, customer analysis, competitor analysis, and stakeholder analysis. The purpose of the brand audit is to provide an overall brand analysis from internal and external sources. By carrying out the brand audit, companies can obtain several benefits, as shown in Table 6.1.

The brand audit provides a structured framework and a firm foundation on which companies can define brand identities and strategize future actions. Companies normally have a wealth of data about their customers, distribution channels, and competitors. This information can be collected through desk research and staff or external stakeholder interviews.

Increasingly, brand audits are focusing on the consistent application of a brand's creative and visual elements (shape and size of logo, fonts used in brand name, colors, look and feel of retail outlets, etc.). Global and regional organizations with brands in multiple countries need to ensure that there is a strong level of consistency and uniformity in the visual elements of brand marketing across countries, regardless of difference in languages.

To obtain an unbiased view of the market and brand, companies can utilize external brand research – usually a combination of qualitative and quantitative techniques. Multiple sets of data are collected through in-depth interviews, focus groups, surveys, and questionnaires. Sophisticated statistical tools like conjoint, factor, and regression analysis are then used to analyze and structure

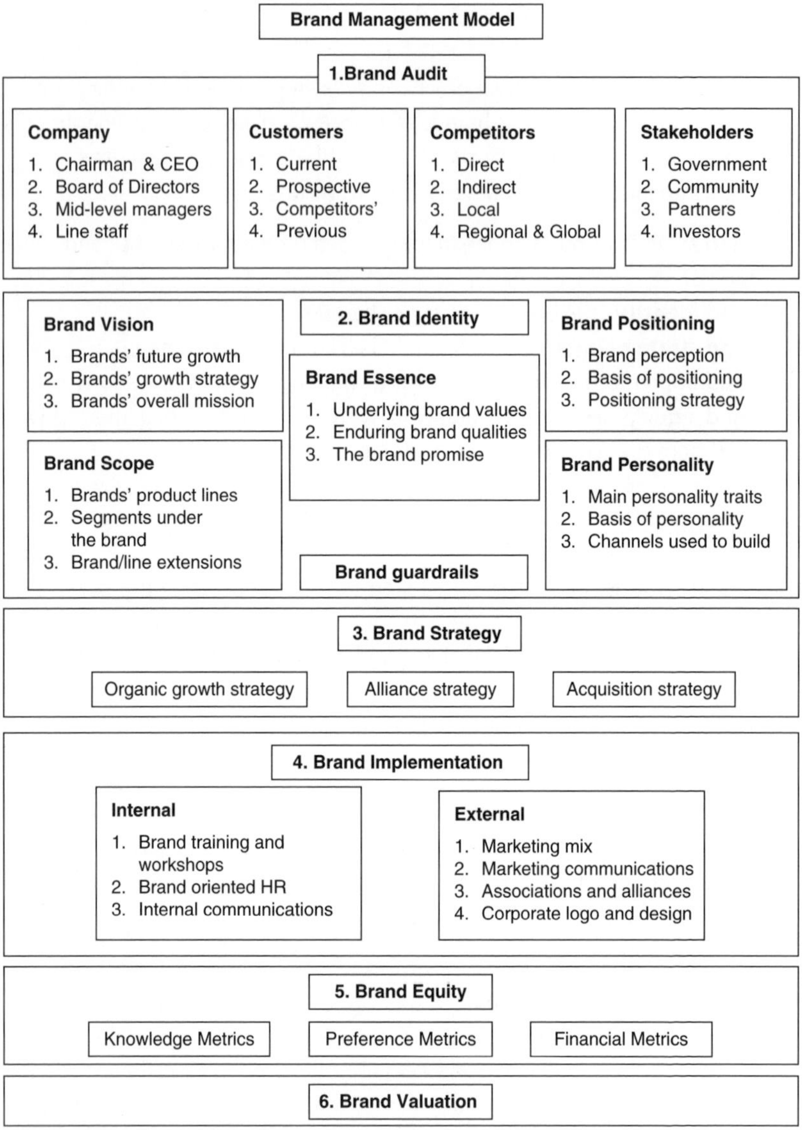

FIGURE 6.2 Brand management model

Source: Martin Roll Company.

TABLE 6.1   Benefits of a brand audit

- Have a better idea about strengths and weaknesses of the current brand portfolio
- Determine their current positioning in the market and formulate the desired positioning
- Evaluate any gap in brand perceptions between internal and external stakeholders
- Determine the relative position of the company in relation to its competitors
- Understand the customers' needs, preferences, and priorities in the specific market
- Build associations and personalities that would be relevant to and desired by the customers' preferences and would strongly resonate with them
- Formulate strategies that will help them outsmart their competitors

Source: Martin Roll Company.

the often-large amount of data to present findings in various user-friendly formats and at various levels of detail. Other commonly used methods are cluster analysis, multidimensional scaling, and correspondence analysis.

Brands can potentially consist of multiple, even innumerable, tangible and intangible features and benefits, and complex interdependencies between them. The most successful brands emphasize features, benefits, and emotional aspects, not only because these are important to customers, but also because they differentiate the brand from competitors. These features are called "brand differentiators" and are critical for building brand equity.

Figure 6.3 illustrates how respondents rank various attributes in decreasing order of importance, and how they rank various brands on the same attributes. The top attributes are the brand differentiators respondents feel are most important, followed by the basic attributes. Figure 6.3 illustrates potential gaps in brand performance as gaps between the importance curve and the brands, and also between the brands themselves. These gaps indicate where a brand can focus to improve customer perceptions and increase competitiveness in the operating category.

Figure 6.3 is just one example of how data can be analyzed and presented to assess and benchmark current brand performance. Other multivariate statistical tools can help identify brand differentiators from basic brand attributes, and how to employ them successfully.

Successful branding is more than gut feeling and great creative ideas. Asian companies can benefit from a rigorous and fact-based branding approach. Cost-effective brand building depends on deep insight into customer needs and preferences and other market insights to tailor the brand successfully.

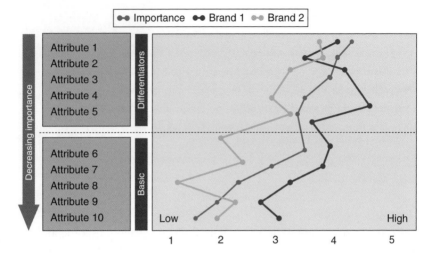

FIGURE 6.3 / Brand performance analysis chart

Recognizing the heterogeneity of Asian cultures, any Asian company with ambitions of high growth and excellent brand building must have a strong understanding of consumer needs and preferences across the multiple markets it operates in or is expanding into.

Brand Identity

The brand identity serves two main purposes. Internally, the identity guides all strategic branding decisions, such as communication, brand/line extension, brand architecture, and association and partnering decisions. Externally, it provides customers with a clear sense of what the brand stands for, its essence, promises, and personality – depending on how well the company expresses and delivers on the promises from the brand identity.

Although many factors influence the creation of a brand identity, the internal processes that create it are as important as the results. The process enables corporate management to discuss and decide the brand's intention and direction. This inevitably leads to discussions about other internal functions and their alignment with branding processes to optimize the delivery of brand promises.

Corporate management should always consider the following six factors when developing brand identity, which will direct actions toward the objective of evoking unique impressions in customers' minds and building competitive advantage:

1. **Brand vision:** an internal document that clearly records the future path and growth for the brand as envisioned by corporate management. It clearly lays down the future direction for the brand and the desired role and status that the brand hopes to achieve in the stated time. It defines the brand's strategic and financial objectives.

2. **Brand scope:** a more specific subset of the brand vision document. This describes in detail the growth opportunities for the brand, in line with the brand vision. Among other information, the brand scope outlines market segments and product categories the brand can enter into.

3. **Brand positioning:** the place that every brand strives to occupy in customers' minds. Positioning is all about brand perception. Companies should decide on the brand positioning based on the targeted market segment, customer dynamics, and competitors' positions in the market. All brands strive to communicate one single idea and occupy a unique position in their customers' minds. Brand positioning enables customers to assess their wants and needs easily, and minimize their risks when selecting the brand.

4. **Brand personality:** the set of human characteristics associated with a brand.[2] Through its own characteristics and features, marketing communications, mental associations, usage patterns, and partnerships, a brand can take on a certain personality, allowing customers to connect emotionally with it. A strong brand personality also helps customers express their own beliefs and attitudes by associating themselves with it.

5. **Brand essence:** the heart and soul of the brand – usually stated in two or three words. It encapsulates what the brand is all about, what it stands for, and what makes it unique. This is an internal tool and never communicated in the external brand-building effort. It serves as an internal anchor in the company and illustrates the meaning and core of the brand.

6. **Brand guardrails:** a simple but clear articulation of what the brand "is" and what it "is not." Strong brand guardrails enable a sharper and more focused brand vision and positioning strategies. An internal tool, they act as a strategic guide for every individual involved in the brand-building process. With ever-changing markets and evolving consumer needs and behaviors, it is important that a brand never loses its strong sense of identity. A comprehensive set of guardrails ensures this.

Brand Strategy

The brand research and identity processes build a strong foundation from which companies can devise suitable strategies for the future growth of their brands.

Before expanding internationally, Asian companies must achieve global standards of competitiveness and distinct capabilities in their core activities. A McKinsey study of global leaders found that their key processes were up to or above global benchmarks before they globalized.

Asian companies are increasingly meeting the pressure of serving the price-sensitive and hard-to-reach consumers, who are more demanding than their peers in developed economies.[3] An example is India's second-largest bank ICICI Bank, which developed the capability to earn profits from small transactions by handling money transfers for a highly-mobile middle class. It later used this capability when expanding internationally. As part of its growth strategy, Uniqlo is offering lower-priced products in outlets outside affluent neighborhoods in China.[4]

Secondly, Asian companies must focus on corporate culture and distinct values in building a strong international brand. Adequate organizational structures and a talent pool of skilled and experienced executives are crucial for expansion into diverse markets. The structure must allow for a certain degree of autonomous decision making to suit specific local tastes and requirements, and yet participate in the overall corporate direction. Employees must be strong brand ambassadors, contributing to overall performance and the local company culture.

According to McKinsey, companies expanding from emerging markets are successful when they first leverage their distinct capabilities and corporate cultures, and subsequently adapt and change where needed.[5]

Asian companies need to resist the temptation to simply imitate the strategies of Western brands. Asian companies have some inherent, unique advantages. Asia is a continent not only of different countries, but of essentially very strong and unique histories, cultures, mind-sets, and practices. Companies need to leverage these and develop strategies to enable them to grow robustly.

Most Asian brands are strong within their countries but not regionally or internationally. These companies can choose between expanding to different Asian countries and then going beyond, or expanding simultaneously to all regions. When deciding on future brand growth strategies, two main challenges confront Asian boardrooms:

- **Management control:** Building a successful brand is about investing resources (financial and organizational) continuously and maintaining brand consistency in both current and future markets. These decisions can easily be made when management has full control over the brand. But when a company operates beyond national boundaries, it can decide to grow its own brand portfolio or ally with or acquire other brands. This alters the level of control that management has over the brand, which can be a great challenge, but is a choice that must be made. This aspect of management control is a crucial factor influencing decisions around formation of joint ventures, majority and minority stake ownerships, franchise decisions, co-branding decisions, and so on.

• **Time-to-market:** With growing competition in every industry and the proliferation of products, services, and brands, the time taken by a company to launch and grow its products and brands becomes extremely crucial for success.

Timing of launch is also important in attaining and retaining first mover advantage for as long as possible in the category. Invariably, imitations will start entering, but if the organization has leveraged the first mover advantage to its best, then it has cushioned itself from future threats.

Figure 6.4 illustrates the possible growth strategies for Asian brands across different markets. The matrix has management control and time-to-market as the main underlying factors. The horizontal axis measures the resource availability of Asian companies (financial and organizational) and the vertical axis looks at

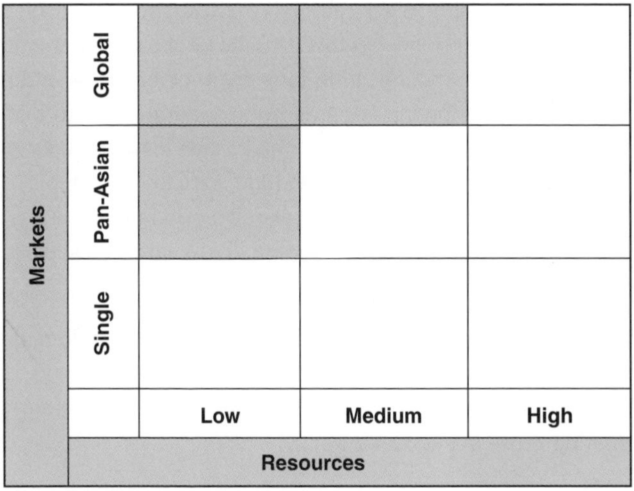

Markets	Low	Medium	High
Global			
Pan-Asian			
Single			
	Low	Medium	High
	Resources		

FIGURE 6.4 Asian brand growth matrix

Source: Martin Roll Company.

the desired market reach. The availability of resources along with management control and time-to-market determines the overall brand strategy.

Challenges in moving along the vertical axis: When companies move beyond their home markets to venture into new territories, it often turns out to be a two-edged sword, with opportunities and challenges. Some obvious challenges include:

Lack of customer knowledge: New entrants must adopt a strong market orientation – usually defined as the organization-wide generation, dissemination, and responsiveness to market intelligence. This not only means the adoption of data analytics and a more prominent role for the CMO and CIO, but sometimes the dissolution of reporting hierarchies so that those at the top can better understand the needs of the organization's front liners.

Global companies entering new markets must leverage the resources of local companies. The combination of the strong brand equity, financial prowess, and business acumen of the global brands with the local networks, established distribution channels, and strong knowledge of local customers of the local companies would offer a winning scenario. Such collaboration would not only facilitate quicker market entry, but also allow the entering company to learn the nuances of the local business market.

Lack of distribution network: Despite Asia's booming growth, distribution is the name of the game. India and China, constituting two of the biggest economies of the emerging block, are very vast countries and distribution holds the key to success in many sectors. Usually local companies would have entrenched distribution networks, with long-term relationships and personal rapport, preventing new foreign entrants from gaining access to distribution networks. Typical strategies to bridge this gap include joint ventures with local players, using an existing player's distribution network to supply products before establishing one's own, or having zero distribution costs all throughout their market presence (having a long-standing tie-up with a local player to use their distribution network).

In many Asian markets, unorganized and traditional retail still dominates, and this is deeper ingrained in local culture than expected. Consumers may also have strong, local preferences for channels, preventing outsiders from successfully penetrating those markets.

International supermarket retail brands have faced these challenges well. Tesco, the largest retailer in the United Kingdom, had to pull out of Japan in 2012 and out of China in 2013 after it struggled to find a profitable position in the tricky Japanese and Chinese markets. The world's largest supermarket brand Wal-Mart pulled out of South Korea in 2006 and sold 16 retail outlets to Shinsegae, a leading department store and hypermarket chain in South Korea owned by Samsung Group. Shinsegae integrated the former Wal-Mart outlets into its highly successful E-Mart supermarket brand catering to local Korean tastes and preferences. French supermarket retailer Carrefour pulled out a few months before Wal-Mart and sold its outlets to local clothing-maker and distribution group Eland.

Increased competition: Expansion into different countries increases competition as the companies would be competing with incumbents. Besides understanding the market and competition, it is critical to understand a country's regulatory and operating environments, which can significantly impact the level of competitiveness of a new entrant.

Challenges in moving along the horizontal axis: When companies decide to extend beyond their national markets, either regionally or globally, it becomes a question of resource availability. Companies either have their own financial resources or seek external funding. Their own resources could be cash assets or strong cash flows used for expansion plans, while companies that choose to raise money externally usually seek public listing or raise money through investors, private equity companies, or funds.

Internal funding and strong resources basically provide better management control. The company can decide with a fair degree of freedom on strategies and objectives, and align their expectations with regard to profitability, growth rates, and time horizons.

In China, government measures intended to cool an overheating economy, such as tightening loans and freezing IPOs, are holding back companies that need capital to grow. Some have turned to overseas exchanges like 58.com (China's Craigslist), which went public on the New York Stock Exchange in 2013; the IPO of Chinese e-commerce giant Alibaba in 2014 was the biggest ever.

External funding can dilute company interests and prove challenging. Success depends on investors' beliefs in intangible assets like branding, and whether they understand its difficulties. Investors also need to understand that it takes resources and time to align the brand promise and its delivery throughout the entire organization. Finally, they need to accept the time horizon required before expecting positive returns from brand investments.

C A P I T A L   A S I A :   B U I L D I N G   A S I A N   B R A N D S   W I T H   G L O B A L   I N S I G H T S   A N D   E X P E R T I S E

L Capital Asia is a private equity group sponsored by the LVMH Group with other investors across two private equity funds. It aims to provide growth equity to private companies and help them build brands. Set up in 2009 to capitalize on the high growth in consumption in Asia, it leverages LVMH's unique experience and resources in Asia and across the globe.[6]

Starting in Singapore with offices in Shanghai, Hong Kong, and India, L Capital Asia focuses on investments in the emerging/fast-growing Asian markets. It specializes in the following sectors: consumer product brands, selective retail and distribution, lifestyle food and beverages, beauty and wellness, boutique hospitality, and media/entertainment.

While LVMH generally focuses on high-end segments, L Capital Asia invests in the layers below luxury, the affordable and aspirational space.

Asian entrepreneurs are generally unwilling to cede control of their business and rarely divest compared to Western businesses. But they are also realizing that expansion into the regional and global markets can be a challenge, so L Capital Asia aims to bridge that gap.[7]

Portfolio companies can benefit from L Capital Asia's expertise by leveraging its global experience in branding and marketing capabilities, and access to distribution channels and partners, including valuable retail locations and reputable franchisee partners, to support the portfolio companies' global expansion. L Capital Asia also helps to improve operations, and shares LVMH's best global practices and know-how to enhance management levels and professionalism in the portfolio companies.

L Capital Asia has invested in 18 companies as of October 2014, including Charles & Keith (Singapore-based shoe, handbags, and accessories brand), FabIndia (natural, craft-based, contemporary, and affordable products from India), Trendy International Group (Chinese fashion conglomerate with brands like Ochirly and Five Plus), Ku Dé Ta (Singapore-based lifestyle, lounge bar, and nightclub) among others.

In October 2014, L Capital Asia invested US$80 million in YG Entertainment, a Korean talent agency and the music label behind famous Korean singers and entertainers including Psy, who went global with the viral spread of the music and video hit "Gangnam Style." L Capital Asia will help YG in its new ventures in fashion and cosmetics. The investment also gives the portfolio companies of L Capital Asia much easier access to Korean stars, who are Asia's major trend-setters.

Greater China will be a big growth area for YG, where the Korean Wave has a huge impact due to Chinese consumers' craze for Korean popular culture and products. An effective way to penetrate China is through Korean celebrity endorsements. Global luxury brands like Chanel, Gucci, and Celine have used product place-ments on Korean TV dramas to broaden their appeal to young Asian consumers.[8]

Charles & Keith retail store at Ion Orchard, Singapore

Source: Courtesy of L Capital Asia.

L Capital Asia company logo

With these opportunities, challenges, and underlying constraints, boardrooms need to decide how to grow their brands, using the following three brand growth strategies:

- Organic growth
- Alliance growth
- Acquisition growth.

Depending on companies' or brands' life-cycle, companies can select one or more strategies in combination to suit their needs.

Organic Growth Strategy

Organic growth is where companies grow their brand portfolios without leveraging another brand's or organization's equity. Companies strive to grow organically by expanding in the same market or other markets with full management control over their brands. As the sole brand owner, the company has much autonomy to decide on its positioning and personality to invest in and continuously manage the brand across all touch points.

The disadvantage of this is that companies potentially might not be able to extend their brand beyond a certain set of product categories and market segments due to high resource requirements. This makes it challenging for companies to launch new brands. In Asia, another challenge is that brands have a very rigid and localized identity and personality, so it is extremely difficult to develop consumer preference and affiliation for brands. This is compounded by diverse Asian cultures with their high degree of heterogeneity. As the outlook of Asian organizations expands regionally or globally, brands need to be ready for successful absorption and adoption in different cultures. This is arguably the most challenging aspect of international brand building strategies.

When South Korean companies first branched out internationally, their early marketing strategies were based on entering other developing countries, which required fewer resources compared to targeting the larger and more developed markets.

Alliance Growth Strategy

Alliance growth is where a company ties up with another in a strategic alliance, whereby both benefit from their combined strengths, with the product or service leveraging both companies' brand names.

A classic example was the motorbike market leader in India, Hero Honda – one of the most successful co-branding activities, made between the local Hero group and Honda of Japan. The Hero group had the local contacts, local market knowledge and distribution networks, and knew how to create the relevant marketing communications with the right feel for the local market. Honda had cutting-edge, Japanese technology and gained access to the extremely lucrative Indian two-wheeler market, leveraging the high brand recognition of Hero in the Indian market. In 2010, this joint venture ended, with the Hero group buying back Honda's stake. Honda now has its own independent fully owned two-wheeler manufacturing and marketing subsidiary in India, called Honda Motorcycle and Scooter India (HMSI).[9]

The alliance growth strategy has inherent advantages and disadvantages. When two companies decide to combine two distinct brands (or a portfolio of brands), both companies enjoy access to new markets, distribution channels, customer segments, and products. However, they face the risk of confused positioning, and ineffective management of the brands' identities. This happens when the two brands stand for two distinct things in the marketplace, catering to two distinct customer groups.

Thus, for a successful alliance strategy, effective brand management practices are crucial. Companies must ensure regular brand tracking procedures assist in maintaining a proper balance in the alliance between the two strong brands, and that customer perceptions support the intentions of the alliance.

More recently, the low cost carrier (LCC) segment of the Asian airline industry has seen a flurry of alliances and joint ventures. Jetstar, the Australian low cost airline owned by Qantas, has a string of partnerships with local investors (either via stakes or outright ownership) in multiple Asian markets. This has resulted in Jetstar's expansion across multiple countries (Jetstar Asia Airways in Singapore, Jetstar Pacific Airlines in Vietnam, Jetstar Japan, and Jetstar Hong Kong).[10]

Without local alliances, some brands are entirely forbidden from entering some markets. For example, the Indian government does not allow 100 per cent foreign direct investment in the retail sector. Starbucks is now operating in India through a joint venture with Tata.

Acquisition Growth Strategy

Acquisition growth is where companies acquire other companies or brands as a means of growth. Many examples of successful and unsuccessful cases of mergers and acquisitions (M&A) exist. As with any business decision, companies need to do a cost-benefit analysis. Retention of key talent, managers, communication, and integration of corporate cultures are four most critical areas for the successful integration of companies engaged in M&A activities.

The acquisition strategy might prove useful for companies that are venturing into new territories outside their home markets. A deep understanding of local practices and market mind-sets would take foreign companies a long time to develop from scratch, thus one of the best ways for companies to leapfrog would be to acquire local firms or their brands. This allows the acquirer to tap into the brand equity of an already established brand, and benefit from its customer base and distribution networks.

An example is Procter & Gamble (P&G) acquiring Gillette Company for a whopping US$57 billion in 2005.[11] Gillette is a powerful branded house (single corporate brand structure) against which P&G is a powerful house of brands (multiple product brand structure). By acquiring Gillette, P&G has obviously gained access into new product lines, market segments and customer profiles – at a high price.

In the global foods industry, Kraft (now called Mondelez SA) bought the biscuits business of Danone for US$7.2 billion in 2007. This gave Kraft control over two of France's biggest biscuit brands, Lu and Prince. Kraft bought the Danone biscuits operations not only in France, but also in 19 other countries, including Belgium, Russia, Poland, and China. By a single acquisition of a specific category, Kraft extended its footprint over a massive geographic area.

There are similar examples in Asia. Wipro Consumer Care and Lighting (WCCL), the FMCG arm of Indian IT behemoth Wipro has been expanding its international presence rapidly via acquisitions. In 2007, it acquired Singapore-based Unza Holdings Limited and launched a range of products from its portfolio in India. Through this acquisition growth strategy, the Indian FMCG manufacturer has extended its footprint to the Southeast Asian growth markets of Malaysia, Indonesia, and Vietnam.[12] In 2013, WCCL acquired Singapore based L D Waxson (S) Pte, which has branded offerings in the skincare market, for US$144 million.

The acquisition strategy will mostly be adopted by companies with strong financial resources. Although at the outset the acquisition strategy seems rosy, it has its own inherent disadvantages, including the issue of integration. This comprises the integration of people, resources, policies, and procedures, and, most importantly, the integration of brands and brand management practices. To reap success, it also requires cost savings and economies of scale.

J O L L I B E E

Tony Tan Caktiong founded Jollibee Foods in the Philippines in 1975 (where he opened two ice cream stores) and it became the largest fast-food chain in the country overtaking McDonald's. Jollibee has more than 750 stores in the country. They also run Chowking (Chinese food) and Greenwich Pizza & Pasta.[13] Jollibee bought the local brand Mang Inasal in 2010 for US$68 million.

Jollibee plans to double its revenues in the next five years, and aims to become a global player.[14] By 2020, the company expects half of its sales to come from overseas operations, up from the current 20 per cent.[15] The company has plans of aggressive expansion in China, by adding another 100 stores to the existing 400 in the country. In China, it owns three brands, Yonghe King in Shanghai, Hongzhuangyuan in Beijing, and San Pin Wang in Guanxi. Jollibee opened its first store in Xiamen in 1998 but had to close it three years later. So instead of building its own brand, the company decided to acquire local popular brands and improve their strengths and operations in the local market.[16]

Jollibee is also actively seeking more acquisitions to expand its brand portfolio. In 2014, Jollibee planned to spend US$2.1 billion on new stores and other expansion plans, more than double compared to 2013.

Jollibee already has outlets in Brunei, Vietnam, Singapore, the Middle East, and the US, and plans to re-enter Indonesia after it withdrew from the country during the 1997–1998 financial crises in Asia. Indonesia is attractive due to its market size of close to 250 million people and a growing middle class.[17] Jollibee needs a local partner in Indonesia to gain a foothold, and with the impending launch of the ASEAN economic community in 2015 allowing for more free movement of labor, it may be easier for the company to bring in experts to advise on local operations. Jollibee may also have to adjust its products to cater to the average Indonesian's spicier taste preference.

American-style fast food chains already enjoy a first mover advantage in Indonesia with global brands like McDonald's and

KFC, together with local brand Es Teler 77, accounting for more than half of Indonesia's fast-food restaurant business.[18] Jollibee will face stiff competition wherever they expand outside their Philippines stronghold, so agility, perseverance, and a long-term view will be the key drivers for long-term success.

Expansion in foreign markets is a fairly slow strategy, requiring time to gain a foothold, effectively learn about operational complexities, and adapt to local consumer needs and preferences. Jollibee entered Vietnam in 1997 and only opened 10 stores during its first five years of operations. Today, there are 48 Jollibee outlets in Vietnam. It also plans to enter Malaysia in the future.

Brand Implementation

The previous two steps of brand research and brand identity will enable the company to establish the brand foundation and its intended direction. The final step in brand building is the brand implementation process – where all the formulated strategies are put into practice in the marketplace. It brings the brand to life and this is where brand associations ultimately start to form in customers' minds.

The brand audit identified the brand differentiators and basic brand attributes on which the brand can be built. These are delivered through many touch points – points of interaction between the company and its internal or external stakeholders. These touch points give the brand multiple avenues to communicate its value proposition to its target audience and make strong impressions if delivered right (Figure 6.5).

It is the sum of all customer experiences through these touch points that ultimately builds strong brand equity. Thus, branding is more than just marketing communications.

Touch points can be defined for each function of the company, for example marketing, sales, HR, finance, and purchase. All these functions interact with stakeholders at some point in time.

As represented in Figure 6.5, touch points are classified into four phases: pre-sales, sales, post-sales, and retention. These phases represent the customer purchase life cycle. Each phase provides a unique occasion for the brand to make an impact. As each phase has different levels of awareness, involvement,

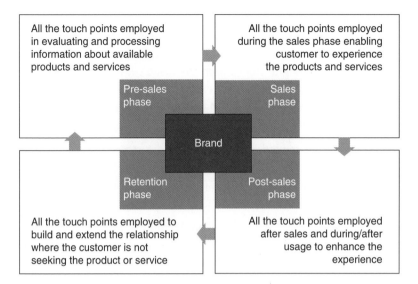

All the touch points employed in evaluating and processing information about available products and services

Pre-sales phase

All the touch points employed during the sales phase enabling customer to experience the products and services

Sales phase

Brand

Retention phase

Post-sales phase

All the touch points employed to build and extend the relationship where the customer is not seeking the product or service

All the touch points employed after sales and during/after usage to enhance the experience

FIGURE 6.5 / Strategic touch point model

Source: Martin Roll Company.

and significance for customers and stakeholders, companies need to choose the right way of delivering the touch point depending on the occasion.

Brand consultant Denise Lee Yohn describes in *What Great Brands Do – The Seven Brand-Building Principles* how business strategy, brand experience, and culture must come together coherently to drive sustained success.[19]

Internal Implementation

The company can implement the following measures to align the organization around the brand:

On-brand recruiting and hiring: HR's leadership role in brand development begins by attracting the right people. Skills can be developed over time but behaviors are hard to change, so interviews must zero in on these abilities. By fiercely protecting their corporate culture, selective brands will attract more of the right candidates, who are proven to improve financial results. Companies with a high percentage of enthusiastic, committed, and engaged employees outperform their competitors in customer satisfaction, productivity, and profitability.

Brand training and workshops: Internal stakeholders, from senior management to frontline staff, must understand and buy into the brand for a successful delivery of the brand's promises. Structured training programs and brand workshops where employees are educated about the company's mission, vision, values, and brand promise can enable this. Employees need to know in detail meaningful stories from the brand's history and legacy, who the target customers are, what they expect, their needs, desires, and, most importantly, how their role contributes to delivering the differentiated, critical customer experiences.

Brand-oriented HR rewards: Contribution to the overall brand growth and profitability is key when defining job profiles and responsibilities, and for all appraisals and performance purposes. This will ensure commitment from the entire organization as performance is linked to financial rewards.

The "carrot-and-stick" system of reward-and-punishment is no longer effective in today's complex organizations. Brands must reward employees beyond monetary compensation. Rewards should increasingly speak to the individual's emotional needs.

Brands may also need to rethink exactly how they define "top performers." Prior to 2011, the bonus pay for pharmaceutical sales professionals of GlaxoSmithKline (GSK) was tied directly to prescriptions sold. GSK now rewards representatives for patient focus, customer understanding, problem solving, and scientific knowledge. With more positive feedback from physicians and financial results to back it up, GSK is now extending these incentives to all 140 countries it serves. You get the behavior you reward.

Internal communications: No matter how perfect a recruitment process is, not everyone will be an ideal brand- or customer-oriented employee. To ensure the success of internal brand alignment, all employees must be informed and updated with the brand, its intention, challenges, and external status and image. The entire organization must be aware of the brand promise, its market positioning, the entire marketing communications package, and the latest strategic and brand updates. By being on the same page as external customers, every employee will be able to act in tandem with the brand identity and contribute to overall success.

External Implementation

Externally, the touch points provide companies with structured plans about multiple avenues where the brand is in contact with customers, and how the brand can make an impact by choosing the right channel and message.

Marketing mix: Externally, all marketing elements should be in line with its overall brand identity. This includes the product quality, price points, and choice of distribution channels, among other elements. Companies must ensure that all these aspects are constantly monitored, adjusted, and optimized for better impact.

Marketing communications: Brand success will depend on how effectively the message is conveyed to customer segments, distribution channels, and many other stakeholders.

The brand positioning, personality, and values will prove futile unless they are communicated through the right media channels, making use of a comprehensive mix of verbal, visual, and audio conduits to make a strong impact. Companies should select from various communications channels available to ensure that brand messages reach customers, despite the high level of competing messages and noise in the marketplace.

INNOVATIVE COMMUNICATIONS

English Premier League football is one of the most watched foreign sports in China – 100–360 million people watch the games on TV. In 2003, the mobile company Keijian, from Shenzhen, aimed to position its brand as healthy, energetic, and upmarket. I decided to sponsor Everton Football Club from the Premier League[20] and was also involved in a player exchange program involving players like Li Tie.[21] It was not new to have Chinese football players in foreign leagues, but it was the first time a Chinese brand had sponsored a club in a foreign league. Everton players had the Keijian name and logo on their shirts, and the company attached football to everything, building up to the Beijing Olympics in 2008. Instead of buying expensive TV advertising, Keijian hired a Chinese journalist in Liverpool to produce football stories for distribution to Chinese TV stations and sports websites.[22] Everton had always been mid-table and with a limited fan base. But overnight, they became the most popular British football team in China.

Associations and alliances: Every entity that a brand interacts with will have an influence on its image. Therefore companies should ensure proper evaluation when selecting partners through associations and alliances. The outcome can be effective leverage of brand equity from partners that five well with the brand, while being cost-effective compared to traditional communication channels.

Corporate logo and design: A brand must have a simple, appealing, exciting, and durable visual aspect. The entire design scheme, including corporate and brand logos, plays an important part. The design and logos must be relevant to the target customer base, reflect the brand's aspirations and effectively convey the brand identity, personality, and values in a clear manner. Strong design schemes and logos serve as important brand identifiers when brand associations and values are attached to them over time, as evidenced by the enduring nature of Nike, Coca-Cola, Mercedes-Benz, and McDonald's.

Brand name: An effective brand name can be a means of communicating what makes you different from competitors and valuable to consumers. Stand-out brand names can even become synonymous with a category itself. Rollerblade, Bubble Wrap, and Band-Aid are now all part of the vernacular. Few brands can ultimately have this kind of success, however. For most brands, the goal must be to simply create a name that is vivid, descriptive, and memorable.

For the successful implementation of brand identity, both internal, and external factors must be carefully monitored and managed. Figure 6.6 is an example of how the touch point model can be developed and implemented in an airline company. It illustrates where and when a given customer interacts with the airline.

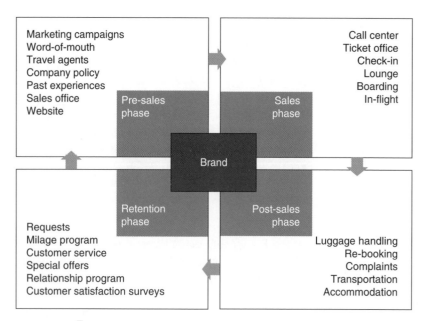

FIGURE 6.6 **Example of a touch point model for an airline company**

Source: Martin Roll Company.

By utilizing different channels to communicate the brand proposition and effectively reach the customers, the airline can use the touch point model to offer optimum and consistent brand experiences across its customer segments and markets.

As the entire interaction cycle between the customer and brand is structured into four different stages, it enables companies to manage a focused and actionable approach. It helps companies optimize their resources by aligning brand promise with brand delivery.

In Asia, organizations have the ability to influence a critical touch point via their marketing and communication strategies. This specific touch point is "word of mouth," which organizations cannot control directly. But through a consistent brand implementation and delivery process and by remaining true to the brand identity, organizations can positively influence this touch point.

Many global organizations have successfully harnessed the power of word of mouth in their marketing strategies in Asia. P&G introduced its Whisper brand of sanitary napkins in India by first introducing them to local communities through training and offering free samples to adolescent girls in schools. After successfully influencing and generating positive word of mouth in these communities, P&G expanded the campaign to reach 2 million girls at 150,000 schools.[23]

GUIDELINE: BRAND NAMING TECHNIQUES

Before considering a verbal identity for a company or product, a brand must first be clear of its promise to customers and its unique points. Brands must begin with the end in mind, working backwards from the selling proposition by asking themselves: What is our purpose? What makes us different? What is the source of our sustainable competitive advantage?

Despite the wide variety of name-types, the common trait is memorability and ability to communicate important brand characteristics. Whatever the technique, the name should be short. If the name is long, consumers will shorten it for you. The less explanation required the better.

Types of brand names in Asia

Visual names conjure an image we associate with certain characteristics:

- Samsung is the Korean Hanja word for "three stars." The character three is meant to signify something numerous or powerful, while stars mean eternity

Expressive names cite the psychological state a consumer will feel:

- Pure Yoga
- Shangri-La Hotels and Resorts describes a utopia
- Aman Resorts uses part of the Urdu and Sanskrit words for "peace"

Promissory names communicate a promise to the consumer:

- NTUC Fairprice
- Forever 21 is a Korean-American fast fashion brand that aims to make everyone feel young

Neologisms are new words created by respelling existing words or by combining words:

- Uniqlo (Japanese fashion brand) is a contraction of "unique" and "clothing"
- Sony was chosen as a mix of the Latin root "sonus" for sound, and the American slang for boy, "Sonny"

Geographical names associate a brand with its origins or a region's characteristics:

- Temasek Holdings is the government of Singapore's investment company a named after an early city on the island of Singapore
- Many banks and airlines are named after their country of origin: Credit Suisse, Deutsche Bank, Singapore Airlines, Emirates Airlines, and BMW

Many brands name themselves in their own language, but foreign language names can also be used to make brands sound exotic, authentic, or superior:

- AmorePacific is a fast-growing Korean cosmetics brand which combines the Italian word for love with reference to its Asian heritage
- Royal Barrel, an Indian-made whisky, uses an English name and branding to associate itself with Scotland

It is vital that a brand name be consistent in its meaning in the language of its target markets. In some cases, this might an entirely new name. In China, for example, the best localized brand names have translations which not only sound similar to their English name, but tell the brand's story as well:

- In China, LinkedIn calls itself Lingying, which translates as "Lead Elite"
- BMW's translation "Bao Ma" means "precious horse"
- Reebok is known as Rui Bu, which means "quick steps"
- Tide detergent is known as Taizi, whose Chinese characters mean "gets rid of dirt"

Truly understanding your brand's purpose and essence will help eliminate some of these options and settle on the right brand name. It is also crucial to check for cultural biases and potential misunderstandings to avoid consumers' negative perception of the brand name. Business history books are full of examples of brands that failed because they had not checked upon the local meaning of the brand name.

Brand names must also create a meaningful digital space through obtaining their domain names, checking the legal implications of brand names in all markets, and ensuring that the brand names can be registered and owned fully as trademarks.

Source: Martin Roll Company.

Brand Equity

There is no universally accepted definition of brand equity. The term means different things for different companies. Many are focused primarily on consumer responses, but can benefit from being attached to the financial performance, and hence reflect the sole purpose of branding – to drive a profitable business and provide shareholder value.

However, there are several common characteristics to the many definitions used today. Professor David A. Aaker defines brand equity as:

> *A set of assets (and liabilities) linked to a brand's name and symbol that adds to (or subtracts from) the value provided by a product or service to a fi s and/or that fi set customers.*[24]

The Marketing Science Institute defines brand equity as:

> *The set of associations and behaviors on the part of the brand's customers, channel members and parent corporation that permits the brand to earn greater volume or greater margins than it could without the brand name and that gives a brand a strong, sustainable and differentiated advantage over competitors.*[25]

There are other definitions of brand equity, but the above two more or less capture its overall essence.

Several stakeholders are concerned with brand equity, such as the firm, the customer, the distribution channels, and the media, as well as other stakeholders like financial markets and analysts, depending on the type of company ownership. However, the customer is ultimately the most critical component in defining brand equity as it is his or her choices that determine the company's success or failure. Customer knowledge about the brand, its perceived differences, and its effects on purchase behavior and decisions lie at the heart of brand equity. The knowledge and associations attached to the brand result in choices, which directly impact the brand's financial performance.

Brand equity is the combined measure of brand strength and consists of three sets of metrics – knowledge, preference, and financial. The brand equity model in Table 6.2 is a useful guide for corporate management to benchmark the objectives and performance of their own brands as well as competitor brands.

TABLE 6.2   Brand equity model

Brand Equity Model		
Knowledge Metrics	**Preference Metrics**	**Financial Metrics**
Brand awareness	• Familiarity	• Market share
• Recognition	• Consideration	• Price premium
• Unaided recall	• Purchase	• Revenue
• Aided recall	• Usage	• Transaction value
• Top of mind recall	• Loyalty	• Lifetime value
Brand associations		• Growth rate
• Functional		
• Emotional		

Source: Martin Roll Company.

Knowledge Metrics

Brand knowledge refers to brand awareness (whether and when the customer knows the brand) and brand image (what associations customers have with the brand). These metrics capture how customers perceive the brand (awareness, feelings, and perceptions). As discussed, a brand would select and use the relevant communication channels and touch points to successfully communicate its brand identity to its customers. The direct result of these activities would be to create brand knowledge.

Brand awareness can be measured through brand recognition and brand recall. Knowing about the brand as a result of many past actions, interactions, and experiences with the brand is referred to as "recognition." Relating and recalling the brand from memory whenever any related dimension is mentioned, such as the product category, usage occasions, and so on, is referred to as "recall."[26]

As basic brand knowledge drives all other customer interactions, customers must be aware of it. But mere awareness is not sufficient to drive brand equity. Customers should be able to relate the brand to product categories, the needs it fulfills, the occasion of use, and so on. This ensures that the brand is in the customer's repertoire. Simply put, recognition without recall is less efficient, and companies must seek high recall for their brands. Recall is usually measured on three levels:

Aided recall: customers recall the brand when prompted with some cues. Customers are aware of the brand but are not readily able to relate it to any specific dimensions (product category, needs, usage). Companies need to effectively communicate the brand message and its value propositions so that it becomes one with its dimensions and customers can recall it without cues.

Unaided recall: customers recall the brand without the help of any cues. Whenever the related dimensions (product category, usage, needs, etc.) are mentioned, customers can relate them to the brand. This reflects a higher level of recall. Companies can achieve this by constantly communicating the brand relevance and delivering the brand promise to keep it in customers' minds.

Top-of-mind recall: the ideal stage of recall that all brands aspire to achieve – the brand is at the top of customers' minds in the respective product categories. Without any cues, they are able to mention the name of the brand as the first choice when the category or other cues are mentioned.

In his book *How Brands Become Icons*,[27] Professor Douglas Holt describes how four different "authors," namely companies, popular culture, customers, and other influencers (like media, opinion makers, etc.) shape opinions about the brand and fill it with meaning. A brand culture is established as the "authors" use, discuss, and monitor the brand as part of their daily lives and as they interact with it at various levels of involvement over time. A brand can therefore be viewed as the *culture* of a product or service, and products and services can become cultural artifacts. Hence brands play a strong role in society and in popular culture.

Brand audit research will help companies identify the brand differentiators and basic brand attributes to obtain a relevant and optimal mix. Successful branding means emphasizing those features, benefits and emotional aspects that are important to customers, while differentiating them from those of competitors.

Functional associations are connections that brands build with customers based on certain tangible and basic attributes that constitute the brand. For example, BMW's functional associations could be German engineering, precision technology, tested quality, and long-term durability. All these are attributes that make up a BMW car. They are tangible and can be measured and evaluated in quantifiable terms.

Functional associations are relatively easy for competitors to copy and they would often be able to claim the same for their own brands. Therefore brands must aspire to create additional associations that appeal to human emotions to ensure a stronger bond with the customer.

Emotional associations are connections that brands establish with customers based on factors appealing to their own mind-sets, beliefs, and personalities. These associations are intangible in nature and relate to factors like status, prestige, aspirations, values, and personality types. In the BMW example, the emotional associations could be prestige and social class, and the status associated with owning a BMW. The brand could fit and support an individual who is in charge of his life. Hence the brand plays an important role for the customer to express his personality, beliefs, and desired status.

Emotional associations are much stronger than functional associations because they tap into the customers' emotions, but they take longer to get established. Brands with strong emotional associations create switching costs for customers by becoming part of their lives and experiences. It is relatively complicated for customers to switch brands as it could mean abandoning shared conventions in their groups and networks.

Emotional associations need to be built up carefully as these are sensitive and have a strong impact on a brand's market success. Also, because they have stronger impact, it is more challenging to have clear emotional differentiators. Brands need to occupy an emotional space that is in sync with the brand identity and develop and enhance that space in the consumer's mind. Success might even involve creating a new set of emotional needs that never existed. Creating a new set of needs is the highest echelon in terms of success of branding strategies.

Knowledge metrics form the initial component of brand equity, with their focus on awareness and the associations created around the brand. They lay the foundation for further interactions with customers and other stakeholders – a strong connecting link between marketing actions and various customer responses.

Preference Metrics

These metrics describe and track customer actions based on the awareness and associations created in the previous phase. Preference is a generic term that refers to the level of liking toward something and it can range from mere liking to a deep loyalty with repeat actions over time. Preference metrics include all those different levels of liking and actual customer behavioral patterns as a result of the awareness and associations that are created:

Familiarity: a level of awareness where customers are more knowledgeable about the brand than, for example, just the brand name itself.

Consideration: customers are interested in purchasing the brand, after acquiring basic brand knowledge and evaluating the brand benefits and attributes against other brands in the same category.

Purchase: the brand is sought and purchased. This may also be referred to as trial.

Usage: customers decide whether to stick with the brand or switch to a different one. This is crucial and depends on the usage experience that customers have.

Loyalty: the ultimate testimonial for any brand seeking to create loyal customers. The loyalty stage is where customers have deep and meaningful relationships with the brand. Measures of loyalty are customer satisfaction and retention.

Preference metrics help a company to assess the brand equity in terms of marketing metrics. Additional metrics could be customer leads and acquisitions to illustrate the pipeline of future revenues.

Figure 6.7 illustrates how preference metrics could be applied to three different brands. The brand funnel shows the value of each of the preference metrics, and also tracks the conversion rate between the various stages. A benchmark

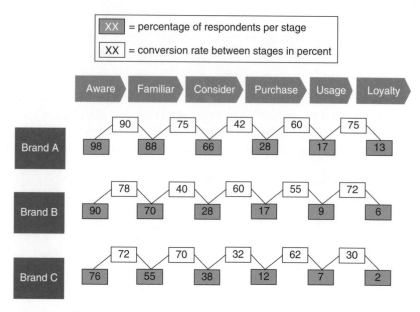

FIGURE 6.7 Brand metrics performance model

Source: Martin Roll Company.

of conversion rates is important as it indicates possible bottlenecks, which need to be addressed with specific marketing actions. It could also highlight stages where certain touch points have to be evaluated for future relevance or emphasized more. For example, brand B has a lower conversion rate from the familiarity stage to the consideration stage compared to the two other brands (40 per cent against 75 and 70 per cent respectively).

The chart can be used for other variables and could include customer segments, distribution channels, and other factors, which can help create a complete picture of the preference metrics and their impact on business. Benchmarking against brands, segments, and distribution channels is important as it reflects dynamics over time and will track the level of progression.

The brand funnel is undergoing an evolution to effectively capture consumers' journeys in a sophisticated world as the concept sometimes fails to capture all the touch points and key buying factors resulting from the explosion of product choices and digital channels, coupled with the emergence of an increasingly discerning, well-informed consumer. A more sophisticated approach is required to help marketers navigate this environment in a less linear fashion. McKinsey has done research in this area and calls this circular approach the consumer decision journey.[28]

Financial Metrics

These metrics measure the financial implications of brand equity linked to marketing metrics:

Market share: quantifies the brand's share of the market and can be divided into customer segments, product segments, and geographical markets. It is an indication of the brand's ability to retain and, more importantly, attract new customers.

Price premium: the financial advantage of a strong brand is its ability to command a price premium in the market. Measuring the differential price points between the brand and competing brands indicates the level of value creation and the premium adds to the overall brand equity. Price elasticity measures can also be included.

Revenue: the average annual revenue per customer divided into segments, product segments, and geographical markets. The trend of this metric illustrates whether the brand extracts more value from customers on an annual basis.

Transaction value: the average transaction value per customer divided into segments, product segments, and geographical markets. The trend of this metric shows how well the brand develops its customers, for example, in the form of cross-selling and/or upselling to other products and brands.

Lifetime value: the average customer lifetime value, divided into segments, product segments, and geographical markets. The trend of this metric illustrates whether the brand extracts more value from customers throughout their entire life cycle with the brand.

Growth rate: the level of brand strength and its equity in the market, along with the level of loyalty among customer segments and the pipeline of prospective customers, determine the brand's growth opportunity. The brand's ability to drive growth adds to its overall equity.

Financial metrics measure the overall value that a company generates from investments in building and managing brands. Companies need to make sure that business drivers and marketing metrics are aligned, to maximize the impact of brand equity on financial outcome.

Based on the detailed analysis of brand equity, it should be quite clear that brand equity is not just about top line growth but also bottom line. Although brand equity gives companies tools with which to measure overall equity, the actual brand value, considered for accounting and M&A purposes, is based on different methods. The final step of the brand management model covers this aspect.

Brand Valuation

Brand valuation is a relatively new development in the practice of brand management. For most of marketing history, marketers were not able to justify fully the financial implications of marketing and branding-related expenses. Until the 1980s, tangible assets like manufacturing plants, land, property, and financial assets were perceived as the main source of business, which could be accounted for in financial terms on the balance sheet. There was a common acceptance that intangible assets like brands generated a large part of shareholder value, but there was no generally accepted method of how to account for these assets on the balance sheet.

During the 1980s, two major factors drove the increasing recognition of the intangible assets valuation. Firstly, the gap between company book values and market value in, for example, stock listings was continuously widening. Secondly, multiple M&As in the 1980s saw a huge increase in the premiums paid for companies, over and above market value. A leading UK food conglomerate was one of the first companies to independently assess its brand value in order to fence off a potential hostile takeover attempt, and in 1989 this early method of valuation was endorsed by the London Stock Exchange by allowing the inclusion of intangible assets in the class tests for shareholder approvals during takeovers.[29] This led to the development of more sophisticated methods during the 1990s and the discipline is still a work in progress among academics and practitioners.

The purpose of these various methodologies, all with different steps, has been to put a financial value on the brand. One method is based on predicting the future earnings derived from the brand and capitalizing the earnings by applying a multiple in the form of a discount rate, hence calculating the net present value (NPV). This approach combines brand equity measures and financial measures, and has become the most widely recognized methodology for brand valuation.

The brand equity measure relates to how brands drive customer demand and also influence long-term loyalty (as discussed earlier in this chapter). The financial measure is the NPV of expected future earnings, a common concept in business and within the financial community. This method includes the following three steps for brand valuation (Figure 6.8).

Financial analysis: identifies and predicts revenues and earnings from intangibles related to individual brands or the entire brand portfolio. The analysis can be further divided into various segments, such as types of customers, distribution channels, markets, and so on, and then calculated into a total

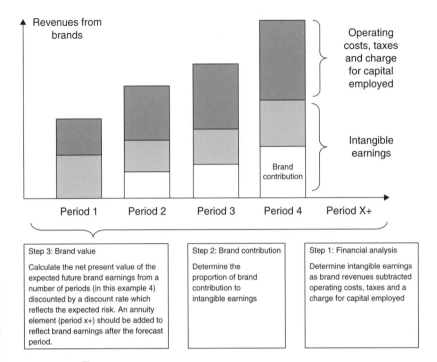

FIGURE 6.8 Illustration of the net present value brand evaluation method

Source: Martin Roll Company.

sum. The intangible earnings are calculated as brand revenues minus operating costs, a charge for the capital employed and taxes. This method is similar to the net economic value added (EVA), which represents the cash flow from an opportunity, adjusted for the cost of resources used to generate the cash flow.[30] Therefore, a capital charge is included in the calculation.

Brand contribution: assesses how much the brand contributes to driving demand, thereby measuring the extent to which the brand contributes to intangible earnings. The brand contribution can be measured in various ways, but the association and preference metrics discussed earlier are the most common factors for determining the proportion of intangible earnings related to the brand. The brand earnings are calculated by multiplying the brand contribution (for example as a percentage or an index factor) by the intangible earnings from the fibut the analysis.

Brand value: calculates the NPV of the expected future brand earnings discounted by a discount rate that best reflects the risk of the future brand earnings. In other words, the discount rate takes into consideration the strength of brand equity and its expected potential to generate future brand earnings.

The brand discount rate is estimated as the current, risk-free rate adjusted for any risk involved in the form of the expected volatility of future brand earnings. In principle, strong brand equity can accelerate and enhance cash flow, and can lead to less volatile and vulnerable cash flows, and vice versa.[31] Brand value is a calculation of the NPV of the expected future brand earnings from the selected periods, discounted by the brand discount rate. As the brand is also expected to generate earnings after these periods, an annuity component should be added to reflect this. The annuity estimates the value of brand earnings after the forecast period.

Conclusion

Over the past decade, brand valuation approaches have been developed by different brand and management consulting firms. Interbrand was one of the first consultancies to develop and refine the principles of the valuation method of discounted brand earnings. It has almost become the industry standard, used by many global corporations and recognized by the US GAAP (Generally Accepted Accounting Principles) and The International Accounting Standards. Appendix A describes in detail the brand valuation method proposed by Interbrand, and Appendix B shows Interbrand's 2014 Best Global Brands.

Recognition by the above standard accounting procedures extends credibility to the various brand valuation methods. Therefore, any boardroom can commission a brand valuation study in the knowledge that accounting companies, auditors, local accounting standards boards, tax offices, and stock exchanges will accept the calculated brand value when it appears in their financial statements.

Despite these developments, all valuation methods, including brand valuation, have an inherent element of subjectivity. Several factors, like the length of the time horizons for future earnings, size of operating costs, how much the brand contributes to intangible earnings, and estimation of brand discount rate, are subject to individual assessments.

Brand valuation can be applied for two major purposes. It provides the company with an internal tool and framework for strategic brand management and determines the financial outcome of the marketing actions, hence helping to assess profit generation. Brand valuation is also applicable for accounting and financial activities, such as M&As, licensing, joint ventures, alliances, collateral for debt, and many others.

chapter 7

Successful Asian Brand Cases

Branding is the Face of a Strong Business Strategy

Brands will become a prominent business driver and a strong source of sustainable competitive advantage and financial value in Asia during the next two decades for the reasons discussed so far. The region is going through an era of renewed growth, development, and prosperity. This has resulted in a new and profound confidence throughout Asia, and resulted in the emergence of millions of middle-class consumers. This rising disposable income will not only buy them basic products but will also enable them to buy brands. This potential consumer power can serve as a strong platform for building and managing brands in the region.

This chapter looks at some of the successful Asian companies which have established themselves as strong brands throughout the region and many of them well beyond Asia. By combining a classic Asian business heritage with unique insights into their industries and strong management, these companies have built successful brands which others can learn from.

The different brands portrayed in this chapter are inspiring examples of how companies from highly diverse beginnings and heritage have created successful brands. It describes their brand journey, their reasons for treading this path, their brand management processes and the major challenges they face in the future.

There are many factors (internal, macroeconomic, market, and industry issues) that determine the success of brand strategies. As discussed previously, successful brands are dependent on the right mindset, beliefs, skill sets, and resources. But the one single issue that stands out amongst all is the commitment and dedication of the boardroom in creating, managing, and nurturing brands as part of driving shareholder value.

Despite the individual character of the boardrooms of the companies portrayed in this chapter, they share one common theme, which is also one of the strongest reasons for their success: their commitment to branding. These boardrooms strongly believe in the importance of branding and brands, the ability to drive value from brand strategies, and the criticality in managing branding processes at the boardroom level led by the CEO and corporate management.

Another common characteristic of the brands depicted in this chapter is their strategy of using branding as one of the key strategic pillars right from their inception. This is in great contrast to the usual Asian bottom-up approach to marketing and branding. The difference in beliefs, style, strategies, and results among the two types of boardrooms clearly suggests that a management-driven approach to branding is a key success factor. Any Asian company that aspires to build strong brands can indeed learn a thing or two from the following case stories.

Singapore Airlines – An Excellent Iconic Asian Brand[1]

Singapore Airlines logo

Think about one of the strongest brands from Asia, and chances are that Singapore Airlines (SIA) and its long-serving, iconic Singapore Girl easily comes to mind. SIA has consistently been one of the most profitable airlines globally, and has the reputation of a trendsetter and industry challenger. There are several good reasons for this. Most relate directly to strong brand management driven primarily by the SIA boardroom and top-management, and healthy brand equity as the result of a dedicated, professional brand strategy throughout a diversified, global organization.

The SIA brand has been instrumental since the start. It serves as one of the leading Asian brand cases for other established and aspiring brands. The SIA brand is unusual in the sense that the boardroom takes dedicated leadership of the brand strategy, unlike many other Asian companies.

Such leadership is reflected in SIA's ranking of 18th in the 2014 list of Fortune's "World's most admired companies," and the only Singapore-based brand and highest-ranked Asian company.

Furthermore, SIA was Asia's first and the world's third airline accredited by IATA with the IOSA (IATA Operations Safety Audit).

The Singapore Airlines Brand Story – Brief Timeline

The maiden flight of Malayan Airways Limited (MAL) took off from Kallang Airport in Singapore to Kuala Lumpur, Ipoh, and Penang on May 1, 1947.

In 1966, the Governments of Malaysia and Singapore acquired a joint majority control of the company and it changed its name from MAL to Malaysia-Singapore Airlines (MSA) in 1967.

In 1968, French couturier Pierre Balmain designed the legendary sarong kebaya – the traditional Malay dress – as uniform for MSA stewardesses.

Differences in operating outlook and priorities between the Malaysian and Singapore governments led to a mutual agreement to set up separate airlines.

In October 1972, MSA split into Malaysian Airline System (MAS) and Singapore Airlines (SIA), and the Singapore Girl icon was created.

SIA was in a different position than most other airlines then. Without domestic routes to serve, it was immediately forced to start competing with international airlines for routes, getting access to airports, securing flight slots and landing rights, and attracting a new customer base. Unlike most state-owned entities, SIA faced heavy competition from the onset and this tough start created a driving spirit to compete and also a dedication to branding, especially in the boardroom.

These factors have prevailed within SIA since, and served the airline very well.

SIA moved into the new Changi Airport, which opened in 1981, and launched KrisWorld, an advanced inflight entertainment system, across all classes in 1995.

SIA was the first airline in the world to fly the Airbus A-380 in 2007, the world's largest airplane, which was bound to take over the Boeing 747 – one of the most legendary aircrafts in modern aviation.

Today, SIA flies to over 250 destinations in 59 countries including services by SIA Cargo, SilkAir (regional airline of SIA launched in 1989), Scoot (low-cost medium to long-haul airline of SIA launched in 2011), and codeshare partners under the global airline partnership and network Star Alliance.

SIA is 56 per cent owned by Singapore state investment firm Temasek Holdings.

Building the Brand

SIA decided on a fully branded product/service differentiation strategy from the beginning. Innovation, best technology, genuine quality, and excellent customer service were to become the major brand drivers.

Throughout their 42-year history, SIA have remained true to their brand attributes. Having pioneered many in-flight experiential and entertainment innovations, SIA was the first to introduce meal choices, free alcoholic and non-alcoholic beverages, free headphones, hot scented towels, personal entertainment systems, and video-on-demand in all cabins. The company keeps driving innovation as an important part of the brand, and the cabin ambience and combined experience are key success factors.

On the technology side, SIA still maintains one of the youngest fleets of aircraft amongst all major air carriers, and keeps to the stringent policy of replacing older aircrafts for newer and fuel-efficient models. Always first in line to take delivery of new aircraft types like Boeing 747 jumbo jets and the Boeing 777, they were the first airline to fly the Airbus Super jumbo A-380 in 2007. In earlier years, the aircrafts have been sub-branded, like 747-Megatop and 777-Jubilee, to further distinguish SIA and its brand.

SIA and British Airways launched the Concorde service between London and Singapore via Bahrain on December 9, 1977. This supersonic service was suspended after six flights due to environmental objections from the Malaysian government, but was restored on January 24, 1979. However, rising costs such as fuel, en route navigation, and landing charges forced SIA and BA to terminate the service with its last flight on November 1, 1980. The aircraft was painted with SIA's colors and logos on one side, and BA's on the other, and it carried crew from both airlines.

Today, passengers board planes via aerobridges. However, in the early days, passengers boarded the planes via a passenger step. Hence, it was a marketing coup that when the passengers boarded the Concorde via the passenger step they could see SIA's colors and logos painted on the aircraft's vertical fin on the port side, and BA's on the starboard. The Concorde carried crew from both airlines.

Singapore Airlines advertisement

Source: Courtesy of Singapore Airlines.

Keeping in line with its strategy to be the pioneer in every aspect, SIA was the first airline globally to fly Airbus A-380 on October 25, 2007 between Singapore and Sydney, Australia. Delayed by almost a year and a half, this first A-380 flight, named flight number SQ380, garnered a tremendous amount of worldwide publicity. It further helped SIA's brand image that all revenue generated by flying 455 passengers on this first flight was donated to three charities in a ceremony the next day in Sydney. SIA later started to fly the A-380 to London, Tokyo, New York, Hong Kong, and other destinations as Airbus delivered new aircraft.

The strategy behind the technology program is clear: Besides enhancing cost efficiency by using the latest aircrafts, SIA uses these events for marketing purposes. The non-stop services to Los Angeles and New York, launched in 2004, attracted huge publicity in global media and kept the innovation promise of the brand alive. The special aircrafts for these long-range routes (Airbus 340-500) were sub-branded – for example, Leadership – to further differentiate the brand promise. Due to rising fuel costs, the direct route to Los Angeles was terminated on October 20, 2013, and the direct route to New York was terminated on November 23, 2013.

SIA recognizes that each innovation has a relatively short life span. Once other airlines adopt it, it is no longer considered "innovative." Therefore, SIA continues to invest heavily in R&D, innovation, and technology as an integrated part of the business strategy to further differentiate itself.

Singapore Airlines' Aircraft Fleet

SIA has 105 aircrafts in its fleet (November 2014). The average age of its aircrafts is seven years and one month, making the fleet one of the world's youngest and most fuel-efficient.

SIA has the following aircraft in its global fleet (as of November 2014):

- 19 Airbus A380-800, and five on order
- 29 Airbus A330-300, and five on order
- 29 Boeing 777-300, and six on order
- 28 Boeing 777-200.

SIA was one of the first customers of the Boeing B-777 during the 1990s and has used the aircraft consistently on most global routes. The aircraft has one of best safety records in the industry, and is a very reliable long-haul workhorse for global airlines.

SIA placed its first orders for two Boeing 747–200s in July 1972 even before the airline commenced operation in October 1972. The two Boeing 747-200s were delivered at the end of September 1973. In 1994, SIA became the world's biggest B747-400 operator when it took delivery of its 23rd of the type. By 2003, SIA operated a record of 51 Boeing 747-400s, comprising 39 passenger variants and 12 freighters. They flew the last flight with the Boeing B-747 on April 6, 2012.

The Singapore Girl

Ms See Biew Wah, SIA check and training stewardess, gets that Balmain touch from the French couturier and Madame Madeleine Kohler

Source: Courtesy of Singapore Airlines.

The personalization of the SIA brand is in the mixed male and female cabin crew, where the flight stewardesses are commonly referred to as the world-renowned Singapore Girls. In 1968 MSA engaged French haute-couture designer Pierre Balmain. He designed a special version of the Malay sarong kebaya as the uniform, which later became one of the most recognized signatures of the airline – a very specific and visual part of the entire brand experience.

When MSA was replaced by MAS and SIA in October 1972, the Singapore national airline retained the sarong kebaya uniform, marking the birth of the Singapore Girl, the gentle hostess.

The Singapore Girl strategy turned out to be a very powerful idea and has become a successful brand icon with an almost mythical status and aura around it. The Singapore Girl encapsulates Asian values and hospitality, and could be described as caring, warm, gentle, elegant, and serene. It is a brilliant personification of SIA's commitment to service and quality excellence. The icon has become so strong that Madame Tussaud's Museum in London started to display the Singapore Girl in 1994 as the first commercial figure ever.

SIA also runs one of the most comprehensive and rigorous recruitment and training programs for cabin and flight crew in the industry to ensure full and consistent delivery of the SIA brand experience. The training program for new crew is 15 weeks long – twice the length of the typical programs in the industry.

Singapore Airlines' Crew Guide

SIA employs both female and male cabin crew, though the Singapore Girl is probably the most recognized face of the airline. There are four operating ranks on board any SIA flight: Flight Stewardess, Leading Stewardess, Chief Stewardess and Inflight Supervisor (same rank equivalent for males).

Some senior cabin crew like the Chief Stewardess and the Inflight Supervisors are trainers and mentors from the SIA Academy flying alongside the operating crew. Inflight Supervisors work like any other cabin crew, but they also function as mentors and trainers on board any flight. They ensure that practices and standard operating procedures with regard to service, safety, and governance taught in the academy are implemented consistently.

Their function is also to observe any insights on how service and safety levels and standards can be improved as they watch actions and behavior onboard the flights and feed it back to the operations and training departments. Inflight Supervisors – and any cabin crew – are one of the most important assets for SIA as they constantly seek to innovate and take their brand to the next level.

Communicating the Message

SIA has been as consistent in its communication vehicles as in its brand strategy. The primary message "Singapore Airlines – A Great Way to Fly" has been consistently conveyed in exclusive print media and selected TV commercials of very high production value to underline the quality aspirations of brand since 1972. All communication messages are featured through the iconic Singapore Girl in different themes and settings.

When SIA launched their comfortable SpaceBed seats in business class, they ran a 60-second commercial of a highly emotional and mythical character to underline the brand aspiration and the Singapore Girl, to differentiate itself.

Interestingly, SIA has chosen to focus on one aspect of the experiential brand strategy – in-flight hospitality and warmth featuring the Singapore Girl – rather than communicating entire brand benefits. It is a dangerous trap, which many other brands often fall into, to try to communicate everything at once. This has led to a focused and consistent message for SIA during the last 42 years. This in itself is a great achievement for any brand.

The Singapore Girl has contributed immensely to the success of SIA's brand strategy and its entire positioning around customer and service excellence.

In April 2014, SIA signed a deal with Formula One Group to become the title sponsor of the Singapore F1 race for two years. The Singapore F1 race was named "The 2014 Formula 1 Singapore Airlines Singapore Grand Prix" and it took place September 19–21, 2014 at the Marina Bay street circuit in Singapore. Singapore has hosted F1 races since 2008, and became Asia's first street circuit and the world's first night race.

Using the Brand to Drive Revenues

While other airlines have also pursued high service/quality brand strategies, none has been able to match SIA in consistency, commitment, and true brand permeation in every facet. SIA has been able to maintain their brand advantage by not wavering from their brand strategy. This is particularly difficult to maintain in a highly cyclical industry where competition seems to react daily to changes in performance. This type of commitment takes dedication from the board, CEO, and senior management team, and strong faith in the brand's ability to pull through bad times. The management team and shareholders must maintain a longer term outlook to avoid making short-term, reactionary decisions which dilute the brand.

For example, the pressure on US airlines stemming from low-cost carrier competition has caused a number of the full-service airlines to begin charging for onboard services that used to be free. Historically, business travelers were willing to pay a premium for full-service airlines, essentially because they provided these services. By abandoning their customer service strategy, even on restricted flights, the premium US airlines are diluting their brand in search of short-term profitability. This is creating a circular effect where the premium airlines are losing cost-sensitive customers to low-cost airlines, which causes them to reduce price to retain these customers, which in turn creates more cost pressure, causing them to start reducing the premium services that differentiated them from the low-cost airlines in the first place.

SIA has been able to deliver some of the best results in the industry by avoiding this type of reactionary behavior. The company competes in the low-cost carrier space through their investments in Tigerair and Scoot.

Global airlines are facing increased competition from low-costs carriers and airlines from particularly the Middle East (Emirates Airlines, Etihad Airways, and Qatar Airways), which has put pricing pressure on premium, full-service airlines. SIA has mentioned plans for rolling out premium economy seats during 2015 to boost its attractiveness. Many competitors have already rolled out premium economy seats but SIA has been careful to follow due to potential cannibalization of its full-fare business and first class products, and overall considerations for the implications for the SIA brand. SIA offered premium economy seats on the non-stop flights to Los Angeles and New York between 2004 and 2008, but later converted their entire aircraft to business class configurations. Non-stop flights were terminated in 2013.

Developing Cost Advantages

SIA's brand strategy is, in theory, a relatively high-cost strategy. Each brand benefit requires significant investment, careful management, and detailed implementation programs to live up to the brand promise. SIA has carefully built a financial and fixed cost infrastructure, allowing them to continue investing while challenging the competition on costs.

First, the strong cash position allows SIA to internally fund purchases of new equipment and airplanes, and limit interest costs. SIA is not locked into long-term leases, and can easily accommodate newer, more efficient equipment, which minimizes maintenance costs and avoids aircraft downtime.

Second, SIA maintains the youngest generation of aircrafts, which provides it with some of the lowest fuel costs in the industry. This is very significant since up to 40 per cent of an airline's total costs derive from fuel. Furthermore, SIA carefully hedges up to 60 per cent of their fuel requirements two years in advance to avoid cyclical and often large volatility in fuel prices.

Finally, SIA's financial and cash position has allowed it to weather the short-term dips in the industry better than the competition.

The Brand Delivers Results

SIA has maintained its position as one of the best-known and best-performing Asian brands, and remains one of the few consistent performers in an industry where established brands are struggling to stay alive. SIA has followed a simple management formula to achieve outstanding results:

Revenues: Command a price premium through consistent brand benefits and avoid reactionary pricing behavior in order to condition the customer not to wait for price matching.

Costs: Tight control of costs though ownership of the most cost-efficient air-crafts, hedging against fuel price increases, and agile corporate management.

Profits: Run the business with a long-term outlook. Be consistent. Stay true to the brand.

SIA has also contributed immensely over the years to the branding of Singapore as a nation. Approximately 50 per cent of SIA's passengers are transit passengers who do not immigrate into Singapore, but get an overall perception of a service-oriented, efficient, clean, and caring country – from the brand elements of SIA.

What is Next for Singapore Airlines?

Recent years have seen a dramatic shift in the global airline industry. There have been major shakeouts and loose consolidation amongst premium, full-service players and a wide expansion in the low-cost carrier market – also in the closely regulated Asian airspace. Air travel has become a commodity and most major routes are saturated with fierce competition.

SIA is facing major challenges and the following are the key strategic issues that the airline needs to monitor and constantly address proactively in the coming years.

Rise of the Middle Eastern carriers: New competitors from the Middle East have been rising rapidly over the last decade. Airlines like Emirates, Etihad Airways, and Qatar Airways are changing and disrupting the global aviation landscape with their onslaught of new destinations and capacity – often competing on price for more price-savvy customers. This is putting global full-service airlines under pressure to keep up as the competitive landscape is evolving from new airport hubs in the Middle East.

Fierce competition from low-cost carriers: Low-cost carriers have significantly influenced consumer behavior for cheap price bargains among leisure travelers and increasingly among business travelers. SIA has already jumped ahead by launching their own three carriers for regional and medium- to long-haul routes. SilkAir is a regional, full-service carrier serving the region around Singapore. Tigerair is a low-cost carrier competing directly with other low-cost carriers. Scoot is a medium- to long-haul, low-cost airline launched in 2012. All the airlines feed traffic between them, and they share a large number of connecting passengers with SIA. 60 per cent of SilkAir's passengers come from SIA.

The aim of this strategy is to avoid dilution of the core premium brand, SIA, and ensure all brands are well-positioned for their distinct segments.

Building traffic from new geographies: Singapore has only about 5 million people, and is geographically situated where SIA may not be able to tap traffic that is not originating from or destined for that part of the world. For example, there is huge traffic demand between India and Europe, which prompted SIA to launch a new airline called Vistara together with the Indian business conglomerate Tata, serving traffic from a hub in Delhi in India. The Indian aviation market is tough with high taxes, over-regulation, and insufficient infrastructure, so SIA needs to manage this new venture with care and diligence to succeed.

Keep innovation as a strategic driver: Innovation is key in the global airlines industry, where the race to present the latest in seats, service, inflight entertainment, lounges, and so on provides a constant pressure on all airlines. Customers expect more with quicker updates. SIA focuses on three pillars to compete effectively: products, services and networks, and innovation have always been leading priorities since SIA was launched. For example, the company is launching a premium economy class in 2015, upgrading lounges across global airports, and revamping seats in all cabin classes.

Conclusion

SIA's strongly embedded positioning and commitment has placed it well to compete in the new landscape. The challenge is to stay true to the brand and keep delivering on the fairly high-cost promise of quality, innovation, and service. This requires heavy, ongoing investments and healthy cash-flows, which can only be achieved through a continuous price-premium strategy and satisfactory passenger load factors.

Thus, customers' perception of the price/value equation, their future buying behavior (partly to be influenced by the low-cost carriers), and loyalty are crucial for the future.

In most industries, there are always segments willing to pay for quality brands. Therefore, the question is not whether there are customers in the market, but rather the ability of SIA to constantly nurture the brand promise, keep innovating, and capture the overall brand value in customers' minds.

SIA's strong brand equity is one of its most valuable assets on its cash-rich balance sheet. SIA is a leading business case from Asia that demonstrates the importance of strategic branding, and it should serve as a great inspiration for other Asian boardrooms building and managing their own brands. SIA is among the top companies globally that is truly able to control the brand through every interaction and experience despite intense competition. SIA has become a hugely rewarded innovator and industry leader: A great way to fly.

Aman – The Unbranded Luxury Resort Brand

Aman logo

Aman is an iconic luxury resort brand that emerged from Asia.[2] Widely acclaimed as the best luxury resort brand globally, Aman is known for ultra-premium service and luxury, high profile clientele, and the most exotic locations. True to the meaning of its name – Aman means peace in Sanskrit – Aman has a reputation for providing a divine and peaceful experience by maintaining exclusivity and being totally discreet about its clients, who count among them many famous celebrities. A magazine once referred to Aman as "faultlessly discreet."[3]

Despite not following the trodden path of traditional brand building, Aman has managed to build one of the strongest brands in the hospitality industry worldwide. Creating a perfect blend of resort experience with local history, culture, and heritage, Aman has been able to create a real-world paradise. As with most iconic global brands, Aman was also guided from the start by its visionary founder and chairman, Dutch-Indonesian Adrian Zecha, and his clear-cut business strategy.

The brand equity was built by creating a very strong and distinct personality in line with the organization's philosophy. The management team, led by Adrian Zecha, has ensured a continuous investment in all branding aspects to ensure consistent delivery of Aman's brand promises. The brand has had ongoing ownership challenges, with the management and control shifting hands quite a few times, but Adrian Zecha has always been able to make the brand stick to its core philosophy by working closely with every new owner.

Adrian explains the discrete way of brand building exemplified by Aman in a beautiful way in an interview with Ralph Lauren magazine, in which he mentions: "We followed the example of good restaurants, which only rely on word of mouth. Or to put it another way, when a restaurant advertises, one knows it is usually not wise to eat there."[4]

The ethos of Aman is founded in simple luxury that is afforded by an exceptional location harmoniously blended with a unique environment, resulting in contemporary and finely tuned resorts that offer, with outstretched arms, an enriching, enlightening, and rewarding "lifestyle" experience in which to willingly surrender.

Background

Aman was born out of Adrian Zecha's strong contempt for the corporatization of the hotel and resort industry. The first of the Amanresorts was opened in Phuket, Thailand in December 1987 and was called Amanpuri. Based on its founding philosophy, Amanpuri had fewer than 50 rooms, compared to the more than 400 room norms of the big hotel chains. This was a part of the strategy. By having fewer than 50 rooms in each of its properties, Aman has been consistently able to provide a world-class personalized service to every guest. Aman runs one of the highest yields per room in the entire industry.

The strategy has been so successful that today Aman has its "pieces of paradise" spread across 19 countries – Bhutan, Cambodia, China, France, Greece,

India, Indonesia, Italy, Laos, Montenegro, Morocco, the Philippines, Sri Lanka, Thailand, Turkey, the Turks and Caicos Islands, the United States of America, Vietnam, and most recently Japan.

Right location is the key success factor in the hotel industry, especially for a luxury brand like Aman. Adrian Zecha is known for being a great site locator and has an impeccable nose for future sites. He said Croatia would become the next hot destination in Europe while the Balkan war was still tearing countries apart. Many of the greatest and often hidden locations globally reside with old families who only rarely consider selling their heritage jewels. When they do decide to sell, it is very likely Zecha will get the first call due to his reputation and exclusive network.[5]

The Brand Philosophy

Amankila in Bali, Indonesia
Source: Courtesy of Aman.

Aman has emerged as one of the iconic brands of the global hospitality industry. Apart from a pro-active and supportive top-management, a dedicated alignment of the corporate vision with the branding strategies and programs has contributed to the brand's success. Aman's corporate strategy, and hence its branding strategy, has been built on four main pillars:

- Keeping the resorts non-institutional
- Providing guests with a luxury private home and not a mere hotel
- Offering visitors a holistic holiday experience by combining luxury with the unique heritage and culture of the resort location
- Maintaining a very high level of exclusivity.

Right from the start, Aman has strived to be as far from a typical commercial resort chain as possible. The owners' aversion toward to corporatization of the hotel industry has led to a very unique work culture and atmosphere within Aman. With an objective of providing an excellent personalized service to all guests, staff members are constantly urged to be as innovative and creative in their service as possible to make every interaction with the guests a memorable experience. Most of the managerial and other staff that Aman recruits are people who have had no experience in the hotel industry but possess the right attitude and the ability to conform to the Aman culture. This is very strictly adhered to as Aman believes that people with no experience come without any hang-ups about doing things in a particular way, without any pre-designed mind-sets. This fits in very well with Aman's philosophy of creative and innovative service.

The right attitude was the key point when Adrian Zecha once stumbled upon a great front office desk clerk in a Sydney hotel, whom he subsequently hired to run Amanpuri. The clerk developed later into one of the best performing managers at one of the resorts.[6]

There is no written manual describing Standard Operating Procedures nor are there any set ways of doing things. Managers and staff are asked to run the resorts as if they were their own companies. This unique work culture has enabled Aman to continue to delight its high-paying guests since the inception of the brand.

When Adrian Zecha started Amanpuri with just 40 rooms, it was evident that it was going to target the ultra-premium customer segment of Hollywood stars, pop singers, sports icons, and wealthy business people. Given the limited number of rooms and the very expensive luxury facilities provided, it had to be priced at the very upper end. This justified its target customers.

Another main attribute was the strategy of providing ultra-premium and extremely personalized service to the few guests at each resort. At some properties, Aman maintains a 6-to-1 employee–guest ratio, something rare in the hotel and resort industry.

With such a high commitment to delivering its brand promises, it is not surprising that Aman has maintained a highly loyal customer base that keeps returning to one of the many properties to experience the paradise again. They are also referred to as "Aman Junkies" and would come back year after year and/or try the latest resort regardless of its location.

The next main pillar of the branding strategy has been the holistic holiday experience offered by blending comfort, personalized service, and luxury with the culture and heritage of the local place. One of the main characteristics of any Aman hotel is the historical background and importance of the resort.

Aman offers special guided tours to the areas surrounding the resorts to explore the local traditions and cultures through interactions with the local population. It also takes its guests on unique travel journeys around the resort.

Before the opening of Aman-i-Khàs in India, the French manager spent six months exploring the neighborhood to a radius of some 20 kilometers around the resort on a motorbike. He showed Anil Thadini, the co-founder of Aman and himself a native Indian from the region, an abandoned village from the 12th century that everyone had forgotten about.[7]

The affluent guests at Aman are used to all sorts of daily haute cuisine and most travel extensively on business while staying at hotels and eating at restaurants everywhere. Therefore, Aman provides no fancy food, but instead simple local cuisines prepared with fresh ingredients served by local cooks to maintain the authenticity of the local place – and to the great satisfaction of the guests who finally get a "home-cooked" meal. Most guests do not leave the resorts to eat outside.

The final brand pillar has been the exclusivity of Aman. Given the high profile of Aman's clientele, it could have been very easy for Aman to capitalize on the presence of the celebrities to gain wide scale publicity and media coverage in the global press. But in line with its overall strategy Aman has refrained from doing so. Aman was never meant for the mass public and will never become so. It has been created for people who pay an extensive premium to have an experience of a lifetime. So the company has maintained a strict policy of exclusivity.

The company has put in place a system whereby all employees act as brand ambassadors. It has managed to do this not through any brand manuals, but by being a very responsive and caring employer.

Aman has also invested a lot of time and effort in nurturing the leadership in its organization through regular training programs. In fact each resort manager has become so attached to the resort and wider location that a self-fulfilling culture has been created. Often multiple generations of families from the local area are part of the team at each property. With these measures, the management has been successful in aligning its entire staff with the organization's activities.

By religiously practicing and consistently delivering on all four of its brand promises externally and aligning the commitment of its staff to its brand promises internally, Aman has been able to build an almost iconic brand with a very loyal customer base without resorting to the traditional brand building techniques. Think of the group of "Aman-junkies" as the brand's unpaid global ambassadors, who promote and market the brand in their own exclusive, high profile, and discrete circles. These are the individuals that Aman wants to target, who become its next customers – and what better platform to reach them than through their own friends, families, and relatives?

Although the chain operates with a fair degree of independence, with each resort manager having the freedom to run a resort in his or her own way, there is still a strong sense of conformism and adherence to the brand values of Aman. The founder Adrian Zecha has to be credited with instilling a strong sense of ownership of the brand in each and every Aman employee. This in turn is reflected by the commitment and zeal shown by each employee in running and maintaining the exclusive edge of the Aman brand.

The chain's website contains a quote from Adrian Zecha that captures this unique relationship Aman has with its employees. The quote reads: "I would like to express my admiration for and heartfelt thanks to our staff: our chambermaids, drivers, cooks, cleaners, gardeners and guides. Most have been with us since the beginning. In the end, performing their invaluable small roles, pleasing you, they are the true Aman."

Brand Communications

Aman is probably the world's only resort brand to have achieved this iconic status with absolutely no advertising since its inception. True to its underlying philosophy of exclusivity, Adrian Zecha and his team decided against any form of advertising from the start. The main brand communication that Aman has made use of since its inauguration in 1988 is word-of-mouth. Ninety days before the opening of every Amanresort, the company sends out a press release to its recipient list.

In addition, Aman invites a close circle of top "Aman-junkies" to experience the resort before it opens. This way news about the resort spreads quickly within the target segment of Aman's customers and would also reach very exclusive travel media like Condé Nast Traveler and Andrew Harper's Hideaway Report. The exclusivity in itself draws more customers toward the Aman brand. Having the leading Hollywood stars, pop singers, and sports personalities visit these resorts is a very desirable attribute for the brand in the eyes of prospective customers. Aman has won numerous global awards, including Travel+Leisure 2014 World's Best Awards Top Hotel Brand.

Aman is an example of superior brand building made completely through word-of-mouth and recommendations. Its clientele has always preferred to stay away from the media and the public eye when they stay at any of the Aman properties worldwide. The brand has recognized the sensitivity of this need and has stayed close to it in its development and expansion. The fact that no mainstream media channel is used to promote the brand gives it the discrete image that its clientele needs. Many celebrities and successful businesspeople have stayed at the chain's resorts, including the likes of Bill Gates and Mark Zuckerberg, and both Novak Djokovic and George Clooney got married in 2014 at Amanresorts. The brand has stayed away from benefiting from and gaining any form of celebrity mileage from these stays.

Future Challenges

Company culture as driver: With its iconic status and following from all over the world, and with the cream of society being the die-hard patrons of the brand, nothing seems to be challenging to Aman at the outset. The biggest challenge will be to sustain the unique company culture and commitment to delivering the brand promise without manuals and detailed management practices. With success comes the obvious threat of copycats – different hotel and resort chains starting their own version of Aman in an effort to give a similar paradise experience. Although no other resort chain has yet been mentioned in the same breath as Aman, it will indeed be a threat worth keeping an eye on.

Leadership transition: Leadership succession for the aging founder Adrian Zecha (born 1933) has been probably the most important challenge for the continued success of Aman. Olivier Jolivet was appointed CEO in August 2014 after having worked very closely with Zecha for years. Most "Aman-junkies" shudder at the thought of Adrian Zecha not being at the helm of the luxury chain. Adrian Zecha personifies the brand. The resorts' niche clientele has come to see Zecha as a living legend,[8] with his creative vision being the cornerstone of the Aman brand offering. The upmarket and highly personalized lifestyle strategy personified by Adrian is highly prized by Aman's discerning patrons.

The second challenge is to nurture a solid lineup of capable and passionate managers who are well-equipped to carry on the organization's unique culture and philosophy after the first generation of managers led by Adrian Zecha fades out. A new Executive Management team with veterans of the travel industry was put in place in July 2014.

Turbulent ownership: Despite Zecha's incredible leadership at the helm in terms of keeping the Aman brand a potent force, maintaining and managing exclusivity, while still expanding globally, the company has had a long history of ownership troubles. The latest series of ownership troubles continuing in 2014 is the ugly spat of lawsuits and counter-lawsuits that has continued between a Russian billionaire and an American entrepreneur, who are the newest owners of Aman.[9] This constant challenge in terms of finding and maintaining a stable set of owners has hampered the growth of the chain and has thrust itself into the eyes of the international media and law, a situation which goes completely against the brand's ethos and philosophy of remaining discreet. The chain definitely needs an owner who has a long-term interest and vision for the brand.

Brand innovation: Adrian Zecha's impeccable penchant for hand selecting exotic locations for Aman virtually makes him the inventor of the concept of the luxury hideaway resorts. The heady Aman success "formula" is comprised of unspoilt remote locales, minimalistic architecture, local cuisine, and a super-lative guest experience. This innovative offering has gained much adulation over the years.

Oscar Wilde said that "Imitation is the highest form of flattery." Aman's con-cept of a luxury hideaway resort has been copied by many hoteliers, which include Richard Branson's Necker Island and five-star developments of major hotel brands. Although Aman may have pioneered this ultra-niche luxury hotel segment, the competition is catching up fast. On the other hand, the tastes of Aman's main client group (high net-worth individuals) are fickle and varying. This high-flying customer base continually seeks new experiences that their money can buy and create and latch on to new trends.

Conclusion

With a savvy customer base and heightened global competition, Aman can only maintain its elite status through market-leading brand innovation.

With the turbulent ownership challenges of recent times, focus on brand innovation could easily have taken a secondary place on the management agenda, which may be detrimental to Aman's market positioning and status among their loyal customers.

Aman hired a very experienced CMO in July 2014, who reorganized the marketing department to include a director of marketing, and three managers handling brand, digital, and CRM. The hires will ensure that marketing continues to take center-stage at the luxury brand.

Aman continues to have very strong brand equity, dedication to innovation and passion for quality in all aspects of their operations – driven by a new strong management team. Aman is a true iconic luxury brand with Asian roots, and the legacy of Adrian Zecha seems to continue with velocity toward new horizons.

Shiseido – The Iconic Asian Cosmetics and Skincare Brand[10]

Shiseido company logo

Of the handful of Asian brands that make it to any global brand rankings, it is most likely that some of them originate from Japan. For a long time, Japan has been known for its prowess in technology, production efficiency, and superior quality. So it is quite natural that one of the strongest Asian skincare and cosmetics companies – Shiseido – also comes from Japan. Shiseido has been one of the very few non-technology Japanese brands that has made it big in the Asian and global fashion, beauty, and cosmetic scene. Leveraging its unique Japanese heritage and its positive country-of-origin effects, Shiseido has been able to penetrate markets globally by offering high quality, relevant, and exciting products. Shiseido had earlier realized the importance of offering customers a highly differentiated experience and exciting them constantly through innovative and high-quality products.

There are several reasons for Shiseido's enduring success since its inception over a century ago. But in the recent past, one of the main reasons for its success is its well-managed brand management practices. The commitment from the company's management has seen a continuous investment in brand-building activities.

Introduction

Shiseido was started in 1872 by Arinobu Fukuhara as Japan's first Western-style pharmacy in Ginza, Japan's fashion and cultural hub. Shiseido started out as a pharmaceuticals company when herbal medicine was the order of the day in Japan. But it outgrew its initial business quickly when it formulated the winning concept of blending Eastern wisdom and aesthetics with Western technology and science. This combination became a strong advantage for Shiseido right from its early days. Soon Shiseido diversified from its pharmaceuticals business.

As early as 1888, it launched Japan's first toothpaste, and in 1897 it ventured into the cosmetic business by launching Eudermine, a softening lotion with moisturizing properties. In 1918, Shiseido launched its first perfume, and by 1937 it came out with its first cosmetic line. Since then, Shiseido has transformed into a full-fledged skincare and cosmetics company with a wide product line encompassing specialty cosmetics, skincare, beauty products, and general cosmetics. In the 1930s, Shiseido began its international business, selling cosmetic products in selected Asian markets and by the 1960s invested in overseas affiliates in the US, Taiwan, and Italy to start with. The company continued penetrating foreign markets with specific product lines, and today counts 89 markets for the Shiseido brand and over 120 for its group brands.

Although blending Eastern aesthetics with Western science provided Shiseido with a strong differentiating factor, it had to extend this beyond a mere concept. Shiseido relied on its core philosophy for guidance. The corporate website lists three core values that guide brand-building efforts throughout the portfolio:[11]

- Rich – defined as the pure, holistic experience of beauty with uncompromised detail
- Human science – going beyond chemistry and biology and extending into physical, mental, emotional, and spiritual sensibilities
- Omotenashi – the Shiseido spirit of hospitality that welcomes you with an open mind and cares with an open heart.

From the very beginning Shiseido based its philosophy on five core management principles that were enunciated way back in 1921. They were: quality first, co-existence and co-prosperity, respect for customers, corporate stability, and sincerity. Shiseido also crafted brand identities for all its products and positioned them toward different customer segments.

Shiseido has based its brand-building on five key principles:

- Creativity and innovation in all its product offerings
- Unique blend of Eastern wisdom, aesthetics, and sensitivity with Western fashion values
- Application of clinically tested formulae to create products that would enhance skincare and beauty
- Ability to customize its offerings to its different markets by constantly analyzing market trends
- Strong distribution strategy.

Shiseido has been one of the first Asian brands to adopt the acquisition strategy to grow beyond its home market. Acquiring rival firms in global markets has served two purposes. First, it gained market entry, and second, it helped Shiseido gain customer acceptance.

Japan's annual beauty and personal care market is still largest in Asia at about US$50 billion, second globally only to the US (US$70 billion), according to Euromonitor International. But China's 150 million-strong middle class is closing the gap fast.[12] Global markets outside Japan provide slightly more than 50 per cent of Shiseido's overall sales.

Cosmetics and fashion companies are realizing that the senior segment is becoming a significant potential market. In Japan, where this shift is profound, retailers are altering retail stores to mirror this change. Aeon, Asia's biggest retailer, is widening aisles in malls, installing more seating facilities, and adopting a more upmarket feel. In 2015, Shiseido will launch a range specially designed for seniors.[13]

Its regional growth plans in Asia are also ambitious. In 2014, it expanded its Indonesian operations by forming a joint venture with PT Sinar Mas Tunggal, to form the new PT Shiseido Cosmetics Indonesia.[14] In 2013, it focused its attention toward the massive potential of the hugely lucrative Indian market by targeting the "masstige" segment – characterized by beauty and cosmetic brands that are priced lower than prestige brands but have an aspirational value for the burgeoning Indian upper middle and middle class with significant disposable incomes.[15]

Brand Philosophy

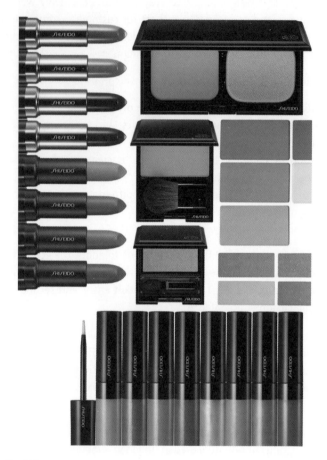

Shiseido lipsticks

Source: Courtesy of Shiseido.

Right from its inception, Shiseido has managed to build its image as an innovator and a market leader. When it ventured into the cosmetics business from its core pharmaceutical business, it leveraged this very perception to the fullest. As the first cosmetic manufacturer in Japan to create fragrances and cosmetics made out of natural flowers to maintain its uniqueness, Shiseido earned a high level of acceptance in its domestic market as the heritage of the brand was well known.

Shiseido started its international expansion as early as 1931. Following this, it expanded into several new markets like Hawaii (1952), Taiwan (1957),

Italy (1963), US (1965), Singapore (1970), France and Germany (1980), and China (1981).

The company faced many challenges when it decided to venture out of Japan in the early 1950s, when brands like Sony and Canon were still establishing their brand names globally. Moreover, Japan was more known for its production efficiency, technological prowess, and high-quality electronics, than for cosmetics and beauty products. This made it quite an uphill task for Shiseido to establish its reputation and quality perceptions. The fashion, beauty, and cosmetics business was dominated by brands from Europe and the US. Shiseido therefore had a dual challenge of breaking into the global cosmetic industry and gaining consumer acceptance while building a strong brand.

From the beginning of their expansion, Shiseido took the innovation route. The same strategy was extended when Shiseido entered the cosmetics business. One of the strongest advantages for Shiseido was that it was an Asian brand venturing into Western markets. It used the mystique and aura of a distant land with its Eastern tradition, color, smells, and aesthetics as an advantage. Its first product for the global market was named Zen, and was launched in 1964. Shiseido packaged it using traditional lacquer designs from 16th-century motifs of Kyoto temples. Besides a distinct appearance, it also created an aura of mystique around it.

In 1997, Shiseido was awarded the US Fifi award, the most authoritative fragrance industry award for a new fragrance, which it had created using aromacology.

Shiseido has always used its research and development to introduce products based on clinically tested formulae. The vision behind Shiseido's R&D has been "Creative Integration" – which called for an integration of function with sensitivity. In line with this, Shiseido introduced many products aimed at enhancing customers' beauty. An example is Shiseido's first anti-aging skincare line called Benefiance, a relaxing fragrance cultivated with new aromacology, introduced in 1982. This initiative has given Shiseido credibility in new markets. By bringing together rational elements backed by scientific proof, and aspirational and emotional elements backed by a strong brand image and personality, Shiseido has been successful in positioning itself in many markets globally.

Another important pillar of Shiseido's brand philosophy is its flexibility in modifying and customizing its offerings. It not only does this in different markets in line with its unique needs and cultures, but also in its brand management practices. One of the reasons for Shiseido's success is that the brand has been able to span markets from the premium segments to the value segment by creating distinct brand identities and personalities for its product lines. When it entered China in 1981, it introduced a sub-brand called Aupres, and positioned it as an elite brand. It was catering only to the top 1 per cent of the market. Later on, when Shiseido decided to target the mass market, Shiseido leveraged the masstige brand extension, Za (pronounced "zee-a"), available throughout Asia.

By tracking customer trends and the associations that they had for certain products with certain places, Shiseido created distinct stories. For example, for makeup products, customers preferred a good and elite image and that was conveyed by creating a brand personality with an American undertone. For skin-care products, customers preferred quality and reliability, which were conveyed by creating a brand personality with a Japanese undertone with the brand Pure & Mild. This flexibility in its brand management model has helped Shiseido to take on different market segments in different markets quite successfully.

Finally, Shiseido has developed a very strong distribution network in Japan, across Asia and in all its major global markets. Shiseido adopted three main channels:

• Department store for luxury products along with personal counseling to customers
• Shiseido licensed store (chain store) selling luxury and middle-level products along with personal counseling to customers
• Convenience and drug stores selling middle to mass market products by launching self-selection cosmetics (no counseling provided).

This strategy has proven very successful for Shiseido as it has been able to market the entire product portfolio through leveraging multiple channels.

Brand Strategy

Shiseido has followed a corporate strategy uncommon for Asian brands expanding beyond the region, by using acquisitions as a main channel to gain foothold in the crucial cosmetics markets of Europe and the US. As cosmetics is an industry primarily driven by aspirations, lifestyle, and images, Shiseido incorporated the acquisition path along with organic and earned growth to gain visibility, acceptance, and access to established customer bases in new markets.

To expand its presence in the French and European markets and gain entry into the professional category, Shiseido acquired the Carita brand and prestigious salon on the Faubourg St. Honoré in Paris in 1981. The salon, with its distinguished and rich clientele of royalty and celebrities, commanded a unique position in the French market. To gain entry into the North American market, Shiseido acquired Unilever's Helen Curtis in 1996. These acquisitions gave Shiseido an opportunity to build on already-strong brands in those markets.

In 2000, Shiseido welcomed NARS to its portfolio, bolstering the color category and adding a top-ten makeup brand to the roster. In 2010, Shiseido bought Bare Escentuals, one of the biggest players globally of mineral makeup, for US$1.7 billion.[16] The acquisition strategy also benefitted the company in that it added knowledge and other soft assets that can be synchronized across brands and regions.

Coming back to markets closer to home, the company's Asia expansion and consolidation strategy is also unique, and in many instances secretive. It lost a sizeable amount of market share in China in 2012 due to anti-Japan protests and was unable to fully recover from that shock. Because anti-Japan sentiments have simmered for a long time, the company has followed a stealth-based approach to recovering lost ground in China. The key elements of this approach include investing in and developing local China-based brands like Aupres and Urara and reducing inventories. The third element of the strategy has been to bump up online presence to increase online sales. This is quite unique because Chinese women understand the value and equity of Shiseido products but dislike being seen buying them from physical stores. So the company has simply provided them with an online channel for buying discretely.[17] Despite this, the battle for regional supremacy is going to be a long and hard one, with global giants like P&G, Estée Lauder, and L'Oréal increasingly making their regional business models very focused toward local needs. P&G is opening an innovation center in Singapore and Estee Lauder has already launched a new brand (with a range of products) specifically for China.

With its diverse brand portfolio, many of which have regional focus, the company has also adopted a strategy of screening and getting out of businesses that are not core focus areas anymore. The sale of the Europe-focused skincare brands Carita and Decléor to L'Oréal in 2014 was driven by the need to concentrate only on core businesses that will drive future growth.

Overall, the company follows the strategy of developing individual brands to gain a foothold and eventually market share in the price tier of the specific segment. Direct and explicit association with the corporate brand, Shiseido, is avoided at all times. The company name is used unchangeably (Shiseido) as the brand for a premium skincare and makeup range only.

Brand Communications

Shiseido made headlines when the company featured Japanese women in ads for shampoo brand Tsubaki accompanied by the slogan "Japanese women are beautiful." Shampoo advertising in Japan had typically featured Western models and Japanese beauty standards had been influenced strongly by the West. But as Japanese women increasingly looked for role models from their own culture and started to gain self-confidence, Shiseido made a communication hit with Tsubaki. Shiseido did not promote the features of the shampoo but promoted the brand in very aspirational and emotional terms. Tsubaki (pronounced tsooh-bah-key) emerged as the number one shampoo in sale rankings compared to the traditional competitors Unilever, P&G, and the Japanese rival Kao.[18]

As the company pursued a global expansion strategy, it realized the importance of having local celebrities as brand ambassadors. This form of marketing is nothing new in the beauty and cosmetics segment. American actress Jennifer Connelly and Chinese model Sui He became global brand ambassadors in 2012. For the first time in its 140-year existence, the company signed American sportswoman and Winter X Games champion Hannah Teter in 2013 as the company's spokesperson for its suncare, skincare, and color range of products in the US.[19] This is an example of celebrity endorsement that associates the brand's offerings with a lifestyle choice that the celebrity feels very strongly about. Hannah Teter had continuously championed the need for skincare and sun care protection among athletes specifically and among women in general. This made her an obvious fit for promoting Shiseido's brands in these segments.

Shiseido has its own internal "Advertising and Design Department," which according to the company has "100 creators," who are involved in creating not only advertisements for the brands, but also product packaging and retail outlet designs.[20] The company also effectively uses advertising, media planning, and PR agencies to plan and implement communication strategies. It has increasingly started to utilize the services of specialist agencies to better engage with the digital and social media world and its immense possibilities for brand building.

Future Challenges

Despite Shiseido's enduring success for more than a century, Shiseido faces a new set of challenges as it travels ahead into new markets with different demographics, increased competition, and multiple segments.

Continue the Asian-Western blend: One of the main challenges for Shiseido going ahead will be to maintain the blend between Eastern wisdom and aesthetics, and Western cosmetics science and technology. It becomes significant as Shiseido has been acquiring brands in the US and Europe with its own heritage and unique brand stories. Given this, it will be a challenge for Shiseido to continue with the blending as that is one of its strongest differentiation factors.

Keep up with the Korean beauty role model: Driven by Asia's appetite for Korean popular culture, including TV drama series and their celebrities, Korea has become a preferred role model for Asians in terms of beauty and grooming. Korean competitors are perceived as having special expertise in innovation of beauty products, and Korean women are beauty role models for many Asians. This is a challenge for Shiseido as Japan has traditionally been a stronghold for trends, popular culture, and beauty.

Consistency in positioning: Predominantly, Shiseido has been positioning itself as a high-end premium and luxury brand in the US and European markets across the entire market spectrum from low-end, value, and middle to luxury segments in Asia. With customers traveling globally, a global media landscape, and the Internet easing information flow across countries, Shiseido should take steps to ensure that it conveys its varied positioning carefully in its different markets. The omnipresent nature of social media leads to a constant information exchange about brands among consumers.

The increasingly mobile nature of the global consumer: It is a very common phenomenon these days for women from Hong Kong to travel to South Korea to buy cosmetics and for Chinese women to buy Shiseido hair care products in Paris. Consumers are aspirational and do not want to be treated with low importance. Shiseido has to avoid a situation of getting into a "positioning mismatch." For example, a Chinese woman who perceives Shiseido to be a value brand, suddenly sees high-end cosmetics from the brand in Paris. In short, her first reaction will be that Shiseido treats Chinese women as "low-value consumers." These positioning challenges can be avoided by being more efficient and prudent about product lines to enter and the brands to launch and acquire. Proactive communication and advertising of what the company sells in Europe and the US are important to generate equity for the company as a global player, but they must be managed and implemented carefully.

Maintaining a strong brand architecture system: Managing the brand architecture can be very challenging for Shiseido. Shiseido has been engaged in three main activities: acquisitions of brands in Europe and the US, importing new non-Shiseido brands into Japan through the brand holding company, and introducing multiple brand extensions in the market. The obvious advantage of a "house of brands" architecture framework and a tiered pricing system is that due to weak relationships between individual brands, one brand's performance doesn't impact the other. This means that even if some of the company's mid-tier brands fail, they will not impact the company's premium image driven by a separate set of brands. But all these advantages also come with their own set of challenges, which is essentially around micro-management of each brand as a separate P&L account.

Given the diverse market segment Shiseido's brand extensions serve, these brand extensions will obviously have their own brand image and personalities. Integrating them with the parent brand and managing their interactions with the parent brand are quite challenging. In some respects, keeping some of the brands and their associated identities separate from the parent brand works to Shiseido's advantage, but eventually, too many brands with a wide performance score range becomes difficult and challenging to manage. There are two ways by which Shiseido can maintain a strong brand portfolio with a consistent and coherent architecture:

- Be more prudent and selective in terms of acquisitions and also in terms of launching new brands in different segments (at different price points)
- Have a regional strategy in terms of brand portfolio management and segments it wants to focus on – this automatically leads to a more manageable and efficient brand management system and will result in moving the focus away from everything.

Developing the corporate brand in the Western world: Even though Shiseido has been quite successful in following the acquisition strategy, it has yet to build a very strong corporate brand in the US and European markets. As it has been acquiring brands with a loyal customer base, modifying the brand identity and personality of the acquired brand to suit the overall Shiseido brand architecture can prove to be quite challenging. Developing a strong corporate brand with a unique identity and personality will be very crucial for Shiseido's long term success.

Become a truly globalized company: If Shiseido aspires to become a truly global company, it needs to appoint more foreign executives and hire diverse talents across the global organization. The challenge is the Japanese culture, which involves strong personal relationships. Top managers at Japanese companies usually have attended the same elite universities and joined the companies after graduation. Therefore, it can be hard for outsiders to become part of the culture.[21] If Shiseido wants to become a global company, it needs to act and look like a global company. This requires a more international management team and corporate culture, which will enable Shiseido to compete effectively across many diverse markets and cultures globally.

Samsung – The Global Asian Brand

Think of any high-end consumer durable like a camera, MP3 player integrated mobile phone, plasma television, or even camcorder, and it is only natural that Samsung comes to mind. Samsung, the South Korean behemoth, was ranked the seventh most valuable global brand in 2014, with a brand value of US$45 billion, by Interbrand, an international brand valuation firm, in its annual ranking of the world's top 100 brands.[22] Samsung has a diversified empire with interests in electronics, heavy industries, financial services, and trading. Envisioning itself as a global leader in most industries, Samsung booked record profits of more than US$22.25 billion in 2012, on revenues of US$187.9 billion.[23]

These achievements are outstanding testimonials to Samsung chairman Lee Kun-Hee's vision of taking Samsung from a manufacturer of cheap versions of Japanese products to a global digital leader. With a business strategy spun around building a top-notch brand, the company invested billions to reposition itself as a respectable brand, with innovation, cutting-edge technology, and world-class design as trademark characteristics. From being on the verge of bankruptcy during the 1997 Asian financial crisis, Samsung has become a truly world-class business empire.

Introduction

Samsung started as Samsung General Stores in 1938 in the Northern Province of Kyungsang in South Korea. Until the early 1970s, it was involved in businesses ranging from commodities, wool, and insurance to fertilizer manufacturing and broadcasting. Samsung was best known for producing cheap copies of Japanese electronic goods.

The current chairman Lee Kun-Hee laid the foundations for today's Samsung when he took over its management in 1993. His declaration of new management principles emphasized intellectual capital, organizational creativity, technological innovation, and employee empowerment. Samsung Electronics is one such key business unit that produces world-class mobile handsets, wide-screen plasma television screens, digital camcorders, and other household appliances. Established in 1969, it generated an operating profit of US$27.2 billion in 2012.[24] This has been the flagship division within the Samsung Group. *Bloomberg Businessweek* ranked Samsung Electronics first in its information technology global ranking in 2002. In 2003, Samsung Electronics was ranked fifth in *Fortune* magazine's Most Admired Electronics Company list.[25] With US$216.7 billion sales revenues in 2013, Samsung Electronics is the world's largest electronics company by revenue.[26] Samsung's success is largely based on its brand management processes. From its early days of repositioning the brand from a cheap manufacturer to a brand of class and quality, Samsung has had a consistent policy of basing all activities in line with its brand strategy. The company has set an example for the whole industry in brand stewardship, with the chairman himself constantly managing and nurturing the brand.

Brand Philosophy

From the beginning, Samsung had to fight hard to change customers' perceptions of it as a manufacturer of cheap electronic goods. Since 1993, Samsung has adopted an aggressive branding and advertising strategy.

Samsung's branding philosophy is built on five main pillars: innovation, cutting-edge technology, world-class designs, recruitment of the world's best talents, and internal branding.

For the previous five decades, Sony was the undisputed brand leader in the consumer electronics industry worldwide before a period of rapid decline, which it is yet to exit. When Samsung began its branding journey, one of its initial goals was to emulate Sony. In a competitive industry, Samsung had to capture customers' attention by inventing innovative products, as Sony did with its Walkman and PlayStation (which launched in 1994). With standardized products and relatively short product life cycles in the consumer electronics industry, Samsung Electronics wanted to put its innovation into building new features, creating new appliance categories and usage. Samsung understood early on that successful and profitable innovation had to be constantly backed by superior technology and the best designs.

Samsung has invested heavily in R&D to churn out new technologies. In Strategy&'s (formerly Booz & Company) 2013 annual study on Research & Development expenditure, Samsung was the second highest spender with US$10.4 billion in R&D spends.[27] In 2013, the company announced an additional R&D spend of US$4.5 billion with five new R&D centers in its home country.[28] The company has more than 40,000 people working in R&D globally, spreading out across 26 R&D centers in 11 countries.[29]

These figures exemplify Samsung's total commitment to developing cutting-edge technology to ensure a competitive advantage (noting that it is competing with Apple in multiple categories). Another commitment to technology was that Samsung had the second highest number of patents (5,043) in 2012 awarded by the United States Patent and Trademark Office (USPTO), a rank consistently maintained since 2006. IBM continues to top the number of patents awarded to it annually in the US.[30]

Samsung increasingly realized the need to be the best in product design. Backed by innovation and cutting-edge technology, the latest, trendiest, and coolest designs have uniquely positioned Samsung in both the market and consumers' minds. With cut-throat competition, the visual treat of Samsung's products has been a marked differentiator from its rivals. Consequently, Samsung started the Innovative Design Lab (IDS), an in-house academy to teach and study design. With Chairman Lee's support, this served as the design laboratory for future Samsung product designs. Samsung also started comprehensive training courses for all its design employees to learn the latest trends in designing, along with courses on ergonomics and mechanical engineering. By looking at the art, culture, and sculpture of many countries, the design lab trained its design engineers to be the best. The IDS concept expanded into Samsung's current global design centers. More recently, after Samsung's significant foray into the mobile electronics space, where it competes directly with Apple, design has received a renewed focus. In a 2013 interview with *Forbes* magazine, Dong-hoon Chang, Head of Design Strategy Team, Corporate Design Center, talked about the philosophy of Design 3.0, which is encapsulated in the slogan "Make it Meaningful." He summarized Design 3.0 as:

> "Design 3.0" is a third-phase design strategy aimed at creating new and meaningful product-service experiential value and lifestyles for users, thereby going beyond exterior style and convenient use.

In short, Samsung's design focus has now moved from a product-focused philosophy to a service-focused one.

The emphasis on and seriousness of design are characterized by the fact that the Corporate Design Center, which manages and coordinates the five Global Design Centers in London, San Francisco, Shanghai, Tokyo, and Delhi, reports directly to the CEO.

For Samsung to lead in either cutting-edge technology or designs, it needed the best talent available. Acknowledging this, Samsung has been a leading recruiter from many top-tier global business schools. This was evident when Hak Soo, former COO and vice president of Samsung once said: "People are Samsung's biggest challenge. We need to hire and train the best global talents because we are a global company, not just a Korean company."[31] Samsung has come a long way from a point when hiring talent used to be a challenge.

By practicing its five-pillared brand strategy, Samsung has been successful in repositioning its brand globally. Samsung products like the Galaxy smartphone series and the Smart and Curved televisions are perceived to be technologically sophisticated and innovative. Though the repositioning strategy has been successful, it shifted focus away from the creation of a distinct identity. The company's biggest competitor now is Apple, whose corporate and product brands enjoy strong emotional connection with its consumers, besides being innovative and technologically advanced.

Samsung's business and operating environment has changed significantly in Asia and globally. The company needs a holistic, structured, and integrated brand philosophy that can successfully link the corporate brand with the product brands in the brand portfolio through efficient brand architecture and brand portfolio strategy. Samsung must emphasize its emotional and intangible brand elements to build strong connections.

Brand Communications

Samsung has used all possible communication channels to convey its brand's positioning and personality. Mass media advertising, public relations, event sponsorship, sports sponsorships, product placements, the Samsung experience gallery, and Samsung experience retail stores have been its major brand communication channels.

The brand communication had two main objectives. Firstly, to reposition Samsung as a premium, world-class brand offering quality, credibility, and design, and, secondly, to be seen and accepted on a par with the likes of Sony and more recently to be the top consumer electronics brand globally. After Sony's decline and Samsung's aggressive entry into the premium smartphones category, Apple is now Samsung's biggest competitor in the high growth categories of smartphones, tablets, and smart wearables.

With these two huge objectives and formidable competitors, Samsung has to use all possible channels to communicate its superior positioning.

Samsung used its technological prowess with its design and innovation to gain industry attention. Products like the world's first wristwatch clamshell rotating camera phone, the largest plasma TV, the largest LCD display, and the color wrist phone, all conveyed Samsung's technological leadership globally. After the company's entry into smartphones, its Galaxy phone series tried to push design boundaries and user experience. They also gave Samsung a lot of media coverage in international business magazines like *Bloomberg Businessweek, The Wall Street Journal, The Financial Times, Forbes, Fortune, and Marketing Week* and technology magazines and websites like CNET.com and others. These, along with numerous awards Samsung won for its design and use of technology to create better products, acted as credible third-party endorsements. Samsung wanted to take advantage of the technological breakthroughs of the 1990s, mainly digital convergence. With its leading technology in the fields of wireless communication, memory chips, and plasma screens, Samsung wanted to position itself as a leader in digital convergence – making products that combined wireless communication with photography, music, and video. This philosophy has guided Samsung in all its communications for the past seven to eight years. The connectivity experience its Galaxy phones provide (in terms of content, apps, and social media sharing), smart remotes in televisions, and wifi, apps, and touchscreen functionality in refrigerators are a continuation of its digital convergence philosophy.

The year 1997 saw Samsung's first global campaign: Challenge the Limits. This aimed to position Samsung as a leading company aspiring to reach heights beyond mere technology. With the same aim, Samsung sponsored events such as the Olympics, winter games, and extreme sports. In contrasting, other global brands like Nike sponsored individual sports personalities. Samsung wanted to convey a team spirit, healthy competition, and global convergence. The next major global campaign was in 1999 when Samsung initiated "DigitAll: Everyone's Invited."[32] Through this campaign, Samsung reiterated its leading position in the digital convergence era. It wanted the world to see it as a company that had the capabilities to provide the best digital products and experiences.[33] In 2013, it launched the "Design Your Life" global campaign, designed to promote connectivity of its Galaxy series of smartphones, tablets, and wearables.[34]

Samsung's first serious, global push to enter the smartphone market and challenge Apple happened in 2009, when the Samsung i7500 was launched as the Samsung Galaxy. This was the beginning of the long series of Galaxy phones, which has recently challenged the Apple iPhone's popularity. For its entire Galaxy range, Samsung has successfully utilized digital and traditional channels in the communication programs. For the 2012 US launch of the Galaxy SIII, it reportedly spent more than US$300 million through using innovative media channels like 3D games in movie theatres, short 3D films, and free content download from kiosks and posters, combined with traditional channels.[35] This has continued in subsequent Galaxy series launches. For the Galaxy S4, it used innovative techniques like crowdsourcing, social media engagement, and content sharing, in combination with TV ads to drive awareness.

These campaigns signify Samsung's desire to remain in the forefront of embracing new channels, media, and platforms for communication and marketing. It has continually embraced and actually created groundbreaking interactive and immersive consumer experiences. It has also not downplayed the importance and the reach provided by traditional media channels, seen by its staggeringly high levels of advertising spends dedicated to TV, print, cinema, and outdoors.

Event Sponsorships

Samsung has used international electronics, games, and technology events to showcase its product range and offer the Samsung experience. Events like the World Cyber Games (until it closed in 2014), CeBIT, Comdex (until it closed in 2004), IFA, and the Consumer Electronics Show allowed Samsung to educate and entertain its core target customers – businesses and consumers. At the Consumer Electronics Show (CES) held in Las Vegas, Nevada in 2014, Samsung unveiled its curved TVs. CES 2014 attracted more than 155,000 visitors over 4 days.[36]

In 2013, Samsung sponsored The Life is Beautiful Festival in Las Vegas, attended by more than 60,000 music fans. In 2014, it reportedly spent more than US$20 million running ads during the breaks in the live telecast of the Academy Awards (the Oscars). Besides getting mileage and exposure, it also generated massive amounts of awareness through the infamous "Oscars selfie," which the host Ellen DeGeneres took with a host of leading Hollywood actors. In addition to TV advertising, Samsung integrated its Galaxy smartphones by giving handsets to American Broadcasting Corporation (ABC) for use during the show, and by running a clip of six aspiring filmmakers using Samsung devices. By acting as the chief sponsor at such events and integrating its products into the event, Samsung has consistently projected and bolstered its brand image.

Sport Sponsorships

To become a global leader in consumer electronics, Samsung had to communicate globally. What better way to achieve this than by sponsoring international sporting events? Samsung has been the chief sponsor of the 1988 Seoul Olympics, the 1990 Beijing Asian Championship, the 2000 Sydney Olympics, the 2002 Salt Lake Winter Games, the 2004 Athens Olympics, and the 2012 London Olympics. In 2014, it announced a strategic extension of its Olympic sponsorship up to 2020, making it a chief Olympic sponsor for the 2016 Rio De Janiero Olympics, the 2018 PyeongChang Winter Olympics, and the 2020 Tokyo Olympics. By setting up a 1,064 square meter entertainment complex within the Olympic sports complex at the Vancouver 2010 Winter Olympic Games, Samsung attracted over 300,000 visitors to showcase its current product portfolio, offer the Samsung experience, and display its futuristic, pipeline products.[37] Samsung's affiliation with international sporting events has added positivity to its personality, with a spirit that challenges world-class competitors on a global level.

Besides associating with global sporting events like the Olympics, Samsung has increasingly sponsored niche and regional sporting events. In 2013, it signed a three-year deal worth US$100 million with the National Basketball Association (NBA) to become its official handset, tablet, and television provider.[38] It is the principal shirt sponsor of football club Chelsea FC in the English Premier League in a deal worth US$16 million annually. In February 2014 it became the title sponsor of the World Surfing Tour, comprising 21 events, with the tour now being called "The 2014 Samsung Galaxy ASP World Championship Tour."[39] In October 2014 in the UK, Samsung signed a three-year deal to become the official Consumer Electronics, Smartphones and Home Technology Partner to the Rugby Football Union (RFU).[40] These sponsorships have increased Samsung's awareness levels in prospective sports-loving consumer groups worldwide.

Samsung Experience

The North American market is important for Samsung. Being the most important playground for all major global players to prove their mettle, winning the markets' and consumers' minds in the US is crucial. This is particularly important as Samsung is competing against Apple, a leading iconic brand.

With this intention, Samsung created the Samsung experience in New York City. It opened a 10,000 square feet gallery at the Time Warner Center in

Manhattan in September 2003 full of its latest technology. Until it closed in 2011 after the lease expired,[41] Samsung operated it as a pure gallery – to offer customers an experience, not to sell products. Besides specific experiences created in major global cities, the chain of exclusive Samsung retail stores have been branded "Samsung Experience" stores worldwide, allowing consumers to browse and purchase the full range of Samsung products (smartphones, tablets, laptops, cameras, and accessories). In 2013, Samsung entered into an agreement to open Experience Stores within 1,400 Best Buy outlets across the US.[42] In January 2014, it announced the opening of 60 Experience Stores across seven European countries (UK, Ireland, Germany, Spain, Portugal, Sweden, and the Netherlands) in collaboration with the erstwhile electronics retailer Carphone Warehouse.[43] The global expansion strategy of Samsung's stores has one key objective – increase high street visibility to compete effectively with Apple.

Product Placement

With movies reaching a global audience, Samsung successfully managed to place its high-tech gadgets in the cult movie *The Matrix*, creating an excellent opportunity to gain the attention and curiosity of millions worldwide. With its emphasis on technology that appeals especially to youngsters, teenagers, and young adults, the association with movies like *The Matrix*, released in 1999, has helped Samsung convey its positioning strongly to a potential customer base. In 2012, Samsung signed a product placement deal with the popular reality TV series *The X Factor*, thereby placing its mobile phones and tablets in the judge's house section of the series along with dedicated apps, online content, and display advertising.[44]

With such dedicated and targeted brand communications, Samsung eventually overtook Sony as the world's largest television brand. In September 2014, Sony announced a loss of US$2.1 billion for that fiscal year and layoffs of 1,000 workers out of the 7,100 employed in its smartphone division.[45] Yet although Samsung has been doing all the right things, it will be a challenge to maintain consistency. Apple's iPhone 6 and 6 Plus achieved record sales, with the company selling more than 10 million units in the very first weekend after launch.[46] Though initial sales figures of Samsung's Galaxy S5 smartphone were encouraging, eventually the model could not exceed sales figures of the Apple iPhone 5S in the first two months after launch.[47]

In contrasting, Chinese manufacturers like Xiaomi and Huawei are gaining traction by launching cheap entry level Android handsets. Google has also started collaborating with Indian manufacturers to roll out Android handsets that cost less than US$100.[48]

Future Challenges

As the market leader in semi-conductor chips and the largest global manufacturer of flat display screens, Samsung has indeed come a long way from its humble beginnings of 1938. In 2012, it officially replaced Nokia as the world's biggest mobile manufacturer by shipping 93.5 million handsets compared to Nokia's 82.7 million handsets.[49] But Samsung faces some tough challenges.

A critical challenge is to become a truly, global iconic brand that resonates strongly with global consumers and stakeholders. The company needs to enhance its brand architecture, portfolio, and identities, and work on strengthening the emotional elements.

In its smartphone business, which has been the driver of overall handset sales, it faces a resurgent Apple, which had a hugely successful iPhone 6 launch in 2014. Not only is the premium handset segment becoming more competitive, Samsung also faces increasing competition from Xiaomi, Huawei, and Google at the lower end of the handset market.

In 2014, Samsung announced a weaker-than-expected profit forecast, driven by a slowdown in mobile phone sales and intensified global competition from new and old competitors.[50] For Samsung, ensuring the healthy and profitable growth of its mobile phone business is key. Additionally, it needs to build up brand equity in other product categories like tablets and accessories. Its recent push into smart wearable accessories (Samsung Gear) attempts to strengthen the brand beyond televisions and smartphones.

Maintaining Consistency

Samsung has invested billions in global advertising and brand building activities. Given its presence in multiple industries and consistent investment in R&D, it will be difficult to sustain branding investments. But Samsung has not yet reached a position where the brand can live independently of its products as Sony did, even though it is now a bigger organization than Sony with stronger brands. It is important for Samsung to constantly build its corporate brand value, which does not have strong equity and suffers from a confused image. In other words, current and prospective customers of Samsung lack a clear differentiated image about Samsung in their hearts and minds. This is in contrast to Apple, which enjoys strong emotional and functional bonding with its customers. Samsung's image is driven strongly by its product brands while Apple's is driven by its corporate brand.

Spreading the Corporate Brand too Thinly

Managing and building corporate brand equity is critical for Samsung. Even today, the Samsung name is found on literally everything from ships, to memory chips, mobile phones, and camcorders. Although the company is leveraging its brand to build new businesses and gain considerable advantage in existing ones, this can prove dangerous. Samsung has been trying to position itself as a premium lifestyle brand worldwide, but many businesses in the portfolio do not match this positioning. Therefore, although it might appear an advantage, spreading the corporate brand too thinly across a wide array of businesses might prove costly to Samsung in the long run. At one stage in its global expansion path, a decision on the corporate brand positioning needs to be taken. The five-pillared branding philosophy has been successful in giving Samsung a global edge, but key competitors like Apple still have stronger brand equity at the premium end of categories. Samsung's challenge is to create and maintain a high level of premium, innovative, and lifestyle-driven corporate brand image, and to clarify the roles of the product brands in the overall brand architecture. Apple has always been a lifestyle brand, an image carefully nurtured and developed over the years and supported by the genre defining experiences created by its flagship products.

Local and International Competition

Today Samsung is faced with never-seen-before competition in the consumer electronics industry. Asian mobile handset manufacturers are increasing the competitive threat to Samsung at the lower end of the market. These include Xiaomi, Coolpad, Oppo, and OnePlus from China; Micromax and Karbonn from India; Smartfren, HiMax, and Mito from Indonesia; and I-Mobile from Thailand. In the premium smartphone, tablet, and wearables segment, Samsung continues to fight an intense battle with Apple. Apple's launch of the Apple Watch has taken a direct fight in the smart wearables segment to Samsung.

Though it has overtaken Sony, Samsung still needs to deal with a significant threat from South Korea's LG Group and potential competitors from China and Taiwan. Although Samsung has a comfortable lead-time due to its top-notch technology and constant innovation, this should not lead to complacency. Samsung should continue to invest in technology and design capabilities, and marketing and brand management activities to maintain the lead over its rivals that it has so tirelessly built over the past decade. In 2013, LG Group announced that it would spend US$57 billion on R&D to take on its rivals. A large part of this spending will be focused on smartphone software, HD and smart TV, and next generation flexible and transparent displays.[51]

Managing the Samsung Brand Architecture

Even though the latest trend is to nurture a strong corporate brand, as Unilever and P&G have been doing, Samsung lacks the necessary similarity between its various business units. Therefore, Samsung should develop a strong brand architecture framework, which will define and monitor the interaction of various brands within the Samsung portfolio under the corporate brand. This is easier said than done, given the extremely diversified business units of the chaebols (Korean business conglomerates).

The brand architecture will also guide Samsung in creating new brands as well as acquiring brands to enter the value segments of different markets, as LG has done with the Zenith brand in the US to target solely the value segment. Presently, Samsung lacks value in its brand offering across all product categories. This creates pressure for Samsung to manage its brand portfolio across a wide price range. An example of this brand architecture challenge is the company's situation in India. According to analysts and company insiders, Samsung is struggling in India on two fronts – it is being challenged by low cost brands like Karbonn and Micromax in the low and mid-end smartphones segment and competing with Apple at the high end. Without a strong portfolio strategy driven by a clear brand architecture, the company is fighting a battle to retain market share in multiple price segments, while Apple can simply focus its effort on the premium segment it operates in. With the millions of dollars that Samsung has spent over the past decade to build the brand, it will be a major challenge to put in place a strong architecture system that will help in implementing successful branding practices. The conflict between Samsung's value offerings and its futuristic push toward premium products and to become a lifestyle and experience brand needs to be resolved as part of a broader organizational strategy.

Creating the Samsung Personality – Build Emotional Connections

Most great brands are those that have strong personalities, with Apple iPhone and iPad being the latest proof. But Samsung seems to have ignored this crucial aspect in building its brand. Although Samsung has been doing all the right things in its communications, it has not focused on creating a strong personality for its brand. It does not own anything specific in the consumers' minds, like a Harley-Davidson standing for the rugged independence of western America or a BMW standing for the ultimate driving experience. As has been well recorded in the branding literature, a successful brand provides customers not only with functional benefits, but also emotional and self-expressive benefits.[52]

So far, Samsung has emphasized the functional benefits of leading-edge technology, contemporary designs, and exciting features, but at a product level. It needs to go beyond this and create a cult following for its brands, like the Apple iPhone has done. Samsung needs to ensure that its brand can live independently of its products. As highlighted in the previous point, the Samsung corporate brand needs to be defined and built around a set of strong differentiators, including more emotional aspects of all the brands in the portfolio. This is and will continue to prove to be a major challenge.

Conclusion

Samsung has four critical areas in its branding strategy that it needs to address to remain competitive in the future:

- Strengthen its value brands in the categories they compete in
- Maintain the differentiated image of its premium brands, which have been built up over the years through sizeable financial and manpower commitment
- Define and maintain an image of the corporate brand, which encompasses the company's offerings across the value and premium ends of the categories it plays in
- Put in place a brand architecture in the organization that emphasizes the relationships between the corporate brand and the product brands and how the identity and image of each can help strengthen the others.

chapter 8

Aspiring Asian Brand Cases

The successful case stories of Singapore Airlines, Aman resorts, Shiseido, and Samsung have indeed laid the blueprint for branding success in Asia. As is evident from the brand stories in the previous chapter, the main reason for their success has been the continuous support from corporate management, including the chairman and CEO.

It is indeed good to see these Asian brands becoming successful well beyond Asia. But although it has two-thirds of the global population, growing economies, and a rapidly growing middle class with an increasing disposable income, Asia still boasts only a handful of powerful brands, which is a cause for concern.

Despite Asia's historical focus on manufacturing and trading activities, the global landscape could potentially face a wealth of new Asian brands in the coming years. Every country in Asia has its own list of aspiring brands just waiting to cross the local borders. In literally every industry sector, many companies are realizing the potential value creation that they might be forgoing due to a lack of branding. These companies are gradually making a mark in the region, having been inspired by the industry leaders. But, as yet, not many have managed to attain international recognition.

Even the governments of Asian countries are providing incentives for companies to adopt the right brand management practices to move up the value chain, and a large number of companies across Asia are already somewhere on the branding journey.

In the next 10–20 years, Asia will definitely contribute to the next generation of internationally recognized brands. This chapter examines some of these aspiring brands that could make a mark in the global brandscape.

AmorePacific – The Asian Beauty Creator

Background

AMORE PACIFIC
CORPORATION

AmorePacific company logo

Established in 1945, AmorePacific Corporation is South Korea's largest beauty and health company with over 30 brands of skincare, makeup, fragrance, hair care, oral care, and body care products. The brand portfolio also includes green tea. The company started out as a small family business selling hair oil made from camellia seeds in 1932.

Although AmorePacific has nearly 40 per cent market share in South Korea and been ranked among the top 20 global beauty companies, its foray into global markets is relatively recent. Its premium Laneige brand debuted in 1993 but only became available outside Korea in 2002. With an expected world population of 7.6 billion by 2020, a rising trend in tourist cosmetic purchases[1] and many new Asian consumers, AmorePacific knows that its future success depends on becoming a regional and global brand.

AmorePacific aims to become Asia's number one beauty company, one of the world's top five beauty companies,[2] and generate US$12 billion in sales by 2020 with 51 per cent from global markets, compared to 17 per cent presently.[3]

In 2013, AmorePacific was ranked the 17th biggest global cosmetics company in terms of global sales. L'Oréal was first, followed by Unilever and Procter & Gamble.[4] AmorePacific is the third-largest Asian cosmetics company behind Japanese companies Shiseido and Kao.[5] Its gradual expansion in Asia is highlighted by an increase in its skincare market share in China from 1.2 per cent in 2007 to 2.6 per cent in 2012, putting it above Unilever and Johnson & Johnson, according to global research firm Euromonitor.

AmorePacific operates around 13,300 points of sale across all distribution channels in 14 countries including the US, France, Singapore, and Indonesia.

AmorePacific is headed by Suh Kyung-Bae, who succeeded his father and the firm's founder Suh Sung-Whan in 1997. As the youngest son, he grew up watching his grandmother and father develop cosmetics products. Suh Kyung-Bae is famous for trying all products before their launch – except mascara. He is the company's chairman and CEO.

Today, AmorePacific's brand portfolio ranges from traditional oriental herbal cosmetics to cutting-edge biotechnology cosmetics spanning high-end luxury, premium, and mass-market categories. International success and image likely rest on two of the company's prominent brands – Laneige and Sulwhasoo. While Laneige – "la neige" is "snow" in French – is positioned as a Western skin cream, Sulwhasoo's herbal products, which combine traditional herbal treatments with advanced technology, cater to the demands of ultra-premium Asian consumers.

AmorePacific has a wide portfolio of brands under the group umbrella, including Aestura, Amos Professional, Annick Goutal (Paris), Dantrol, Espoir, Etude House, Hanyul, Happy Bath, Hera, Illi, Innisfree, Iope, Lirikos, Lolita Lempicka, Makeon, Mamonde, Median, Mirepa, Mise en Scene, Odyssey, Osulloc, Primera, Ryo, Songyum, VBProgram, and Verite.

Inner beauty is as important as outer beauty in AmorePacific's brand philosophy. Nutrition, vitality, and cosmeceuticals are part of this belief, as well as a vision of treating obesity, skin diseases, and chronic pain. It is AmorePacific's commitment to innovation, the discerning nature of local shoppers, and Korea's strengthening nation brand that provides it with an enviable platform for global growth. The company's website explicitly mentions that its corporate identity reflects the harmony between inner and outer beauty, traditions and the future, and reason and sensibility.[6]

Brand Philosophy

AmorePacific's vision is to be the "Asian Beauty Creator" in customers' minds by providing total care beauty and health products. "Beauty" is a word that permeates many levels of AmorePacific's brand, including how they refer to creating beautiful relationships with business partners and local communities. The belief can guide social contributions as well. One of their main citizenship campaigns is "MakeUp Your Beautiful Life," whereby confidence is restored to female cancer patients through beautiful changes and the transferal of beauty know-how.[7]

Country-of-origin has always been a prestige indicator for beauty brands. Similarly to how Paris and New York are symbolic capitals of beauty, much of AmorePacific's brand equity will be due to its country-of-origin. Apart from the synonymous relationship between Japan and technology, it is still difficult for many Western consumers to positively associate an Asian country with a competitive advantage other than low-cost. However, just as Korean and Taiwanese technology brands have largely broken this mold over the last decade, Korean beauty brands are following suit. A survey found that women in Southeast Asia and China believe that Korea is now the model for Asian beauty.[8] This is largely because South Korean women emphasize skincare much more than women in other parts of the world.

Between skincare, makeup, and night routine, South Korean women use an estimated 17 products daily. Because appearance seems to be such a constant preoccupation, it is sometimes misunderstood as vanity. There is a buzz word, *ul-jjang*, which literally means "best face," that promotes characteristics of the ideal Korean face. While this has contributed to South Korea having the highest plastic surgery rate globally, Koreans believe that skin is an important area of their overall health – much like maintaining a fit body through exercise and a healthy diet. Many beauty products sold in Korean pharmacies often have health benefits as the most prominent selling features.

The philosophy and concept of beauty in South Korea attract Asian women to the country's beauty industry. AmorePacific has succeeded in leveraging and capitalizing on this increasing interest. According to a report released by the Korea Customs Service in 2013, skincare exports have witnessed an explosive growth of 1,500 per cent in the last 15 years (1998–2012) accounting for 61 per cent of commodity exports.[9] In 2012, it reached US$1.1 billion, exceeding imports for the first time.[10]

The Evolution of Western and Asian Beauty Ideals

As Europe and Asia slowly recovered from World War II in the 1950s, Hollywood cinema became global and American shows were a major source of television programming worldwide. At that time, the US accounted for nearly 60 per cent of the global cosmetics market. With Paris and New York as fashion capitals, beauty also meant "Western." However, even as Asian beauty companies looked to France and the US for inspiration and brand names, differences in beauty standards evolved between East and West.

By the early 1960s an estimated 86 per cent of American girls aged 14–17 were using lipstick while three-fifths of the total Japanese beauty market was held by skin preparations – a preference shared by Koreans today. In terms of cosmetic surgery, Western women typically exaggerate their features with fuller lips or bigger breasts, while Asian women seek to refine their features, with smaller noses or chins, without really changing their features.[11] While Western women use tanning beds and spray to darken their skin artificially, Asian women lighten their complexion by using whitening creams or other cosmetic treatments to lighten their skin.

In the more recent globalization era since the 1980s, the rapid economic growth of China, India, and other emerging markets has raised global awareness of non-Western cultures. The impact is evident in the increasing popularity of non-Western cinema such as Bollywood and the "Korean Wave" (Hallyu) starting in the late 1990s. Through locally-dubbed Korean soap operas, young girls all over Asia now want to look like their favorite actors. The end of the mass-industrialization era has led many brands to rediscover local ingredients and create a strong revival of local traditions and a new confidence in unique Asian beauty.

Brand Strategy

Within its home country, AmorePacific has a broad distribution strategy. Korea accounts for more than 80 per cent of company sales. By channel, door-to-door sales represent almost 22 per cent of total sales, department stores account for 12 per cent and home-shopping/online accounts for more than 10 per cent. The fastest growing distribution channels are digital and duty-free.

From a brand portfolio management perspective, AmorePacific's portfolio can be described as a "house of brands," where a company manufactures and markets a range of brands. A close match of AmorePacific's brand management philosophy is Procter & Gamble's. In this model, each brand competes in a specific segment of a specific category. The markets in which the brand competes can be local, regional, or global. AmorePacific's brands, initially local, are now competing with other personal care and skincare brands regionally or globally.

AmorePacific has a strong brand management philosophy that consistently develops and establishes individual brands. All new brands have no company branding support and have been nurtured individually.

The knowledge of South Korean and Asian beauty consumers about AmorePacific lends credibility and prestige to any brand from the AmorePacific portfolio. Even then, there is no direct use of the company's name in individual advertising and communication strategies for the brands.

As it positions for growth in major overseas markets, especially China and South East Asia, AmorePacific is replicating this approach. While standard practice in Asia Pacific is to open shops under individual brand names, the strategy in the US is different. American luxury shoppers prefer high-end department stores for convenience and because they can touch and feel the products.[12]

Today, AmorePacific brands are sold in almost 200 specialty stores, including Bergdorf Goodman, Holt Renfrew, Neiman Marcus, Nordstrom, and Sephora. The luxury Sulwhasoo brand recently made its American debut at Bergdorf Goodman in New York City. As a soft-entry strategy for the US, AmorePacific launched a Beauty Gallery & Spa in SoHo, New York, to create a high-end footprint in the lucrative market and serve as a creative center to understand American consumers. The spa blends AmorePacific's cultural and scientific philosophies, promoting Korea's unique oriental sensibility with cutting-edge technology.

The most unique aspect of their Asian strategy is the shift toward indirect distribution via duty-free channels. As air travel expanded in the 1950s and is now undergoing a second wave of growth driven by Asia, travel retail provides exposure to many new potential customers with less distribution costs. Fittingly for AmorePacific's luxury brand image, the exclusivity adds some allure while and makes the tax-free products more affordable. In fact, the 2008 debut of Laneige outside South Korea was at Singapore Changi Airport's Terminal 3 mega-store. Singapore is a major hub for regional luxury shoppers and Laneige has been seeing strong growth in travel retail ever since. The brand quickly proceeded to secure a listing onboard the in-flight shop on Singapore Airlines.

Today, Laneige counters are in 34 regional airports and its products are available on 17 airlines. In 2010, Sulwhasoo was also launched in Changi Airport. AmorePacific has credited the boom in duty-free business as a key growth factor.

Sustainability Initiatives

To become a company that global customers love, AmorePacific believes it has a role to play in environmentalism – an important consideration for Korean consumers. In 2012, AmorePacific announced its intention to become an "evergreen company" by promoting sustainable product lines and focusing more R&D in the areas of biotechnology and green research projects. From these initiatives, AmorePacific achieved a 35 per cent reduction in carbon dioxide emissions by instituting a low temperature production process, and aims to reduce the amount of packaging used per product by 25 per cent by 2020.

AmorePacific created the Beautiful Fair Trade program in 2010, a purchasing program consisting of agreements with towns, villages, and local agriculture associations in Korea to source raw materials such as nutmeg, bamboos, lotus seeds, ginseng, and lilies without pesticides or chemical fertilizer. The plan is also to expand Beautiful Fair Trade overseas.

Innovation is Key to Success

South Korean beauty consumers are constantly looking for something new and are willing to pay a premium for it. A prime example was when LG Household & Health Care introduced the world's luxury chilled cosmetic, Frostine. Since the ingredients required cold storage, LG introduced a specialized cosmetics fridge called an Icemetic Cellar. Despite the exorbitant price tag, LG's overall cosmetic sales recorded 300 per cent growth in a month after launching. Similarly, when Sulwhasoo's Dahamsul Cream, a super-premium anti-ager with caviar ingredients, debuted on the home shopping channel, it sold more than 2,000 sets within 40 minutes and was frequently sold out for the next six months.

As a competitive necessity, AmorePacific has invested heavily in research and development throughout its history by "contributing to humanity by providing beauty & health through technology and devotion." Since the 1980s, investments have evolved from strictly dermatological research to a total health approach with greater emphasis on health and nutrition. AmorePacific's two main R&D buildings in Korea carry out research in: Cosmetic Research, Skin & Science, Medical Beauty, Health & Science, and Bio Science. Globally, AmorePacific has been developing networks in new markets through alliances with local universities, medical schools, hospitals, and research institutions to gain better knowledge of local women and climates.

In 2014, it opened a new 41,000 square-meters R&D and factory facility in Shanghai (China) to further capitalize on demand for beauty products from China and the Asia Pacific region. The annual production capacity of the factory is 13,000 tons, or 100 million units.[13]

In the traditional makeup category, this innovative approach allowed AmorePacific to break ground in new categories. They spearheaded a form of "nonflowing liquid," called "Cushion foundation (compact)," for sunscreens that is light and easily absorbed after reapplication – a chief complaint for users. AmorePacific also initiated the commercialization of an aerosol foam hair dye.[14]

AmorePacific cushion compound

Source: Courtesy of AmorePacific.

Their prowess as innovators also prevents AmorePacific from losing ground to competitors by missing out on new consumer preferences and fads. In 2012, as Korean women increasingly preferred not to touch cosmetic products with their hands, manufacturers introduced diverse high-tech make-up applicators while AmorePacific's own response, the vibrating make-up sponge, became a sensation as the category exploded. Global research company Nielsen found that Asian consumers are most likely to try new products – meaning brands that consistently do something different that effectively responds to consumer preferences can thrive.

In biotechnology, food, and drug categories, AmorePacific labs are on the cutting edge of stem cell and molecular biology. Aside from rejuvenation and metabolism, AmorePacific dreams of developing cosmeceutical products for weight-loss, disease, and aging. A recent design is a dosage release technology that controls drug absorption, a technique already been used by an arthritis treatment drug. These new innovations are increasingly becoming known as cosmeceuticals.

The company's innovation initiatives are not restricted to its core business of beauty and cosmetics. In line with creating synergy and balance between inner and outer beauty, AmorePacific also has a very successful organic tea brand – Osulloc. The tea leaves are grown in tea fields in Jeju Island, utilizing nature's gifts of rich quality volcanic soil, optimal climate, and volcanic mineral water. The manufacturing system for Osulloc has been certified as the world's best and the brand has won numerous awards in international tea competitions. The brand is also exported to Japan, Germany, the US, Australia, Switzerland, and Canada.

The brand is marketed through "experiential marketing," with tea roasting demonstrations, Osulloc tea classes, and so on. There are Osulloc-branded tea shops, an Osulloc Tea Museum in Jeju Island and the brand is sold in tea houses popular with global tourists. Thus the power of innovation in production, marketing, and various stages of the value chain cannot be undermined.

Brand Communications

In general, advertising for AmorePacific's many brands follows the same strategy as most beauty brands – mainly television and glossy magazine ads. Following the placement of Laneige and Sulwhasoo in major travel outlets, promotional campaigns have targeted groups who most frequently travel to those regions, such as Chinese tour groups to Hong Kong and Singapore. While AmorePacific also participates in a variety of interactive and social communication channels, their most effective communication strategies are via brand ambassadors, thanks to the highly collectivist nature of the Korean culture.

In South Korea, Asian models are often utilized to sell makeup while Western models are used to sell more risqué items, such as lingerie. Three different members of the K-pop group Girls' Generation endorse three different AmorePacific brands. This brand endorsement strategy, enhanced by the global appetite for Korean popular culture, has increased AmorePacific's brand awareness in Asia and globally.

However, AmorePacific must adapt its marketing strategy in China so as not to rely fully on celebrities. Korean women are emotional customers, but the Chinese are more practical, placing more importance on scientific and dermatological testing in beauty products.[15]

To cultivate its brand image, AmorePacific has become a knowledge curator, owning and operating the Amore Museum (once known as the Pacific Museum) since 1979, which specializes in Korean culture, tea drinking, traditional makeup, and other histories. In 2012, AmorePacific published the

Beautiful Story of Native Plants in Jeju. The book not only contributed to conserving Jeju's native plants and traditional knowledge but also included detailed information on the raw materials used in AmorePacific products. As an accompaniment to the launch of an herbal medicinal body care brand, Illi, AmorePacific published Jataebogam Illi, which contained the history and cosmetic effects of Illi's key ingredients, and the traditional beauty methods of famous Korean women.

AmorePacific is increasingly using the digital media landscape to market its portfolio of brands. Facebook quotes AmorePacific's use of the social media-networking platform for brand marketing as a business success case. The company has 19 different Facebook pages dedicated to separate brands, with more than 600,000 fans.

Future Challenges

Major competition from global organizations is always a concern. Together, L'Oréal and Procter & Gamble collectively sell a quarter of global beauty products and have aggressively expanded into the Asian market with acquisitions such as L'Oréal's purchase of the Japanese brand Shu Uemura and Yue-Sai, a local brand developed by a famous Chinese television personality.

Unilever's highly successful skin whitener, Fair and Lovely, launched in India in the 1970s. It still holds over half of India's skin lightening market and has now expanded into nearly 40 countries across Asia, Africa, the Caribbean, and the Middle East.

Luckily, these competitors in Asia achieved success through the lowest common denominators of their products, which are widely distributed and appeal to the majority of consumers. This is not the space AmorePacific occupies.

However, Western brands that have drawn on their expertise with Japanese lightening creams pose the biggest threat to AmorePacific's niche. Lancôme rapidly established itself as the leading prestige brand in China in 1999. Two-thirds of the brand's sales in Asia are skincare products. Procter & Gamble owns the highly successful ultra-premium brand SK-II, which originated in Japan.

Maintain the Edge in China

China is the ideal market for AmorePacific's most differentiated product – the super-premium Sulwhasoo brand. China's share of the global beauty market may seem small compared to those of the US and Japan, but with a population of 1.3 billion, its growth potential is staggering. China now represents 42 per cent of

AmorePacific's overseas sales, followed by France (29 per cent), the rest of Asia (25 per cent), and the US (3 per cent).

The beauty market in China is worth an estimated US$44 billion, and AmorePacific holds 1 per cent market share.[16] AmorePacific expects its China revenues to grow 40 per cent annually to 2020, twice the rate in 2013.[17]

Since entering China in 1992, AmorePacific has operated over 2,900 stores for its five brands: Sulwhasoo, Laneige, Mamonde, Innisfree, and Etude House.[18]

Chinese brands like Shanghai Jahwa are building brands that honor past traditions similar to Sulwhasoo, but AmorePacific holds an edge in terms of cultural influence. Much can be learned from Shiseido's approach in China, where it launched Aupres, a brand specifically for the Chinese skincare market utilizing a perception referred to as "J Sense" by local marketers in China.

Another important aspect is Chinese women's perception toward beauty products and their country-of-origin. Although the company is slowly making gains in the country it needs to account for the stronghold of Asian competitor Shiseido over China. It has long been established that Chinese believe Japanese technology to be the best and Japanese skin to be closest to Chinese skin in terms of makeup and beauty regime requirements. These are important cultural aspects that AmorePacific will need to consider as it implements its China strategy.

The beauty and skincare categories in China will become increasingly competitive. Local Chinese cosmetics brands like Houdy, Caisy, Longrich, CMM, Herborist, and Chinfie are increasingly becoming popular. Shanghai Jahwa United Co., Ltd is slowly emerging as a significant competitor with successful brands like Liushen and Herborist.

Multinationals are also not sitting back. Estée Lauder, the American giant, launched a completely new brand, Osiao, only for Asian markets in 2012, which reportedly contains ingredients like ginseng. The brand was developed after five years of intensive research at the company's R&D center in Shanghai. Every aspect of the brand has a strong Chinese connection. Osiao has five letters, a number considered lucky in China, and the "O" at either end of the brand name is meant to reflect balance in skin.[19]

AmorePacific needs to keep pushing its strategy in China consistently as its market share was less than 3 per cent in 2013 compared to that of L'Oréal (16.8 per cent), Shiseido (10.3 per cent), and Procter & Gamble (9.8 per cent) according to Euromonitor.[20]

Even though it faces an uphill battle in China, AmorePacific seems to be attracting Chinese women shopping overseas. South Korea's scenic Jeju Island is a hugely popular destination for Chinese tourists due to the allure of the fresh air, volcanic peaks, scenic waterfalls, and local dishes like "black pork," but most importantly the duty-free shops. AmorePacific has been the winner in this domain, with its duty-free sales in South Korea to customers from China, Taiwan, and Hong Kong increasing by 184 per cent in the first half of 2014 compared to 2013.

Encountering and Fighting Fake Products

Korean cosmetic products continue to be popular in China, but concern is growing about the online sale of counterfeit products with almost identical brand-logos and appearance. Even fakes of some products not yet officially on sale in China are being offered. Fake versions of AmorePacific's best-selling

Iope lipsticks from AmorePacific

Source: Courtesy of AmorePacific.

items such as Iope's "Air Cushion" are being sold for cut prices on Taobao, a Chinese equivalent of eBay. Korean companies are concerned that the fake products are tarnishing their image and brand equity because they contain different ingredients that may damage the skin.[21]

AmorePacific should continue to fight fake products in China and ensure that their brands are well protected in trademark and patents terms.

Developing Men's Cosmetics

Urban men globally are increasingly investing in skincare products. While Western Europe has a large male grooming market, the latest boom in male beauty products is in Asia, where many men now use foundation with sunscreen, not just traditional aftershave or colognes.

Asia-Pacific is the fastest growing market for men's skincare, accounting for US$2.1 billion (63 per cent) of the global market of US$3.3 billion (2013).[22] China, including Hong Kong, is the largest single market for men's skincare at US$974 million (2013) and is expected to grow to US$1.2 billion in 2014. Asian countries account for five of the top 10 global skincare markets in per capita spending, according to research firm Euromonitor.

Euromonitor estimates that South Korean men spend nearly twice as much today on skincare than they did in 2007. Korean men spent US$635 million on skincare in 2013. Today, TV shows and spas devoted exclusively to male makeovers exist. This style, known as *kkonminam* – directly translated as flower handsome man – has been heavily popularized by Korean superstars, including singer/actor Rain and actor Lee Byung-Hun, who have recently featured in American movies.

AmorePacific's Laneige Homme line for men will face a tough fight for the male skincare market – arguably the industry's most lucrative and untapped. Procter & Gamble is the world's largest men's grooming products company, with strong distribution throughout Asia, but AmorePacific's emphasis on technology and innovation could appeal to many men if it continues to differentiate itself as a luxury Asian specialist brand for men.

The global skincare market for women is still 30 times larger (US$107 billion in 2013) than men's skincare, but men's skincare is growing faster (9.4 per cent) compared to women's skincare (4.8 per cent).[23] AmorePacific has a huge opportunity to tap into men's skincare, but will face tough competition from international brands like L'Oréal, Shiseido, and Estée Lauder.

Continued Innovation

Continuous innovation is critical for success and for staying competitive in fast-evolving product segments like beauty, cosmetics, and personal care. AmorePacific operates in product segments where product obsolescence is rife. The hyper-competitive nature of these categories demands continuous innovation.

AmorePacific's innovative "cushion compact," a mixture of colored foundation, sunscreen, and moisturizer to be applied by touching a foam pad to a spongy, liquid-filled cushion, was developed by AmorePacific research labs in 2008. It has been a huge success, with more than 30 million units sold. The company needs to have more such innovations that are huge commercial successes to maintain its edge against the likes of L'Oréal, Procter & Gamble, and regional players like Shiseido. It is also important to understand that innovation is hugely expensive and AmorePacific should have an innovation strategy focused on core business areas.

Innovation is copied and replicated very quickly. AmorePacific and L'Oréal were early innovators in the development of nanotech-based beauty products, using tiny molecular compounds to improve the performance of creams, sunscreens, and shampoos, but the rest of the beauty industry began to catch up aggressively. From 2000 through the end of 2009, a total of 217 personal-care brands that incorporated the term "nano" were trademarked worldwide. The second half of that period had 575 per cent more registered marks. This foray into technology has even attracted new competition from companies not associated with the cosmetics industry, including Fujifilm and BASF. This shows that an organization can very quickly lose its competitive edge through the sheer pace of innovation replication. Therefore, consumer education must become a central pillar of AmorePacific's communication strategy. This will require disciplined effort, matching and exceeding competitors' innovation budgets and efforts and employing the best in terms of skill sets and capabilities.

Global Expansion Strategy

As it pursues an expansion strategy in regional and global markets, AmorePacific needs to change its thinking and operating model to match a global mind-set for success. For example, the company's brand communication strategy still remains very regional. All of the brand's ambassadors are Korean celebrities. This may be successful when targeting the Chinese consumer, but unsuccessful when targeting consumers in Europe and the US. Elements of Korean culture, including the allure of Korean celebrities, are virtually unknown there. Consequently, a change in brand ambassadors is necessary to increase brand awareness in global markets. Most of the global beauty giants have global ambassadors, thereby having a balance of global versus local appeal.

Secondly, a global expansion strategy requires a strategic rethink of the brand portfolio. Western consumers still have markedly different preferences and attitudes toward their beauty and skincare regimes, and consequently toward products and brands. AmorePacific needs to gain an in-depth understanding of these preferences and position its brand portfolio accordingly. This is also important to give a strategic direction to its innovation roadmap, which should help in developing new products that have a broader market appeal but remain in touch with the AmorePacific brand ethos. Developing and launching brands with global appeal and relevance will help the company develop a coherent brand architecture. A clear brand architecture outlining the relationships between the parent and sub-brands will be crucial for portfolio management and making brand positioning decisions.

Finally, expansion into new markets does not start and end with the launch and development of new brands. To ensure visibility and generate awareness, effective advertising campaigns need to be coupled with efficient distribution strategies. Distribution is the key driver of preference and point-in-time sales in the beauty and cosmetics business. AmorePacific's distribution strategy in the US has been described as "narrow and deep," with the brand's products available in select Bergdorf Goodman, Nordstrom, Neiman Marcus, and Sephora retail stores. The company has plans to further deepen this narrow distribution by adding its range to all stores of these chains. This is crucial because it is operating on the turf of the legendary Estée Lauder and Procter & Gamble.

Global Leadership and Vision

An effective global strategy can only be implemented with a visionary senior management. As AmorePacific expands and takes up a regional and global competitive stance, it needs to have senior management representing diverse cultures, with a mix of strategic experience across multiple sectors, an appreciation of global trends, and an in-depth understanding of the external and internal forces that shape the organization's future.

The success of AmorePacific's perfume brand Lolita Lempicka in France and of its skincare products in the US is attributed to the company's ability to correctly predict future trends and prepare for opportunities. For this to continue to happen, the company must have the right set of people in senior management locally and globally.

Overall, AmorePacific is well poised for growth as it expands into markets outside China and Korea. To sustain this growth and remain competitive in the segments it operates in, AmorePacific needs an aggressive, innovation-driven marketing model with a global mind-set and deep consumer understanding. Going beyond the shores of its home country will be challenging, but with its credentials and past successes in foreign markets, it can be reasonably assumed that the company has the right compass to map a course through new, uncharted waters.

Jim Thompson – The Asian Silk Brand[24]

JIM THOMPSON

Jim Thompson company logo

The Jim Thompson Thai Silk Company from Thailand is a well-known Asian brand with great potential to become a strong international lifestyle brand. Known for its silk fabrics, apparel, accessories, and, recently, home furnishings, it is one of the few brands praised by Thai Royalty, celebrities, and the discriminating public for its quality, designs, and Asian sensibility. From the time it was established in 1951 by Jim Thompson, an American soldier settled in Thailand,[25] the brand has steadily strengthened its reputation.

The company operates 32 retail stores in Thailand, three in Malaysia and two in Singapore. Jim Thompson has showrooms in Paris, Munich, and Atlanta, and it plans to open one in London in 2015. Jim Thompson has established a strong name for itself locally and regionally with more than US$100 million in sales across the group. The company employs 2,433 people across its operations, and the brand is present in more than 40 countries globally.

Evolution of the Jim Thompson Brand

When Jim Thompson resigned from the American armed forces and decided to settle down in Thailand, he spent much of his time initially travelling around the country, particularly the northeast region. He became fascinated with the pervasive rural Thai silk cottage industry, which flourished as most

Jim Thompson – founder of Jim Thompson Company

Source: Courtesy of Jim Thompson Company.

village families had traditional hand looms under their houses where cloth was woven locally for their personal clothing. Jim Thompson astutely realized the potential to bring Thai silk to international attention and acclaim, and to an honored place on the international fabric stage. He took the initiative to "go international" by standardizing the silk woven through the use of chemical dyes. He used his acute sense of style to adapt traditional Thai designs and color schemes to international tastes.

Thompson began his first commercial weaving operation in the Muslim Ban Krua village that now lies just across the canal from his renowned house. He established close personal ties with these village weavers and they became small stakeholders in the Jim Thompson Company.

Jim Thompson was able to produce a world-class silk product that captivated the international community with the charm and feel of a hand-woven product that was far superior to similar products. For example, Thai silk is different from Chinese silk. Thai silk is inconsistent and has "humps and bumps" and iridescent colors (changing colors depending on the light). Also, Thai silk is not only good for garments but also ideal for home furnishing materials.

To ensure 100 per cent quality control of the output, Jim Thompson has a vertically integrated production model. Although 100 per cent of materials were hand-woven silk in 1967, today only 50 per cent are hand-woven silk and the remaining 50 per cent use other materials. But, according to William Warren, a Jim Thompson biographer based in Bangkok, "it took years of experiment, frequent frustration and plain hard work first to persuade a handful of remaining weavers to increase production on better looms, using colour-fast chemical dyes instead of traditional vegetable colors, and then open up foreign markets where none had existed before."[26]

Thompson successfully took Thai silk beyond Thailand by leveraging his contacts in the US and other countries. Thai silk gained international recognition in *Vogue* magazine, and in 1951 it was featured in a Broadway production.[27] The company also benefited a great deal from the personal charisma and personality of Thompson himself. His efforts to establish his Thai silk company proved to be a major profit-earner. This gained him much respect and adulation. In 1967, Thompson disappeared mysteriously in Malaysia's Cameron Highlands and was never found. There has been no proof found to give credence to any of the many theories around his disappearance. Thus, this lingering mystery has added greatly to the brand's legend and myth.

Today, almost 65 years since its inception, the Jim Thompson Company continues to grow with its inimitable zest and passion. Although it started out with just silk fabrics, by leveraging its brand equity and the Thai heritage, the company has now diversified into many other related product lines, the latest one being food and beverages (restaurants) and home furnishings. In 2001, it signed renowned London-based Thai designer Ou Baholyodhin, known for his vibrant designs strongly influenced by Asian cultures, to craft the new furnishing line in collaboration with the in-house design teams.[28] Ou Baholyodhin has over the years advised Jim Thompson, and helped to craft new innovations and designs for the company.

The Jim Thompson Company's strategy going forward is to focus on finished products for the home. The company is focusing on retail products in Asia, where it has strong brand equity. As the brand is strongly linked to the Thai experience, buying Jim Thompson products for a tourist equates to bringing home a piece of Thai culture. This is why a significant proportion of retail customers in Thailand are tourists who buy gift items when returning from Thailand.

However, in Europe and the US, where the company is building its brand, the Thai connection and direct experience with Thai culture is difficult to establish. Therefore, the company is focusing on finished products for the home, which are distributed through local distributors and displayed in Jim Thompson's own showrooms in Paris, Munich, and Atlanta.

Jim Thompson has also collaborated with Ed Tuttle, a leading American designer. Through this collaboration, Jim Thompson provided custom-made fabrics (Rue de la Paix, Vendome, and Chenille Canvas) for his architecture and design projects, which include Aman resorts and Park Hyatt Hotels. As design is a vital part of the company's success, these collaborations with external consultants have also provided the company with valuable insights into upcoming trends in global markets.

Brand Philosophy

The company's brand is primarily built on three pillars. The first is the legend surrounding the founder Jim Thompson. The second is the unique blend of Eastern (Thai) tradition and heritage with Western contemporary designs based on traditional Thai symbols and patterns. The third is the elevation of the brand from a cottage industry product into a fashion and lifestyle concept.

The Jim Thompson Company has built a story of the brand surrounding the founder, his origins, his contributions to the Thai silk industry, and his eventual mysterious disappearance. The founder's journey to take the Thai silk industry global and his drive to involve the weaving community as strategic partners in the business itself is a legend in Thailand. By leveraging this connection, the Jim Thompson Company has been able to blend into the social fabric of the country.

Finally, Jim Thompson has created a lifestyle concept centered on silk and contemporary designs. Although the company started out with silk fabrics, it has successfully expanded into home furnishings and even into restaurants. Jim Thompson runs two restaurants in Bangkok and one in Singapore. These brand extensions have enabled Jim Thompson to create an emerging premium lifestyle concept around the core brand offering.

By developing the brand on these three pillars, Jim Thompson has been able to maintain its differentiation and build a strong brand. The brand is perceived to be highly authentic, and to have high quality and a strong heritage.

In recent years, global competition and customer trends have evolved significantly, and Jim Thompson will have to revisit its brand identity and market position to ensure it stays competitive in this changing global landscape. Jim Thompson has other global brands and their positioning strategies from which to get inspiration. For example, Ralph Lauren is excellent at creating dreams and delivering promises over a complete and distinct lifestyle. French luxury brand Hermès has an uncompromising attitude toward quality and is a very high-end, authentic brand. Bottega Veneta is known for its unbeatable craftsmanship and unwavering belief in a single strong signature product.

Jim Thompson Brand Growth

Renowned for its quality, design, and Asian feel, Jim Thompson has been widely acknowledged by leading brands in the hospitality industry. The brand's furnishing materials have been widely used by many luxury hotels in Bangkok, which include The Oriental, The Four Seasons, Amanpuri, the Regent, Conrad, and the Sukhothai. In Europe, the Park Hyatt Paris and Park Hyatt Milan hotels, among others, have been attracted to Jim Thompson's furnishing materials. The Park Hyatt Paris has used 9,000 square meters of furnishing materials alone. These hospitality industry clients, among many others, serve as very strong testimonials for the Jim Thompson brand.[29]

As it is common for a strong brand to leverage its equity and diversify into related market segments, Jim Thompson has also followed this path. Today, its portfolio consists of many additional product lines apart from mere silk fabrics, including scarves, ties, handbags, textiles, apparel, and accessories for home furnishing.

The company also launched No. 9 Thompson in 2008, an elegant and relaxed brand extension of Jim Thompson. It adopts a new take on Oriental inspiration, staying true to the Jim Thompson heritage while using a lighter, more painterly style for a young, contemporary edge.

Brand Communications

Jim Thompson has selectively used mass communication channels to build its retail brand. The company uses other communication channels like fairs and exhibitions to create awareness about its professional home furnishings brand. It showcases its products during these events and generates considerable interest. By leveraging the unique designs of its retail stores, where it showcases its entire product portfolio, the company offers a comprehensive customer experience. As Jim Thompson does not own retail outlets outside Asia, it works very closely with its international distribution partners.

Many of its resources are focused on internal marketing, which involves educating the channel partners about the brand, product features, and benefits. Jim Thompson also maintains a list of more than 50,000 customer names in Thailand for local promotions. As all of these customers have already purchased Jim Thompson merchandise at least once, they also act as strong word-of-mouth marketers.

In recent years, the company has taken steps to enhance its marketing capabilities and insights to better tackle increased competition and changing customer needs and demographics. Jim Thompson has established a global marketing department as it aspires to become more market-driven and customer-centric. This also includes an enhanced focus on digital capabilities, including a social media strategy and new online properties.

As the brand is strongly associated with its founder, with Thailand, and with the Jim Thompson House in Bangkok, a museum open to the public could not be overlooked. The Jim Thompson House belongs to the legally, but not spiritually, separate James HW Thompson Foundation (a non-profit organization devoted to the preservation and development of art, culture, and heritage in Thailand). It displays a wide range of traditional objets d'art along with the entire product portfolio of Jim Thompson. In 2014, the museum had over 200,000 visitors, adding significantly to the promotion of the brand to foreign tourists, including keeping the mystery around Jim Thompson's disappearance alive as part of the brand story. This not only helps build awareness among the company's prospective customer base but also reiterates its strong link with Thailand's heritage and culture.

The James HW Thompson Foundation also created and funded the Jim Thompson Art Center. Finally, the Jim Thompson Company is engaged in philanthropy, including annual scholarships for children of workers.

Future Challenges

Jim Thompson is faced with many challenges moving forward as several factors like increased competition, evolving global trends, the modernization of Asia, and macro-economic changes will impact the future success and growth path of the company. The Jim Thompson brand has been successful so far and is unique in many ways, but arguably it has grown slowly compared to how Asian and global markets have evolved in the last 20 years. In order to compete effectively, the company needs to acknowledge and tackle a variety of strategic issues around competition and revitalizing brand equity.

Creating a strong brand identity and personality: Jim Thompson's legend around its founder and the brand is popular in Asia among retail customers.

However, in Europe and the United States, the company deals with hotels, designers, and interior decorators. Thus, at an aggregate level, Jim Thompson primarily operates as a B2C (business-to-consumer) brand in Asia and a B2B (business-to-business) brand in Europe and the United States. Thus it needs to create a consistent brand identity that resonates across regions and customer bases, while still remaining responsive to the specific needs of any particular customer segment. Bridging a brand successfully across both B2C and B2B categories is always a challenge that needs dedicated marketing attention.

Installing a brand management system: As the brand grows, it becomes crucial to constantly monitor and hone the brand to reflect market demands. With any retail brand, the brand promise and brand delivery must work in tandem. Customer service, for example, is an important element. Jim Thompson owns retail outlets only within Asia, and in particular in Thailand where the brand is strongest. This necessitates that the channel members are properly trained in executing the brand promises outside Asia. For such a training system to endure, consistent support from the corporate management and continuous investment of resources is required.

Protecting the core Thai market: Thailand provides a disproportionate part of the company's revenues and primarily from retail stores – which is a cause for concern. Recently, the Thai market has been under pressure from the challenging political situation, and the associated decline in overseas tourists coming to Thailand – a major customer segment for Jim Thompson. The brand also seems to have somehow lost touch with the local, affluent Thai population. It thus needs to regain its strong position in Thailand to protect revenues and brand image.

Expansion beyond Asia: Jim Thompson's brand equity within Asia is related to a large extent to the legend of the founder. But outside Asia, this legend is less known and may not be very relevant. Moreover, an Asian brand with a Western name might confuse customers. Given these impediments, Jim Thompson should strive to create a brand with an appealing identity that not only is relevant to customers across regions but also captures its unique Asian heritage.

Taking a brand to multiple markets and sustaining investment in brand building can have a toll on resource capabilities. Moreover, most resources are utilized for operations and production. Jim Thompson needs to consider these factors before venturing into multiple markets and product segments.

Single brand company: Another major challenge will be to leverage the Jim Thompson brand name and potentially introduce new brands into the market.

Until now, Jim Thompson has been a single brand company. Moving ahead, the challenge will be to cautiously leverage the brand equity through brand or line extensions so as to explore new opportunities either by introducing new brands to cater to new segments or by venturing into new product categories. Jim Thompson must be cautious in carrying out this exercise as it might result in a possible dilution of brand equity as a result of brand stretch. Finding the right balance between pursuing an expansion strategy and protecting the brand equity from dilution will prove to be a considerable challenge.

Capture a younger generation: Jim Thompson's core clientele is concentrated among the older age groups, both in Thailand and overseas. The brand does not have a strong image or preference among younger consumers. Targeting the younger consumer and not diluting the brand equity will be an ongoing challenge and balancing act. The product segments are traditionally not those that appeal to youth. Appreciation and sensitivity toward finely crafted silk, homemade furnishings, silks, ties, scarves, and accessories are life-stage driven and generally mature later in life.

Capturing the interest of the younger generation and thereby tapping into the lucrative apparel market will be a matter of careful strategic consideration. Launching a sub-brand (such as No. 9), which can be positioned toward the younger generation, without diluting brand equity, might be a solution.

Having a presence in the apparel segment for youngsters and being successful in it are two completely different stories. The company will come up against sizeable competition in this segment wherever it expands into, as well as in the regional markets where it has a successful presence.

Taking the brand into new product categories either via the use of the existing parent brand name or through a new sub-brand is viable, but only after the category has been rationally selected, carefully researched, and strategically analyzed. Launching into the restaurant business has been successful until now, but it is too far from an "adjacency play" for it to be successful in every market.

The company does have potential to expand its presence in the premium and luxury designer apparel segments by identifying more collaboration opportunities with influential designers. Premium and luxury are age-encompassing and will allow Jim Thompson to get closer to a wider age group of potential consumers.

Evolution of the product portfolio: Jim Thompson needs to streamline its product portfolio in the retail business and ensure a constant evolution of new merchandise in tune with customer needs and global trends. Again, a collaboration pipeline with influential designers can be a key success factor here. This will enable the company to influence trends (and not follow them). However, the collaboration choices need to be careful, strategic, and forward looking. Noting that the company is slowly embarking on a global expansion plan, its collaboration should be with individuals who have at least regional (if not global) appeal.

Jim Thompson has been strategic and sensitive enough to continually expand its product lines, but management of these lines, what to push and what to hold back in different markets, understanding distribution channel nuances, and an in-depth understanding of consumer needs and preferences will be the key success factors.

Globalizing the company operations: Home furnishing is the only business unit operating in Europe and the US. For a company used to operating only in Thailand, along with a few other Asian countries, operating globally can be a strategic, cultural, and operational challenge.

Until now, the company does not have any of its own retail outlets in global markets outside Asia – despite the fact that the Jim Thompson brand has a huge, untapped global potential. The company is solely reliant on its few partners in these markets. Operating via a franchise/distribution model is not a recipe for disaster, but it is not effective for every product category. Jim Thompson operates at the juncture of legacy, tradition, and luxury. These kinds of product characteristics and image require tight control over the whole marketing mix of the brands in the portfolio. That can only come from either full or shared ownership in country-level ventures or operations.

Besides the brand's intangible aspects, there is the challenge of having globally efficient production and distribution models. Because the primary raw material for the company's products is still Thai silk, decisions around locations for manufacturing need to be taken very carefully. The company has two key challenges to address here – one, the export of the raw Thai silk to any global manufacturing site and, more importantly, how to access the skill of the local Thai craftsman in terms of working on the silk. The first challenge may well be addressed, but the second is more difficult.

As mentioned earlier, global expansion and establishing presence in multiple markets require tight control over the brand and its presence. Jim Thompson has to ensure the same level of quality, the same image around legacy and tradition, and the same level of experiential marketing that it has managed to create in Thailand. These cannot be created overnight, but the company has to make visible and conscious efforts and strongly portray its intentions to maintain its legacy and credibility everywhere it has a presence.

Transition of the senior management team: Last, but not least, is the challenge of creating a globally focused senior management team. Not only do the board and the management teams have the responsibility to become more strategic, but also the local teams in the countries where the company has a presence or plans to have a presence need to operate with a global mind-set too.

Expansion of teams through fresh hiring and relocation should keep the trait of strategic thinking and global vision as key success criteria for individuals. Additionally, individuals responsible for shaping and driving the company's global operations should have a deep appreciation of the company's founder, values, contribution to reviving an almost dying Thai silk industry, quality, and manufacturing process.

Alibaba – The Chinese Brand Leading Disruptive Innovation

The world had started noticing Alibaba before, but when the Chinese e-commerce company created the world's biggest Initial Public Offering (IPO), valued at US$25 billion, in September 2014, it raised everyone's eyebrows.[30] Jack Ma, the company's billionaire founder, started the company in 1999 by founding the website Alibaba.com in his apartment.[31]

The company's consumer-to-consumer trading portal, Taobao, features close to a billion products. The company has become synonymous with e-commerce in China, and the group of websites that it owns and operates accounted for more than 60 per cent of the parcels delivered in China in March 2013,[32] and 80 per cent of online sales by September 2014.[33]

Jack Ma thought of the company's name while sitting in a café in San Francisco. As part of his short and focused market research project to validate the attractiveness of the name, he asked one of the waitresses in the café whether she was aware of the name and its meaning. The waitress said yes and that the name meant "Open Sesame."[34] The moment she said this, Jack Ma decided on the name for his company. Trudy Dai, one of Jack's friends and the company's earliest employees, reportedly sent hundreds of emails every night answering queries from American customers without letting them know that she was Chinese, earning a paltry sum of 550 yuan (US$6) per month.[35]

Today, Alibaba is the world's largest e-commerce company, boasting 279 million active buyers using its websites, who place 14.5 billion orders a year, which translate into revenues of US$8.6 billion in fiscal year 2014.[36] Before the record breaking IPO was launched, many analysts had already started sounding the death-knell for Alibaba in terms of it growing its business in the US. But, in spite of all negative publicity and outlook, the company's founder went through with the IPO, which was more than a year in planning.

The attractiveness and potential of the company's business model were never in doubt. In the first two years, it was successful in raising US$25 million in funding from SoftBank, Goldman Sachs, and a host of institutional investors.[37] The company's vision clearly centers on the power and potential of the Internet as a medium for trade and business. The exact wording reads "from the outset, the company's founders shared a belief that the Internet would level the playing field by enabling small enterprises to leverage innovation and technology to grow and compete more effectively in the domestic and global economies."[38] Since the start, it has done just that by providing the Internet platform for facilitating trade between small and medium-sized traders globally.

Jack Ma's vision has constantly evolved and kept pace with the technological changes and innovations in the online space. Alibaba provides not only a trading platform, but also its own online payment system called Alipay, which now controls more than half of China's online payments market.[39] In addition, the group now has a portfolio of Internet-based businesses targeted toward specific segments and niche areas of online commerce. Some of the companies include Tmall.com (online retail platform), Juhuasuan (group shopping website offering "flash sales" items), eTao (comparison shopping website), AliExpress (online retail service for small sellers), and 1688.com (B2B trade in China).[40]

In China, young single Chinese celebrate the loosely defined 11/11 holiday for its four "1s," the number representing their single status.[41] It has become a day for a nationwide shopping spree, attracting enormous e-commerce transaction volumes. In 2014, Alibaba's Single's Day transaction was US$9.3 billion, an increase of 58 per cent compared to 2013 (US$5.9 billion). 43 per cent of all transactions came through mobile devices (up from 21 per cent in 2013), illustrating how e-commerce is changing the retail industry in China, although e-commerce penetration is still low.

Background

As mentioned earlier, Jack Ma founded the company in 1999, leading 18 other individuals who were investors and the company's first employees. Ma always had an entrepreneurial instinct and had founded multiple companies before, one of which was a translation company and the other called China Pages, which allowed Chinese companies to scour for customers globally. Four years after China Pages turned out to be a failure, Ma founded Alibaba.[42] The company's success, although attributed to Ma's hard work and vision, is also equally driven by his distinct personality, his captivating speaking style, his ability to engage and drive employees, and his management and operating style. Ma speaks fluent English, which has worked toward the advantage of communicating clearly to the Western media. He also has a dose of eccentricity, which includes turning up at a company rally wearing a nose ring, dark lipstick, and a blond wig.[43] In short, Ma is Alibaba's brand creator, curator, artist, and communicator.

Within two years, the company achieved profitability. In 2003, Taobao, the world's biggest consumer trading platform was founded. On its 10th anniversary, the company made its foray into the next generation of computing services with the launch of Alibaba Cloud Computing.

Brand Philosophy

Jack Ma calls Alibaba the "everything company." Ma's strategy, right from the very beginning, has been to make a company so diversified that a customer will not have to go anywhere else. In a difficult market marred by global recession, fears of a slowing Chinese economy, fleeing customers, and competitors with deep pockets, Alibaba has been able to grow continuously and expand with the help of strategic partnerships, mergers and acquisitions, and unrelenting leadership from its founder to build a company that truly serves its customers.

The company's philosophy is customers first, employees second, and shareholders third, and is reiterated and re-emphasized by Mr. Ma in most company meetings and public appearances. The brand philosophy is closely tied to this company philosophy.

All its branded digital offerings in the market, which are essentially its family of websites and portals, have a similarity – the strong positioning toward a specific customer segment (be it broad or niche). For example, the corporate website Alibaba.com is targeted toward international importers and exporters. Taobao Marketplace is targeted toward the massive consumer-to-consumer segment while Tmall.com is an online retail platform targeted toward manufacturers.

The philosophy is also driven by constant evolution of the company's capabilities and innovation in its offerings. This is the hallmark of any successful brand with multiple digital properties. The concept of a "one-stop shop" is strongly integrated into Alibaba's business model. From its inception in Jack Ma's apartment in 1999 to its current stature as an e-commerce behemoth, the need to diversify into a conglomerate has been Alibaba's driving force. Going forward, even with its intention to become a global player, diversification is still an essential component of the brand philosophy.

The global ambition is also supported by a strong sense of humility and dedication to wealth sharing that permeates throughout the organization. After the US markets closed after the first day of the company's IPO, Jack Ma hosted a company reception and re-emphasized the company's values and philosophy – Customer First, Teamwork, Embrace Change, Integrity, Passion, and Commitment.[44]

Brand Strategy

Alibaba's digital brand portfolio is organized around a hybrid brand architecture model. This is characterized by two sets of digital properties and services and the extent to which the corporate brand name (Alibaba) is associated or disassociated with the specific digital brand. The properties can be categorized into the following two groups.

Master brand and product family brand architecture: Alibaba, the master brand, lends its equity, promise, and philosophy to all the product family brands. Examples of product family brands in the portfolio are Alipay (third party online payment platform), AliExpress (online retail service), Alibaba Cloud Computing (cloud computing service platform), and AliWang (instant messaging service).

Product brand architecture: The product brand portfolio has been created to communicate a distinct value proposition to customers. Product brands have long-term strategic importance and substantial marketing investments driving them. The most important product brand in the portfolio is Taobao Marketplace, China's answer to eBay. Other product brands include Tmall.com, Juhuasuan, eTao, and 11 Main (US shopping website launched in 2014).

The group strategy has a strong underpinning in driving the equity and simplicity of the Alibaba brand name across product family brands. This serves the dual purpose of extending the equity of the Alibaba brand name across the group offerings and also follows the diversification strategy.

In 2014, this strategy was further extended by the launch of Alimama, the Google AdSense-like contextual advertising program of Alibaba and Alibaba Pictures, a film and TV production company.

The product brands that have operated independently within Alibaba's portfolio have been its biggest success drivers. The digital property Taobao Marketplace has its own mascot, an ant. Ma introduced the platform globally by stating that "we are the ant army." The word "Taobao" stands for "search for treasure" in Chinese, which exemplifies the fact that the website has more than 800 million product listings as of June 2014[45] and was in the top 10 most visited global websites.[46]

The brand strategy across the hybrid architecture model has placed equal emphasis on both the product brands and the product family brands. There are two differentiating features:

Use master brand equity to diversify: The equity of Alibaba as a brand name and the fact that it has a simple meaning and can be easily pronounced by anyone gives it a global appeal. This tenet is being used to expand the name into associated services and products, which are essential for the company's global success.

Strengthen appeal of product brands at a local level: Alibaba does not believe in attaching the prefix "Ali" to every product or service it launches. Jack Ma has been known to say that the company's success is attributed to an "Act Local, Think Global" strategy. Everyone has written reams about Taobao's success in China. But for its US growth strategy, it launched the US-focused shopping website 11 Main in 2014, instead of extending the Taobao brand name. 11 Main provides a platform for US-based specialty goods manufacturers to sell their products and make them visible to the American consumer.

These are two defining aspects of Alibaba's overall brand strategy in its significant growth phase.

Future Challenges

The group faces multiple challenges as it looks to expand beyond China. These challenges are not restricted to global markets, but are also emerging in the increasingly competitive Chinese landscape, which has been Alibaba's growth driver.

Handling the Made-in-China Challenge

Global perceptions of brands are often related to the country-of-origin, which makes it a vital ingredient in a brand. However, brands that globalize often forget about the importance of roots and culture. In this context, made-in-China will eventually become globally accepted and a positive trait for Chinese brands, but until that happens on a broader level, Alibaba needs to work hard to overcome any negative or skeptical perceptions related to its Chinese country-of-origin. Alibaba has to commit itself to excellent quality, reliability, and transparency, and provide good governance in all aspects of operations and business.

Genuineness of Products Sold on Platform

This has been one of the most persistent problems to have impacted Alibaba's equity with the outside world. China, which had a dubious past of being the hotbed of fake products, is still in the process of shrugging off this image. But Alibaba's Taobao platforms (for B2C trade) and other specific platforms for B2B trade, have been plagued by fake product listings, dubious suppliers, and a sustained perception that it has never done enough to increase the level of trust the outside world can place on Chinese suppliers.

This perception needs to be changed rapidly as the company expands globally. If this challenge does not receive the attention it deserves, then the global business community will never treat the portals with the seriousness they need to become a global shopping destination. Alibaba has maintained that it regularly takes down listings selling spurious or fake goods, but the problem and its associated negative perceptions have not gone away.

Lack of Awareness Outside China

Outside China, Alibaba and its portfolio of digital properties have very little or zero awareness. Though it was able to beat eBay in China, it does not have the global awareness and equity enjoyed by the likes of eBay and Amazon. This is going to be a significant challenge for Alibaba to overcome as it plans to expand into global markets. The fact that it is using the product brand approach to extend its presence in outside markets is a good strategy to start with. However, eventually the parent brand equity needs to be associated with the local product brand to give it the credibility it requires. Also, having a multiplicity of product brands focused no different regions or countries leads to inefficient resource allocation and marketing investments within the business. This also leads to more complex brand management processes and fragmentation of brand building and consolidation.

Having locally-focused digital properties (online marketplaces) allows Alibaba to have a stronger cultural impact, but leads to the development of a portfolio where each product brand has a sphere of awareness limited to a small geographic area. This is not a portfolio structure that any company with global ambitions would like to manage.

Increasing Competition in China

Although Alibaba still remains one of the biggest e-commerce players in China, enjoying majority market share both in terms of value and number of shipments, the external environment has not remained the same. Just as Alibaba has expanded and taken a new shape, China has also evolved into a market with a new set of challenges.

Alibaba's biggest competitor in China is Tencent, the technology company that owns the increasingly popular QQ and WeChat instant messaging services. It also owns QZone, one of China's largest social networking services and Tencent Weibo, a micro-blogging service. Alibaba used to have the WeChat instant messaging service as a feature on its portals, before switching to its own messaging service AliWang. Tencent slowly started making strides in the online payments market, by enabling payment features in WeChat. It has started showing ambitions to take Alibaba on in its home territory of e-commerce, by taking a stake in the online retailer JD.com.

Chinese businesses are also increasingly collaborating to take on Alibaba. In August 2014, Dalian Wanda Group (China's biggest commercial land developer), Tencent Holding, and Baidu Inc. formed an US$813 million venture with the aim of seamlessly integrating the physical and the digital worlds these companies dominate.

China is no longer the massive growth juggernaut it once was, with GDP growth rates in 2014 almost half of those recorded immediately before 2008. This could well have been the trigger for Alibaba to open its eyes to international expansion, but it will have a significant impact on the company's business operations, which have been and will continue to be the largest contributor toward revenues and profits.

Huawei – Transforming a Chinese Technology Business into a Global Brand

History

Huawei Technologies was founded in 1987 in Shenzhen, China as a rural sales agent for Hong Kong-based phone and cable network businesses.[47] Between 1996 and 1998 Huawei expanded into metropolitan areas of China as urban populations exploded. McKinsey predicts that China's urban population will hit the 1 billion mark by 2030 and the country will have 221 cities with over

1 million inhabitants by 2025, compared to 35 in Europe.[48] Vast cities require complex communication networks and Huawei has continued to grow at an astounding rate by expanding on this need.

Today, Huawei's products and solutions are deployed in over 170 countries, serving more than one third of global population.[49] The third-biggest global manufacturer of routers, switches and other telecommunications equipment by market share after Alcatel-Lucent and Cisco,[50] it recently joined in the ultra-competitive smartphone race.[51]

For many observers, Huawei has seemingly come out of nowhere to become one of the world's most dominant technology brands. Primarily a business-to-business company (B2B), its biggest gains have been outside of the public eye. Major customers include telephone and Internet operators, who use Huawei's expertise to provide services to customers under their brand name, not Huawei's. The company also lacked worldwide fame due to its origins. With up to one-fifth of the world's population within the borders of its own country, Huawei has been able to grow while still remaining isolated.

Huawei's core business can be dissected into three business groups.[52] The first group, the Carrier Network Business Group, provides wireless networks, fixed networks, global services, carrier software, core networks, and network energy solutions that are deployed by almost all major communications carriers world-wide. For seven years leading up to 2012, the compound annual growth rate of Huawei's managed services division exceeded 70 per cent annually, making Huawei the fastest-growing managed services provider globally. The second business group, the Enterprise Business Group, is a perfect complement. Once information is sent and received through "pipes," it has to be analyzed, trans-lated, stored, and saved by Huawei's data center. The newest business group is the Consumer Business Group, which spearheads the company's push into the personal handset and smartphone segments. Huawei calls this its "pipe strategy," which focuses on information storage and processing, information transportation and distribution, and information presentation and creation.

Huawei's personal handset business has steadily built expertise from a low-cost component and assembly provider to one of the top global mobile phone makers. Although it received no branding benefits, by 2008 it ranked number three in the global mobile equipment market. It has now successfully shed its role as an original design manufacturer (ODM) and begun to manufacture and brand its own smart devices. The movement up the value chain from component manufacturer to self-branded smartphone maker is a major part of Huawei's current and future growth strategy. According to Gartner, the company ranked sixth in worldwide mobile sales in Q2 2013.[53]

Brand Philosophy

Huawei's vision is to enrich life through communication.[54] More people are becoming connected worldwide on ever-faster devices, with greater demands on speed, usability, and a secure and personalized experience. Businesses have their own demands and use technology to manage logistics, operations, and all kinds of consumer data. By 2020, interactions between people, things, and the environment are expected to result in over 50 billion connection requirements from GPS, compasses, cameras, and microphones, not just communications. To deal with these digital floods, Huawei is committed to providing broader, smarter, and more energy-efficient pipes.

Working closely with customers is one of Huawei's greatest differentiators. It has set up 28 joint innovation centers directly with leading carriers worldwide to create customized technologies for each carrier's unique needs and establish their competitive edge for customers.

In 2014, Huawei was ranked the 50th most innovative company globally by the Boston Consulting Group.[55] It ranked second in terms of global Patent Cooperation Treaty patent applications in 2013.[56] With 150,000 employees, Huawei has over 70,000 research and development employees in Germany, Sweden, the UK, the US, France, Italy, Belgium, Finland, Ireland, Russia, India, and China. R&D expenses totaled 13 per cent of annual revenue in 2013. This single-minded dedication to innovation is illustrated by the company's philosophy of "Might from a small hole." Just as water can cut through steel plates once highly pressurized through a small opening, Huawei believes that if its resources remain committed to a sharply-defined purpose of enriching life through communication, it can consistently improve.

After its successful foray into the smartphone business, Huawei has pursued a philosophy of positioning its products as technologically-advanced problem-solvers. It aims to link its solution-providing legacy to the world's biggest telecommunication providers with its future platform of manufacturing and selling the most advanced phones. The transition from a non-visible ODM to a visible manufacturer of brands is a challenging one for Huawei to manage and excel in.

Brand Strategy

Outsmarting current technology and setting industry standards are integral strategies for Huawei. To be the first choice and best partner of telecom carriers, Huawei not only has to master the current technological level, but also anticipate future customer needs. There are almost 200 fourth-generation networks operating commercially across 75 countries today, with another 200 still in planning stages.[57] Meanwhile, Huawei's R&D teams have been working on developing fifth-generation, or 5G, networks for several years, expecting to introduce commercial 5G networks by 2020.[58] Huawei's foresight will make it the first-mover in 5G technology when the time comes. Huawei's rotating CEO Ken Hu suggested 5G will be up to 100 times faster than 4G.[59] In 2014, Huawei set up the world's first 5G phone network on the Isle of Man.[60]

Huawei is taking further advantage of its growth by becoming an international leader in various industrial standards. By June 30, 2014, Huawei had joined more than 170 industry standards organizations, holding more than 180 positions in those organizations. From this leadership platform, Huawei can shape the future of information technology policy and stay ahead of its competitors.

Huawei has taken great strides in aligning its internal leadership and hierarchy to remain responsive in a fast-moving industry. Although a chain of command that promotes uniformity and control quality is vital for branding, it can be detrimental to innovation. Making more decentralized decisions is important, and Huawei has begun delegating decision-making authority to customer-facing roles and field offices, encouraging idea flow.

By far the most risky, and potentially the most brilliant leadership strategy, is Huawei's rotating CEO system, by which a small group of executives takes turns to fulfill CEO duties. Compared to one single CEO who is expected to handle multiple strategies with in-depth insight, a group of rotating and acting CEOs is believed to be more effective as they have time to prepare better for their next term as acting CEO. This ensures that a wider breadth of expertise is present in the most senior leadership positions over time.

Technical prowess, combined with a unique senior management style, allows the company to operate with fresh thinking toward its brand strategy. In 2014, the company launched its corporate marketing and branding theme, "Building a Better Connected World," demonstrating its vision and future positioning. It follows Apple to some extent by presenting glitzy events to build awareness, but it also invests significantly in public relations and lobbying. Its marketing efforts are linked to a strategy of positioning its products (especially smartphones) as epitomizing excellence. The "Excellence with Edge" campaign for its P7 smartphones in 2014 portrayed visionaries or trendsetters.

Huawei has continually leveraged technological expertise in its product positioning. The company does not hesitate to use words and phrases that describe its products as the "best" or the "fastest." The underlying strategy is to attach a very high value proposition to its products. The brand strategy is accompanied by a strong visibility campaign. By 2012, more than 90 per cent of the company's consumer devices were shipped and sold under the Huawei brand. Although this resulted in a backlash from some telecom providers, who stopped doing business with Huawei, the company refused to relent on building its brand visibility.

This brand visibility push has also been aided by the decline of Sony, BlackBerry, and HTC, which has opened up opportunities in customer retail space. Beyond China and the US, the company's smartphone brands have found potentially lucrative opportunities in India, Indonesia, Taiwan, and many African countries. These newfound opportunities have linked nicely with Huawei's status as an entry-level challenger in most markets and enabled it to design and implement a global marketing strategy rather than grapple with the complexities of different maturity levels in different markets.

Brand Communications

Huawei's landmark year on the global stage came in 2005 when international contract orders first exceeded domestic sales. Recognizing that an identity change would be needed to accompany its ascendance on the global stage, Huawei redesigned its corporate identity to reflect principles of customer-focus, innovation, steadiness, and harmony.[61] The new image was intended to balance internal challenges occurring within Huawei – reflecting its transition from a traditional, local brand to a modern, international one.

Huawei officially released its new visual identity and logo on May 8, 2006. By the end of 2006, Huawei had been awarded "Broadband Infrastructure Vendor of the Year in Asia Pacific" by Frost & Sullivan and boasted 31 of 50 top telecom global operators as chosen corporate partners, including Vodafone, BT, Telefonica, Telfort, FT/Orange, and China Mobile. No longer a rising star, it was now a global leader.

To continually re-imagine itself as a mobile brand rather than simply a B2B service company, Huawei unveiled its "Make it Possible" smartphone initiative using story-telling around its products rather than promoting product features in 2013.[62] In technology industries, branding should focus less on superiority claims, and more on understanding customer desires and improving lives.

Brands also communicate through pricing. Huawei's ultra-affordable $80 Android phone has helped it gain footholds in many markets ignored by premium the smartphone makers Apple, Samsung, HTC, Microsoft, and BlackBerry.[63] In Africa, Huawei plans to put tens of millions of smart devices in the hands of African youths and bring 1 million African small and medium-sized enterprises (SMEs) online by 2016.

For consumers in mature markets like the US and Europe, Huawei may have to consider a different pricing strategy. Whether consciously or unconsciously, customers use pricing as a quality and reliability indicator. In these markets, premium pricing implies a premium product. For Huawei to enter as a low-cost provider by such a wide margin, it risks segmenting itself as a low-quality alternative. In 2013, in the US, Huawei made its first formal marketing push in mobile. But due to the US governments' suspicions that the company was acting as a spy on behalf of China, Huawei received continuous rejections, was banned from bidding in government contracts, and its sales and marketing efforts were severely restricted. By the end of the first quarter of 2014, the company had officially and unofficially announced its intention of not pursuing the US as a market.[64]

The company's investments in marketing and communications have paid off in the short term. In 2014, it became the first Chinese brand to break into the top 100 (rank 94) of Interbrand's ranking of the world's most valuable brands.[65] This has been due to continuous investments in improved brand management, glitzy events, public relations, and lobbying. It toyed with the idea of changing its name to ease pronunciation for Western consumers, but eventually stuck with its name.

Because of its global strategy to increase brand awareness and visibility, Huawei's marketing and advertising campaigns are global in nature (launched in 40+ markets simultaneously). It now employs some of the leading global marketing and advertising groups, including WPP/Ogilvy Mather and Saatchi & Saatchi.

Consistent and heavy investment in advertising and communications has been the mainstay of Huawei's brand strategy. This will continue as the company tries to strengthen visibility and awareness of its products globally and remain competitive (in terms of marketing investments) with the likes of Apple and Samsung.

Future Challenges

Continuing the Pace of Innovation

History has shown that monopoly control is temporary. Structural realities in every industry have and will continue to change, as illustrated by BlackBerry's fall from its once dominant height. The biggest mistake of successful companies is complacency. For Huawei, continuing to push forward with R&D is insufficient. As a cautionary tale, Nokia spent ten times more on R&D than Apple between 2004 and 2007, yet Nokia steadfastly built products to satisfy its current key segment's needs, ignoring the small number of consumers who showed great interest in future touch-screens. Similarly, Huawei must continually seek to satisfy and create future consumer needs rather than their current ones.

Although Huawei is an entirely employee-owned private company, it will certainly attract attention from investors looking to latch on to its impressive growth. Should it pursue an IPO and become more widely held, leadership must resist the shareholder value syndrome that has befallen many of tech's greatest innovators. The focus of stock markets on quarterly returns has entrenched a management system in most great companies that discourages dramatic change because game-changing innovations are risky. Stock markets do not initially respond well to disruptive innovators.

Brand Image in the United States

By far the most difficult challenge in Huawei's global strategy is in the US, where a smear campaign is being conducted by the US government.

Huawei has long been searching for an opportunity to expand into North America, which accounts for about 20 per cent of global telecom spending. Ever since a 2007 report highlighted the military background of CEO Ren Zhengfei, Huawei has become a political target.[66] Before he founded Huawei in 1987, Ren was a civil engineering director for the Chinese military. Huawei currently sells telecom equipment to major Internet carriers which, in turn, carry data for practically every government agency. The US intelligence committee said that US telecommunications firms should avoid business with Huawei because of potential Chinese state influence and security threats.[67]

In response, Huawei has started a charm offensive toward analysts, reporters, and politicians to shake suspicions.[68] Huawei also disclosed the names of its Board of Directors. These B2B challenges are partly why the smartphone will likely be the key to Huawei's growth in America.

Mergers and Acquisitions

A significant part of Huawei's leap from regional player to global leader has to do with its astute strategy of brand partnerships throughout its development. In 2003, Huawei established a joint venture with 3Com, a world leader in networking solutions at the time. The venture was called H3C – a conjunction of both companies' brand names. Under the agreement terms, 3Com would simply sell and rebrand products under H3C while reaping the benefits of Huawei's distribution networks and local knowledge. This venture would be extremely profitable for 3Com, but in the long run possibly even more valuable for Huawei who, after years learning from the American giant, eventually moved to purchase their global operations in 2007. Unfortunately, US government regulators stepped in over concerns that the Chinese military would gain access to 3Com's cyber security unit, which sells software to the US military. Eventually, 3Com was acquired by HP in 2010.

However, Huawei succeeded with Symantec. In 2008, it signed a joint venture with Symantec to boost their capabilities in network, security, and storage technologies. More than 50 per cent of Huawei Symantec employees would be engaged in research and development activities, with labs in Beijing, Shenzhen, Hangzhou, and India. Three years later, Huawei acquired all of Symantec's shares in the joint venture. From a company that had only begun R&D in security technology in 2000 and storage in 2004, Huawei was now a global powerhouse in both fields.

Huawei continues to be mentioned as suitors in potential game-changing acquisitions as it seeks to deploy its capital. In 2010, Huawei purchased products and services from American companies totaling US$6.1 billion. In 2012, rumours began to swirl that Google – who had bought Motorola – was in talks to sell the entire Motorola handset business to Huawei.[69]

In continuing to add its expertise, Huawei will have to stay away from the type of mergers or acquisitions that are predicated on cost efficiency and economies of scale. The most meaningful mergers and acquisitions for brand-building are those that truly add to a company's competitive advantage, not just its bottom-line.

Brand-oriented Global Leadership

Asian companies making their mark against Western players share a common denominator – a strong commitment to branding by their boardrooms and senior management. To succeed in building a strong global brand, Huawei should rotate more marketing-oriented personnel into CEO roles rather than traditional experts in finance and operations. Huawei also needs more managers with a global vision, regardless of nationality or background. CEO Ren Zhengfei has admitted that "Time will tell if the rotating CEO system is the right move or not."[70]

The company has started to make a conscious effort to bring more international and diverse experience in its managerial ranks, not only at board level but in multiple senior and mid-management roles. It has also started hiring high-profile Western executives to diversify its senior management team. This strategy should be followed and implemented in a comprehensive fashion so that diverse, global thinking and experience permeate deep into the organization's fabric. A truly global senior management team is essential for Huawei's success in foreign markets.

chapter 9

Ten Steps to Building an Asian Brand

Vision without action is a daydream. Action without vision is a nightmare.

— Japanese proverb

The practice of brand management has gone through substantial changes over the past few decades, and has evolved into a more integrated and visible part of overall corporate strategy. The evolution of the brand equity concept during the 1990s, the development of advanced financial brand valuation methods and their adoption by advisors and their clients, and the emergence of better brand tracking tools have all facilitated the elevation of the branding discipline beyond middle management and into the boardroom.

Asian boardrooms generally lag behind this trend and tend to manage brand management from a bottom-up instead of top-down perspective, as most traditionally manage marketing and brand decisions in mid-level marketing departments. Thus a large emphasis is on tactical marketing activities as opposed to corporate management-led strategic branding approaches. Branding has been widely perceived as being advertising and promotions.

However, several indications show rapid progress in the right direction for some Asian companies that have come to recognize and accept branding as a strategic tool within their boardrooms. This is partly driven by the increasing attention on branding and its value-driving capability among Asian stakeholders, media, and opinion makers. Strategic branding and its implications for Asian companies and governments is a much debated topic, through media coverage and regional conferences and seminars. Asian companies may have great intentions and aspirations to move up the value chain through branding to capture the previously-described financial and competitive benefits. However, they must follow a comprehensive brand strategy framework, supported by a systematic implementation process throughout the organization, which will help them achieve sustainable revenue and future cash flow streams.

The brand vision, objectives, and marketing activities must be closely aligned with the corporate strategy. They must blend together, as they serve the same purpose – driving profitability and shareholder value. Branding is the sum of all the parts and elements involved, so getting the strategic balance right between the brand, the corporate vision, and the entire organization is crucial. The boardroom must ensure that the brand delivers successfully and seamlessly on every customer touch point, so that it supports the overall strategic intention. This is easier said than done. A systematic and dedicated framework and a considerable period of time are required for success.

There are 10 crucial steps to follow when building a successful branding strategy and managing its implementation (Table 9.1). These steps enable the Asian boardroom to focus its attention on the required areas, and serve as check-points that can be tailored to the individual company's specific needs and requirements. Hence they need not be followed strictly or chronologically. As branding is an iterative process, it has to strike a balance between several objectives, trade-offs, resource constraints, and many other factors throughout the organization. These steps are meant as a useful guide for Asian branding projects – irrespective of scale, scope, and time horizon.

TABLE 9.1   Ten steps to building a successful Asian brand

1. The CEO needs to lead the brand strategy work
2. Build your own model as not every model suits all
3. Involve your stakeholders, including your customers
4. Advance the corporate vision
5. Exploit new technology
6. Empower people to become brand ambassadors
7. Create the right delivery system
8. Communicate!
9. Measure the brand performance
10. Adjust regularly – be your own change agent

Source: Martin Roll Company.

The CEO Needs to Lead the Brand Strategy Work

The Asian business landscape requires Asian companies and their boardrooms to follow a different path to be successful. Companies must achieve a fine balance between low-cost production (competitiveness), constant innovation (differentiation), and enhanced customer satisfaction (value capture through branding).

Increasingly, businesses must adapt to meet the growing needs and aspirations of Asian consumers, who have been exposed to Western brand offerings. The explosion of social media and the rapid increase in digital advertising has exposed the Asian consumer to what global brands have to offer.

A *New York Times* article pointed out that the clearest advantage American companies have over Chinese competition is branding. It described how many US firms are powered by "eccentric failed novelists" (meaning former advertising and consulting firm executives with solid brand expertise) and "visionary founders" (like Steve Jobs) who have created exceptional brands, compared to Chinese CEOs who are far more operational and transactional.[1]

Brands are not just built from traditional advertising and promotions, but rather through the use of a comprehensive range of strategic activities delivered by all employees. Therefore, the crucial balance between brand promise and brand delivery has implications for all company functions and it becomes a managerial responsibility that reaches far beyond marketing and communications departments.

Branding can no longer be delegated to the mid-level marketing function in the typical Asian organization. Instead, Asian boardrooms and the CEO must take charge of brand strategy, lead brand development, manage its implementation, and be fully involved in brand performance tracking.

The marketing and communications departments do not have managerial authority over other company functions. The following three examples illustrate this clearly:

1. According to survey data, if the service level of an airline's frontline staff slides, it could quickly harm the brand promise. But the marketing department has little authority to implement any necessary actions, and can only influence the process. Internal political complications could be significant and it may be longer than necessary for action to be taken.
2. Brand success depends on the company culture and the right type of people working in the company. Service businesses, for example, are strongly

dependent on these cultural and people factors. However, marketing people have little power to set guidelines and influence specific types of future talent to be recruited, unless the guidelines are enforced by top management.

3. A brand might have to enhance its visual appeal or innovate to maintain its relevance and stay competitive. Marketing departments have little influence and authority over the objectives and development plans in the R&D department, unless the R&D department has been actively involved and has been integrated into the company's strategic brand driven vision.

The above examples illustrate the conflicts that internal functions face while working with each other. Marketing and communications departments should be enabled to work closely with other functions. Reciprocally, every organizational function should have an in-depth understanding and respect for the marketing and communication function's objectives. The successful implementation of an efficient, process-driven branding and marketing strategy requires boardroom and corporate management involvement, and it carries the great weight when it is led and enforced by the CEO. Therefore, branding should be represented in the boardroom by a person responsible for branding so that he or she is able to participate equally with corporate executives like the CEO and CFO.

Naturally, there is a limit to the direct involvement and supervision of the CEO in managing marketing and branding activities. To ensure his or her continuous involvement in branding despite his or her other responsibilities, the CEO must be backed by a strong brand management team of senior contributors, who can facilitate the continuous development and integration of brand strategy into the organization's operating model. The CMO, who is often missing from the Asian boardroom, can serve as the crucial link in enabling corporate management to design and control the brand strategy directly, and allocating the necessary resources to implement the strategies successfully.

As shown in the brand boardroom model (Figure 9.1), all the different line functions of an organization both contribute to and benefit from branding. The model shows the value that different departments within a company derive from strong brand management. For example, the finance department reports better margins due to strong brand recognition and brand equity, and the HR department gets a better and more talented applicant pool.

The company can also gain significant advantages from creating a brand board chaired by the CEO and led by the CMO. This removes the missing link between the boardroom (corporate management) and the marketing function (implementation of brand strategy). The key people from all relevant

BOARDROOM	**Finance**
• **Enhance shareholder value**	• Positive impact on cash flow • Better margins • Enhanced profitability • Easier collection of receivables • Extended credit terms • Collateral for debt and other loans • Platform for M&A, joint ventures, and alliance activities
• **Catalyst for better leadership**	**Sales** • Better sales pipeline management • Enhanced sales due to better customer perceptions and loyalty • Wider collaboration with distributors
• **Drives a shared vision throughout the organization**	**Corporate communications** • Better opportunities for becoming a thought-leader • Sustained platform for media and stakeholder relations
• **Balances short and long-term perspectives and performance**	**Purchase** • Enhanced bargaining power with suppliers and partners • Better collaboration terms • Platform for long-term partnerships
	Human resources • Strengthen corporate culture • Ease of staff recruitment • Better staff retention and satisfaction • Staff as brand ambassadors beyond their jobs • Support training and motivational programs

Marketing

• Plan, implement, and measure brand equity	• Facilitate strategic alliances and partnerships
• Linking marketing activities, metrics, and performance	• Strengthen co-branding and licensing opportunities
• Enhances cross-functional collaboration tied to the brand	• Platform for internal branding
• Better basis for brand/line extentions	• Brand evaluation and valuation

FIGURE 9.1 The brand boardroom model

Source: Martin Roll Company.

departments should be represented on the brand board, including staff from the marketing department. This ensures that the brand strategy is commonly shared and understood throughout the organization, thereby enabling everyone to take ownership of it.

This proposed reorganization is beneficial for the Asian marketing profession as a whole and will help Asian brand marketers build a reputation for being financially responsible. Shareholders and analysts are pushing companies and boardrooms to deliver on revenue and profit objectives. Therefore the CEO must ensure that marketing expenditures deliver a satisfactory return and help to drive the bottom line.

Elevating the Asian brand marketer to the boardroom creates a new trio consisting of the CEO, CFO, and CMO that encompass both corporate and brand strategy. It is not a question of titles (it could be marketing director, vice-president, or the like) but rather dedication from the senior management to make the brand strategy an integral part of enhancing and accelerating cash flows and financial value throughout the organization.

Build Your Own Brand Model as Not Every Model Suits All

All companies have their own sets of business values and unique operating style, influenced by the company heritage and culture. Many brand models are available and more are being developed annually. Even the best and most comprehensive brand strategy model has to be tailored to specific company needs and requirements. Often only a few but important adjustments are needed to align these models with other similar business models and company strategies to create a simplified framework and toolbox for branding. Branding is the face of a business strategy, and thus these two aspects must work hand in hand for the company to become successful.

Corporate management should set clear and quantifiable objectives for the brand portfolio – and stick to them. Brand building is a long, drawn-out process. Therefore, companies must take a long-term view and not get hold to unrealistic short-term expectations. Brand metrics are helpful here as they are important tools that can measure performance and benchmark several indicators over time.

Corporate management must determine the brand identity, strategy, and implementation plan, and make sure it is aligned with the corporate strategy. The entire process is important in itself, as it forces the corporate management team to discuss and agree on crucial brand issues and their implications for the company. For example, if enhanced service aspects or new innovation capabilities are believed to be future brand drivers, there are implications for several functions and managers throughout the organization and the way service and innovation initiatives are implemented and managed.

Branding requires the right amount of organizational and financial resources. The corporate management team therefore needs to ensure the brand promise and brand delivery are closely aligned. This involves a thorough examination of the entire operational system of the organization and how well it is equipped to deliver the brand promise that is communicated to the market. A comprehensive customer touch point program plays a crucial role in managing and measuring the entire process throughout the company.

INDIGO AIRLINES: MAKING INDIA GO HIGHER

Founded in 2006, the private budget airline IndiGo has topped the leaderboard of India's airline industry, deposing industry heavyweights on its way up. It commands one-third of the market for all domestic passengers and has carried 84 million passengers since its inception.[2] While its competitors SpiceJet and Jet Airways are languishing in the red,[3] IndiGo has made money since 2009. It reported a net profit of US$51 million and revenues of US$1.8 billion for fiscal year 2014.[4] This is no mean feat against a predominately loss-making global aviation backdrop.

IndiGo's enviable market and financial performance is due to unflinching adherence to its first brand pillar: cost consciousness.[5] The group's managing director Rahul Bhatia keeps costs "structurally low" and refrains from emulating competitors' non-core offerings like loyalty programs and hot meals on board.[6] IndiGo believes in keeping things simple, its "do one thing and do it well" approach sees it offer standardized airplane configuration, fares, and customer service that keep waste at bay.[7]

The airline's second brand differentiator is its obsession with punctuality (marketed as IndiGo Standard Time).[8] Its on-time performance and low flight cancellation statistics are industry leading. Even though IndiGo's flights do not have business or first class sections, business travelers are loyal to the brand due to its reliability.

A courteous and hassle-free travel experience is the final pillar of IndiGo's brand philosophy. Its attractive young fleet of 84 Airbus A320-200 aircraft has an average age of three years.[9] The airline's biggest edge is its undiminishing customer focus. The brand believes that low cost should not mean low quality. This is a stand out differentiator to a customer base that has come to expect poor customer service from budget airlines. IndiGo's target consumer is described as "not a demographic but a psychographic."

The branding and advertising uses youthful urban cues, indulging the cool quotient and has great crossover appeal.[10] IndiGo obsesses about details like step-free handicap accessible boarding ramps, "Fragile" luggage stickers showing a heart shape, airsickness bags reading "Get well soon," and reusable pastel color cookie tins.[11]

The three-pillar brand philosophy is aptly summarized by IndiGo's corporate mantra: "Offer fares that are always low, flights that are on time, and a courteous, hassle-free travel experience."[12]

However, aggressive competition from new market entrants (like Tata Group–AirAsia's budget airline, and the new airline from Tata Group and Singapore Airlines called Vistara)[13] puts IndiGo at risk of losing some of its clientele to new upstarts. It is under scrutiny for the legitimacy of its profits, which some people attribute to creative accounting of sale-and-leaseback agreements.[14] With an understated management approach and an inward focus on cost efficiency, the brand should develop attributes of brand charisma rather than just functional appeal for continued success. With a healthy order of 250 new Airbus A320s,[15] a synergistic joint venture with Accor (the group that owns Ibis hotels)[16] and a desirable credit profile that can help secure bank loans and equity financing[17], the future looks positive for IndiGo.

Involve Your Stakeholders, Including Your Customers

Who knows more about a company than its customers, employees, and key stakeholders? This is common sense, but many companies overlook these simple and easily accessible sources of valuable information as key enablers for creating and managing powerful brands.

The value of market research cannot be underestimated. A company should get an external and unbiased view of the competitive landscape, including the current brand image among stakeholders, the brand positioning, and critical directions for the brand identity and strategy in the future. However, its own observations, cultural understanding, and intuition are also important to achieving a well-balanced platform for decisions. For example, it can be difficult to get respondents in research situations to talk openly about their aspirations or imagine things they want in the future as consumers always face difficulties in clearly articulating future needs and preferences.

72 per cent of companies believe their budget for customer insights is too low.[18] A simple rule of thumb is to spend around 5 per cent of the brand-marketing budget on market research and insights to establish a platform for strategy development. Many research-driven organizations invest a sizeable

amount of marketing budget in conducting research. In 2012, P&G spent an estimated US$0.5 billion on market research.

L'Oréal is another organization that invests heavily in market research. It has research centers in China, India, and Singapore. It also has evaluation centers, which keep tabs on local trends and listen to consumer feedback, in South Korea, Thailand, India, Indonesia, and China.[19]

CUSTOMER-CENTRIC AND CONSUMER-DRIVEN BRANDS

In today's ultra-competitive marketplace, luring customers from competitors requires more than the dominant product-centric or company-centric model. Customers demand that brands provide a special experience in return for their loyalty. In fact, customers are becoming increasingly vocal and public in offering their feedback.

In the last decade, CEOs have been ranking customers higher on change-driving factors in organizations. According to IBM's Global C-suite Study, CEOs now place consumers second only to the C-suite in terms of their strategic influence.[20] As a result, tomorrow's CEOs, CMOs, and CIOs are recognizing that they need consumers' help to determine their path forward and are dissolving traditional barriers to engage them.

A customer-centric philosophy is an ideology – a value system in which a company's alignment of operations, production, and internal controls are consumer-centered. These activities include crowdsourcing, co-creation, social science, and data-driven design.

Four reasons why businesses should be customer-centric

Clarity: According to more than 1,500 global CEOs, the biggest challenge they face is complexity. However, less than 50 per cent feel prepared for change, citing a lack of customer insight as their biggest deficiency.[21] Customers are the only ones who can provide understanding about their present and future needs.

Design and development: The holy grail of customer-centric strategy is to anticipate what consumers need before they realize they need it. With this, product development and design will be more in tune with customers' needs, enabling sustainable competitive advantage through consistent innovation over time.

Sales and marketing: Customer insights are enabling organizations to improve the timing and positioning of their marketing. Businesses can now predict customer needs by recognizing behavioral patterns, and then tailoring their brand communication, advertising and promotions to when buyers are most receptive.

Profitability: Ultimately, businesses are not charitable organizations – they exist to make as much money as possible. With data analysis, leaders can now identify high-value and high-renewal-propensity customers and identify micro markets within their previously well-defined customer segments.

Brand-driven business: Asking the consumer

One of the simplest ways to understand consumers' needs and wants is to ask. While most companies would conduct market research via face-to-face interviews, focus groups, or online surveys, some of the most intriguing feedback comes from more innovative sources.

Open innovation has become a great way to bring consumers into the design process by letting them get their hands on designing products, services, and even processes themselves, thus losing nothing in the translation.

Regardless of how brands go about soliciting customer feedback, there are still major drawbacks to asking consumers what they want. Human beings are creatures of habit and can become so accustomed to current conditions that it is difficult to think of radical solutions that do not currently exist.

Steve Jobs never asked global consumers what they wanted. He believed that people would not be able to envision what products and services they aspired for in the future. Because most human decisions are unconscious, brands should independently observe customers to understand what drives them, rather than simply ask.

Business insights: Observing the consumer

Companies must also use more objective data-driven methods to gain business and brand insights. Two main methods of gathering objective data exist: the study of human behavior through anthropological observation, and number-crunching, deep analytics, and big data. A balance between these quantitative and qualitative collection methods is required to become successful.

Anthropological observation: To understand what makes customers tick, business leaders sometimes have to observe them in their natural environment. Lindsay Owen-Jones, the former chairman and CEO of L'Oréal, was notoriously obsessed with multiple customer insights, and spent a significant proportion of his executive time on the road visiting, interviewing, and observing global L'Oréal consumers in their natural environment. This meant visiting not only L'Oréal's typical stores but also other types of retail outlets. These insights, along with visionary leadership, were the two main drivers of the global rise of L'Oréal.[22]

In the early 2000s, Lego's attempts to combat competition by becoming a lifestyle brand led the Danish company to become over-diversified and near bankrupt. When Jørgen Vig Knudstorp was appointed Lego's CEO in 2004, he pledged to get closer to Lego consumers, who had lost their connection with the once famous brand. He realized that Lego needed to better understand the phenomenon of play and creativity among both adults and children. The new CEO dispatched "anthro-teams" (teams of anthropologists) to observe customers in their own homes, shopping with them and listening to their stories. The most vital insight was the realization that Lego users play for the freedom to experiment and achieve mastery of their building skills. Thus began Lego's return to making Lego for people who loved it for what it stood for. By going "back to the brick," refocusing on core Lego products, and divesting the unessential business units, the company began its return to profitability and valuable brand equity.

Technological analytics: The most popular and obvious area for brands to gain insights for better decisions moving forward is intelligence gathered from digital and social media. It is no coincidence that some of the most innovative companies are those that are social media-savvy and have fully embraced the digital revolution. Historically, companies and brands have allocated resources on the basis of gut instinct, emotions, and often anecdotal evidence, but deep data analytical capabilities now provide decision makers with richer consumer and market insights.

The need for greater customer centricity in Asia

Asia is still the world's biggest provider of commodity products. To break out of this commodity-driven thinking and see the emergence of strong, international Asian brands, customer centricity must become the core of Asian brand strategy. Asian boardrooms and executives must step up to the challenges and let marketing take center-stage in their companies. A constant dialogue with customers and attention to their needs is the next frontier to conquer for Asia to compete globally, sustain competitiveness, and master customer loyalty.

Samsung, Hyundai, AmorePacific, and Singapore Airlines are prime examples of Asian brands that are strongly customer-centric and brand-driven, but many more Asian companies must follow suit.

Advance the Corporate Vision

A branding strategy is an excellent reason and channel for advancing the corporate vision throughout the company. It allows management to involve, educate, and align everyone around the corporate objectives, values, and future strategy. It provides a guiding star that leads everyone in the same direction. Internal efforts contribute at least half of a corporate branding strategy's success, and they serve as a platform for communicating the corporate vision internally and externally. By involving all internal stakeholders, corporate management can not only ensure a total buy-in for its branding initiatives, but also use the entire exercise to motivate its employees and rejuvenate the corporate culture.

RED BULL: THE ENERGY DRINK

Red Bull is one of the few brands to have created a whole new category – the energy drink. It has led this category since its inception almost 20 years ago. It commanded a 43 per cent market share worldwide[23] and US$6.24 billion in total turnover in 2013.[24] From a humble start with unconventional marketing tactics, Red Bull has become one of the world's most popular drinks. Red Bull originated in Thailand, where it was known as Krating Daeng, which means "red water buffalo." Red Bull was founded in 1987 when Dietrich Mateschitz, a marketing executive at Unilever and P&G, introduced the energy drink into Europe. He modified the ingredients of the drink to suit Western tastes and this created a new "energy drink" category of its own.

One of the main reasons for Red Bull's success has been its unconventional marketing communications, ranging from creating "buzz" and word-of-mouth publicity to sponsoring extreme sports. The communications have been in line with the overall brand personality of being a cool, hip, rebellious brand. The initial ban on Red Bull from entering the German, French, and other key European markets due to its ingredients also added to the brand's mystique. As of 2014, the brand is available in all 28 member states of the European Union and in 166 countries globally.[25]

Red Bull's initial marketing channel was through opinion leaders in its target segments of students, hip and high-end bars, and athletes in extreme sports. By seeding the product through these groups, Red Bull created a positive buzz for its brand. Red Bull followed this up by sponsoring team events and extreme sports, rather than using celebrities, to build up its personality. From windsurfing, handgliding, a Formula One team, and its own flying team, Red Bull sponsors around 650 athletes around the world.[26] The company spends close to one-third of its total annual revenue on marketing globally. Its expenditure on marketing in 2012 was an estimated US$2.2 billion. Around 20 per cent of this marketing spend, close to US$440 million, was on sports events and athletes.[27] In contrast, Coca-Cola spent US$3.3 billion on advertising in 2013, which was 7 per cent of its net sales.[28]

Despite its Asian origins, Red Bull is headquartered in Austria, and has grown into a brand that spans continents. Red Bull is a classic example of how a long-term vision and strong branding initiatives can turn an ordinary drink into a widely popular brand across the world.

Exploit New Technology

Modern technology must play an integral part in branding strategy as it helps the organization develop, manage, and measure brand activities. Furthermore, technology helps increase effectiveness and improve the corporation's competitive edge.

Much of a brand's future success depends on how it manages the mobile, social, and digital advertising revolution. The rise of Big Data is a paradigm shift for global and local businesses. Next-generation business leaders recognize the need to invest in technology-enabled platforms like e-commerce and Big Data analytics, but spending alone does not guarantee success. In this new age for brands, organizational structures should be changing along with capabilities, making technology and analytics an extension of branding and part of a company's DNA. Smart leaders must recognize the value of information and Big Data analytics. They must manage them like all other assets on the balance sheet, giving those responsible for their gathering, interpretation, and deployment a seat at the boardroom table.

> ### THREE EXPLOSIVE SHIFTS IN THE COMPETITIVE LANDSCAPE FOR BRANDS
>
> Explosion of devices: 75 per cent of the world's population now has a mobile phone and global mobile traffic data is expected to increase 11-fold between 2013 and 2018.[29] Any brand serious about capitalizing on how people buy and interact in the future, must have its marketing and communication strategies optimized for not only online and mobile commerce, but also all forms of digital interaction. Brands must provide fluid experiences across multiple devices from PCs, laptops, smartphones, and tablets to TVs and even in-car devices. Strong brands have serious consumer promises and every contact affects the delivery of these promises. Therefore, as touchpoints proliferate, brands have more opportunities to differentiate themselves from competitors and meet or exceed customer expectations using these touch points.
>
> A company website is a crucial channel for any modern corporation, regardless of industry or size. Many Asian companies still underestimate the power of the Internet as a communication channel for building brands. If a corporation does not have a

strategy for and is not accessible on the Internet or on a consumer's chosen Internet-connected device, it does not exist. Consumers expect companies to have a strong online presence. The more professionally and interactively the website is structured and managed, the better the brand perception among increasingly Internet-savvy customers. Websites provide an excellent platform for micro marketing as they can be used as a targeted communication channel.

A well-designed and constantly updated corporate intranet is a must in today's working environment, which has become increasingly virtual, with employees working out-of-office and traveling across the globe. An extranet can facilitate seamless integration with strategic partners, suppliers and customers. It can help to avoid time-consuming paperwork and manual handling of many issues. Intranets and extranets are critical collaboration platforms for the successful implementation of marketing and branding strategies.

Explosion of social media: People have always been the channel by which a brand's most effective advertising is done. However, today's consumers own and control a brand's message to a large extent. Where the customer was once at the end of the communication chain, simply receiving messages, they are now at the center of a vast network, actively filtering, editing, and disseminating their own messages and experiences. They have become co-creators of brands. Co-creation is also a widely practiced qualitative research technique that fuels innovation strategies in brand building.

Rapidly increasing communication channels like blogs, online forums, Twitter feeds, and Facebook posts are increasingly becoming an important way for customers and other stakeholders to express positive or negative ideas. Monitoring these channels allows company executives to respond to customer feedback and reactions immediately. It provides a conduit to invite customers to share their experiences with the brand, but simultaneously serves as a channel for customer complaints, which must be tracked and responded to. These channels have increasingly started to play a critical role in corporate public relations, corporate social responsibility (CSR), and proactive brand building initiatives.

In addition to blogs, marketing and branding activities on networking and social media platforms like Facebook[30] and Twitter[31] have exploded in recent times.

The way consumers prefer to receive brand messaging has also changed. Too many marketers treat digital and social media like a traditional platform – targeting consumers with ads. A brand's digital presence must be consistent with the reasons consumers use new media – to interact, be entertained, and solve problems. Great brands create content and platforms their followers can share and use as an extension of themselves. This has led to the rise of a whole new stream of marketing called "content marketing."

Explosion of data: Social media and connected devices have led to an explosion of instantly available consumer insight. Software can now not only capture every conversation about a brand in blogs, comments, news, and social media but also use natural language processing to decipher the nuance of language like sarcasm and wordplay (a technique which is called "sentiment analysis" in the world of social media analytics). Newer generations of devices will also collect information from our physical bodies and environments. This potential insight level means that analytical rigor has to become a core competency for brands. Marketers have to become data scientists in order to fuel innovation, improve products and services, generate better retail offers, deliver more contextually relevant ads, and anticipate customer needs before they are actually expressed.

One of the greatest advantages that companies have today is the power of customer databases. The explosion of the Internet and the possibility of recording very specific details about customers, their online movements, and their purchase behavior have only added power to these databases. To move towards market orientation is to optimally leverage these databases. The potential marketing intelligence that these databases offer may allow companies to understand customers' current and potential needs clearly. Such an understanding would bring marketing functions in line with customers' needs.

Empower People to Become Brand Ambassadors

One of the most important assets in a corporation is its human resources. They interact every day with each other, customers, suppliers, competitors, industry experts, and so on. But staff members also interact with an impressive number of people who are totally unconnected with the corporation, like family members, friends, former colleagues, and others. Hence they serve as the most important brand ambassadors of the company as their attitudes, behavior, and recommendations will significantly impact perceptions.

A brand is created by thousands of experiences that people have with its products, services, and systems. Therefore, employees are the driving force of brand strategy and should be the core element in this strategy design. The C-suite vision is useless without the culture, rewards, process, strategy, and structure that effectively support it. The most effective way to turn employees into brand ambassadors is to train everyone adequately in the brand strategy (including vision, values, personality, etc.) and ensure full understanding of what the corporation aims at becoming in the minds of its customers and stakeholders.

Today's best brands have wrapped the company's goals and vision around customer needs, values, and emotions. Therefore, organizations should look for people who are independently driven to want to do the best for customers. This type of customer-centric culture is vital because no matter how well-structured a company's processes and systems are, it is impossible to script every possible scenario. When employees are armed with the right value systems, they are more likely to act spontaneously in the right way.

In 2013, HSBC employees received a total of 988,000 days of online and face-to-face training, which is equivalent to almost four days per full-time employee. From the company's internal HSBC Business School, employees get access to a comprehensive set of tools and learning materials based on their specific role and business area. There is also a specialized International Management Programme that offers successful employees the opportunity to pursue an international career spread over a variety of roles and locations.[32]

While management is about control, leadership is about empowerment. A sense of power and responsibility has dramatic effects on behavior, making people better at focusing on information, identifying patterns, and being decisive, energetic, and optimistic. Empowerment gives people a sense of accomplishment, making their daily tasks intrinsically motivating.

Brands like Nike and Apple are known for their comprehensive company-wide efforts in attracting, developing, and retaining talent. They are aware of the risks in having new talent joining and potentially contributing to their unique and strong company cultures. New applicants have to meet several current staff members who assess how the applicants will fit into the company culture. Much effort is put into the recruiting processes to ensure that new talent fits into their company cultures, which are strongly aligned around their brands. Dedication to HR is an important part of these companies' success.

INTERNAL BRANDING: MAKING THE ORGANIZATION LIVE THE BRAND [33]

Shangri-La Hotels and Resorts is a good example of how a leading Asian hospitality brand practices branding within the organization by aligning its staff and management with the overall brand strategy. Shangri-La's stated mission is to delight its customers each and every time. To protect the brand image, it has to ensure that its staff offer top-notch service and that is consistent across the group's 88 hotels and resorts. With this intention, in 1996 Shangri-La Hotels launched the Shangri-La Care series, an integrated training program to train its managers and staff.

The training program is divided into four modules called Shangri-La Hospitality, Delighting Customers, Recover to Gain Loyalty, and Taking Ownership. The objective of the fourth module, for example, is to have employees understand the positive impact they can make on guests, colleagues, and the company by taking ownership. It is about how every colleague can show genuine care that is self-driven.

The aim is to train staff in improving service delivery. The program includes training on how to live the corporate values, how to offer a memorable experience to customers by personalizing services, and how to retain and recover customer loyalty when uncontrollable mistakes happen.

Corporate management has made it mandatory to allocate a separate budget for training and regularly ensures that the training programs are being conducted. By concentrating on internal branding, Shangri-La has been able to project a consistent brand image in all its hotels across the world. Also, with every staff member acting as brand ambassador, it has been able to deliver its brand promises consistently.

Create the Right Delivery System

A brand is the face of a successful business strategy and it promises what all stakeholders can expect from the corporation. The brand will only add value when these expectations are consistently met. Therefore, delivery of the products and services as promised is crucial for companies, as promise without delivery is worthless. Think of the cradle-to-grave concept of a lifelong customer and the value he or she will provide in such a time span (a concept called Customer Life Time Value (CLTV) in the world of data analytics). Companies should ensure that customers are handled with great care, according to internal specifications and outside expectations. The moment of truth is when the corporate brand promise is delivered well – this is the ideal situation for the brand to exceed customer expectations.

Singapore Airlines has a rigid, detailed, and in-depth description of all customer touch points within the corporation, and resources are spent on making sure touch points are delivered effectively every time to every customer. All Singapore Airlines' employees, regardless of title and geographical location, spend a significant number of workdays every year being trained.

One of the challenges for companies in general, and for diversified or expanding companies in particular, is to put in place a systematic structure to deal with multiple factors and considerations associated with brand strategy. To ensure consistency in delivering brand promises, companies should establish some benchmarks and guidelines. These should guide all the different functions within the company. The guidelines just provide the blueprint; the important aspect is to drive these initiatives to their logical conclusion. By implementing and managing the customer touch point model discussed in Chapter 6, companies can ensure that both internal and external stakeholders are adequately aligned in the overall process.

Ever-changing market trends and customer mind-sets make the brand management process an ongoing and evolving one. The process should act as a loop by constantly taking in inputs from the market and customers and evolving the branding processes.

The company also needs to decide on the structure of the marketing organization, that is, whether it should be centralized or decentralized. An example of a central marketing organization is the case of Samsung, which aims to build a premium brand positioning. The company wanted the brand to be managed in a unified manner with a long-term horizon. Prior to Samsung's decision to manage the brand image through a central marketing organization in its Seoul headquarters, many of the marketing activities were localized across regions, which fostered brand dilution and a misconception of the corporate identity.

> Mercury Drug is the Philippines' largest drugstore chain, with more than 900 stores. It was started by Mariano Que, who sold drugs from a pushcart in Manila before opening his first store in 1945. In 1960, the Ayala Group gave Mercury Drug the option to lease a space in a new shopping mall in Makati, which led to the opening of the second Mercury Drug as a self-service pharmacy. Innovation has always been a part of the brand, and Mercury was first with a delivery system (1948), 24-hour stores (1965), and drive-through pharmacies (2012).[34]

Communicate!

In the 2013 Sales Performance Optimization Study from Accenture, made in collaboration with CSO Insights, 70 per cent of organizations admitted that they are yet to develop strong customer relationships.[35] Gone are the days when a good product would sell by itself in the marketplace. With the ever-increasing number of products, proliferation of brands, and over-communication in the markets, creating the right perception has become as important as the product itself, if not more so.

Bill Bernbach, founding partner of advertising agency DDB Worldwide, was clear on brand impact: "Nobody counts the number of ads you run, they just remember the impression you make."[36] Asian companies must realize that communication is not just about creative advertisements. Instead, it is a more comprehensive exercise, encompassing the entire mix of communication channels, with the sole goal of connecting with customers at both the functional and emotional level.

Throughout the 1980s and 90s, the Hong Kong Shanghai Banking Corporation grew rapidly through organic growth and acquisitions. In 1999, the company decided to use HSBC as its brand name and international symbol. The rebranding exercise involved 19 different banking brands in 79 countries.

HSBC developed a unique positioning around "The World's Local Bank," with tailored advertising to different markets and cultures, which has been successful in differentiating the brand.

After a long successful run, HSBC's new CEO Stuart Gulliver moved the bank away from "The World's Local Bank" positioning in 2011 in the face of sluggish growth, mounting job losses, sub-scale operations, and increasing regulatory pressure. The focus of the new HSBC has now changed to "going back to its trade finance roots" and investing in high growth markets like Brazil, Turkey, India, and China.[37]

Companies should ensure that through their integrated marketing communications, the brand is brought to life and made to resonate with customers. All brand messages should be consistent, clear, and relevant to the target audiences and easy to comprehend.

More often than not, companies are focused on buying advertising campaigns. Instead, they should buy marketing effect that will add brand value. By focusing on value creation, companies can establish long-term relationships with the right communications partners like ad agencies, PR and media agencies, and so on. These partners should be made strategic partners with the brand and held responsible for their results.

The following are guidelines for effective communications:

1. Explore multiple ways of marketing communications like public relations, interactive online advertising, event sponsorships, and others, instead of just mass media advertising
2. Involve society gatekeepers and opinion makers in the communication process
3. Never let the ad agencies and other parties decide the communication strategy – this should be decided by the company but in consultation with the agencies
4. As strong brands reflect happenings in society, maintain a balance between being consistent with the message and being relevant by adopting the latest trends and ways to communicate
5. Adopt an integrated marketing communications approach by using fully all the available channels to communicate effectively.

BRITISHINDIA; A BRAND BUILT ON A DISTINCT BRAND IDENTITY AND PERSONALITY [38]

Originally from Malaysia, BritishIndia has carved out a niche for itself in the lifestyle segment of the Asian retail market. Since its inception in Kuala Lumpur in 1994, BritishIndia has built a retail chain of 40 stores in 4 countries (Malaysia, Singapore, Thailand, Philippines) offering fashion apparel, home accessories, and related products.

BritishIndia was founded by Pat Liew, Group CEO and a veteran in the Malaysian retail industry, who oversees the brand's creative direction and soul. The company has its 100,000 square feet open-faced brick headquarters including a design studio with 70 designers and a large warehouse in Kota Damansara, Selangor, Malaysia. BritishIndia is privately held.

BritishIndia started its branding strategy with its name. By naming the brand BritishIndia, the goal was to evoke nostalgic memories and the colonial feel of the British Raj era, and to call upon the rich heritage that the British Empire left behind. This was in line with the initial strategy to differentiate itself in the marketplace. To sustain this differentiation, the company had to come up with a strong identity. It created an exciting blend of British heritage and its timeless elegance, and a distinct personality that would be relevant to the current customer base.

BritishIndia is a classic example of how a start-up company became a strong Asian brand by practicing classic brand management. The brand owes its success to its distinct brand identity and personality that have been created and communicated consistently. Created for the tropics and inspired by the grand romance of the colonial era, BritishIndia stores offer timeless designs created with the philosophy of comfort and effortless dressing for both men and women in mind. The typical customers are well-traveled, socially active, and culturally aware.

BritishIndia has optimally used its retail outlets to communicate its personality and positioning by creating an exciting and unique atmosphere. It has created visual treats in terms of decor, music, lighting, scent, and the materials used. This has enabled the brand to extend this identity to both the main brand and its brand extensions. The BritishIndia Apparel lines have expanded into a brand architecture of six sub-brands, each aiming to capture different lifestyle demands: Classic-Black, Classic-Blue, Pure, Traveller, Adventurer, and Travel & Yoga. A younger brand, Just B, was also developed to cater for the whimsical female clientele.

This strategy of creating a strong brand identity and personality has been so successful that the brand has a following of loyal customers. Another clear advantage of building a unique Asian brand identity and personality has been the ease with which BritishIndia has been able to position itself as a lifestyle brand, a level above a mere fashion clothing brand.

BritishIndia was established as a premium tropical lifestyle brand offering quality apparel designed for the tropics. The fashion company launches six collections per year for every line, and every line averages around 20 styles per collection to keep the merchandise in the retail stores fresh.

Since its inception, the BritishIndia brand has attracted both locals and foreigners. Holistic living, natural fabrics suited to the tropical climate, and superior quality are some of the core values of BritishIndia that are imbued in all its merchandise.

Unlike the usual way of leveraging the Asian tradition as done by many Asian brands, BritishIndia has been successful in evoking nostalgic memories of a bygone era through the colonial decor of its "Asianized" Western designs, backed up with a high-quality product with a sophisticated, elegant, and timeless appeal. It is indeed a commendable task for an Asian company to establish such a strong brand in a category that has world-renowned names as competitors.

Since 2005, the typical BritishIndia client base has been growing more affluent and been demanding higher quality products. As part of this evolution, the creative and design teams helmed by its founder Pat Liew have solidified their product range to focus on being the masters of linen while developing an increasingly unique product range that is quintessentially suited for a luxury tropical lifestyle.

The rapid expansion of fast fashion retailers across Asia has forced BritishIndia to focus more on its existing premium positioning to distinguish itself from global fast fashion retailers. Even with limited distribution, BritishIndia continues to achieve high brand recognition in Asia, and provide an alternative to consumers who are seeking alternatives to widely available brands.

Interior from a BritishIndia retail store

Source: Courtesy of BritishIndia.

BritishIndia logo

Merchandise at a BritishIndia retail store

Source: Courtesy of BritishIndia.

Measure the Brand Performance

Brands, like organizations, must deliver shareholder value and be accountable. How much value does the brand provide to the corporation and how instrumental is it in ensuring profitability and competitiveness? These are some of the questions that must be answered as part of a constant commitment to implement corporate strategy successfully.

As shown in Chapter 6, brand equity consists of various tailor-made metrics (including the brand value in financial terms), and these must be tracked regularly. A brand scorecard can help with an overview of the brand equity and the progression of brand metrics as the strategy is implemented. Also, the company should have the right combination of qualitative and quantitative research tools to measure the brand equity.

For example, one important marketing metric is the lifetime value of a customer, which indicates how much revenue a company can expect from him or her. Research once estimated that a BMW customer was worth an estimated US$143,500 and a Coca-Cola customer was worth US$1,200.[39]

Customer satisfaction is another important metric related to lifetime value. Brand success turned this into a difficult problem for Starbucks. Customers experienced long waiting times for service, thus reducing overall brand satisfaction. An analysis found that unsatisfied customers stuck with Starbucks for just one year, made 47 visits and spent US$200, whereas highly satisfied Starbucks' customers patronized the brand for more than eight years, made 86 visits per year and spent more than US$3,000 during the period. The results provided by improving customer satisfaction were so convincing that Starbucks decided to spend US$40 million adding staff in order to reduce waiting times.[40] Market research had also shown that 75 per cent of customers valued friendly, fast and convenient service. But only 54 per cent of customers were being served in less than three minutes. This figure increased to 85 percent when new staff joined and the company introduced the Starbucks Card to speed up payment. Customer satisfaction also increased 20 percent.[41]

These examples illustrate the need for marketing decisions to be elevated to the boardroom for two important reasons. The marketing metrics convey a powerful message to the CEO about the ability of branding to drive profitability, and also because a decision of that level of strategic importance can't be taken within the limited scope of the marketing department. Marketers must become more cross-functional and work in teams within the organization.

To elevate the discipline of branding to boardroom level, companies must accurately assess and measure the financial implications of branding investments and their contribution to overall company growth. Currently, many measures are used by companies to put a value on the brand and track the return from branding initiatives. Over the long run, companies should adopt a method of tracking brand returns based on certain company and industry-specific parameters instead of merely adopting some proprietary tool, as discussed in Chapter 6.

With the emergence of digital and social media marketing channels, getting an accurate measurement of ROI is an increasingly challenging task. A 2013 McKinsey analysis of client cases revealed that around 15 to 20 per cent of marketing budgets could have been reinvested in other activities or returned to the bottom line without losing marketing ROI.[42] The inability to show tangible returns from marketing and branding investments has been the main problem of marketing executives. However, by adopting one of the measures detailed in Chapter 6, this problem can be effectively tackled.

Nike, the sports goods giant, evaluates CEO performance on factors like market position and brand strength, which are clear indicators of company success.[43]

Only if business leaders are held accountable for their actions will they take the reins and dedicate efforts to build strong brands. This issue relates to investor confidence and corporate governance, which is only slowly being adopted in Asian boardrooms. It is the trend especially among listed companies and companies owned by financial shareholders who increasingly scrutinize Asian boardrooms for strategies leading to better shareholder value.

Adjust Regularly – Be Your Own Change Agent

The business landscape is changing almost every day in every industry. Hence corporations need to evaluate and possibly adjust their branding strategy on a regular basis. Obviously, a strong and resonating brand should stay relevant, differentiated, and consistent over time, so it is crucial to maintain a balance between all the parameters. The basic parts of the branding strategy, like vision, identity, personality, and values, should not be changed too often. Instead, the changes are rather small and involve the thousands of daily interactions and actions throughout the organization, which corporations employ as part of their brand marketing efforts.

A key factor in ensuring corporate management success is to make sure that complacency doesn't take root in the organization and impact goal setting. Strong brands are driven forward by leaders who never get tired of raising their own bars of excellence. They become their own change agents – and champions for building great brands.

The troubled path of a once-great company often starts with a high dose of success. As managers focus on efficient execution of strategies that brought them success and minimize share price volatility by focusing on short-term goals, an extended period of mediocrity sets in. Eventually, complacency is replaced by urgency when competitors gain ground. Rarely does true innovation result from urgency – especially when management is driven to protect what it has become attached to.

Building any successful brand is dependent on the buy-in from company shareholders, who must in the end allocate the necessary resources needed for branding as well as evaluate the ROI. This raises questions about the type of non-executive directors and their knowledge of and beliefs in branding as a strategic discipline. Most executives in Asian boardrooms have been elevated from technical, operational, or financial career tracks, and hardly any from the brand and marketing tracks. Asian shareholders and companies can benefit significantly from having one or two non-executive directors on the board with brand knowledge, tools, and international experience as a balance to the traditional over-representation of technical and financial experience. Discussions between non-executive directors about brand strategy and its resource needs versus profitability and performance will then become more qualified and nuanced with details.

There has been some good progress in Asian boards along these lines. A 2013 Accenture study found that 84 per cent of Asian CMOs feel that they are well equipped to achieve the marketing objectives of the organizations with the right set of people, tools, and resources at their disposal. This is higher than the global average of 60 per cent observed in a global Accenture study. The research also identified the progressive thinking of Asian CMOs, who have a strong level of commitment towards embracing and implementing digital capabilities.[44]

Branding is a potentially strong tool for realigning a corporate strategy and ensuring that the corporation, regardless of industry and size, is leveraging its untapped internal and external resources. A strong CEO and a dedicated management team are always seeking to raise their own bars and be change agents for their corporations, backed by a strong corporate branding strategy. Moreover, these teams also act as active brand mentors by instilling the same commitment toward brand building throughout the company.

A well-drafted and professionally managed branding strategy and implementation plan can become a significant part of the Asian boardroom set of tasks in the future. It can help to drive profitability and shareholder value, aligning the interests of stakeholders, the management, and the company. The good news is that Asian boardrooms are increasingly showing signs and the openness to embrace this strategic change.

WHY INNOVATE? THE MODERN BRAND AND THE BUSINESS IMPERATIVE

In a world of abundant choice, the purpose of branding is to guide consumers through a dizzying array of alternatives. True innovation can be the most powerful differentiator of all. Rather than leave differentiation to marketers and creatives, innovation creates unique value by satisfying consumer needs in a way competitors cannot – by creating an uneven playing field.

Relentless entrepreneurial spirit is the driver of long-term growth – the "soul" of the enterprise. But innovation remains the exception in most industries rather than the rule. Opportunity and fear must motivate leaders to pursue innovation as the ultimate differentiator.

Innovation makes competition irrelevant: When organizations operate on a competitive plane by bringing similar products to market, they compete only by making incremental improvements that are easily replicated, or by decreasing their value. On the other hand, organizations that operate on the creative plane develop products that redefine their category, delighting customers with the unexpected, cementing emotional bonds and making competition irrelevant.

Scale no longer provides insulation from market forces: History has shown that every monopoly comes to an end as structural and technological realities change over time. At faster intervals, we are witnessing giants fall while billion-dollar companies ascend. Upstarts can now access cloud infrastructure, outsource manufacturing, and crowd-fund capital while venture capitalists everywhere seek new ideas to put their resources behind. Very few industries still have significant barriers to entry.

Copy-based strategies may keep you in business, but will erode brand value unless true innovation takes place: In most industries, survival hinges on a cycle of product, service, and process mimicry – one company crystallizes a unique offering, then everyone rushes to duplicate it. Why work so hard at innovation when it can become commoditized so quickly and first-mover benefits last for less and less time? For the answer, look to Apple – beloved for over a decade for creating products consumers never knew they wanted.

No matter what motivates today's business leaders to create a culture of innovation – whether fear of failure or drive to capitalize on opportunities – it has become a modern business imperative to constantly pursue radical new ideas. Game-changing innovation is the ultimate differentiator.

chapter 10

Asian Brands Toward 2020 – A New Confidence in the Boardroom

Imitation can be commercial suicide.
—Bill Bernbach, founder, DDB Worldwide

Implications for Successful Brand Strategies in an Asian Context

The Asian business landscape will change rapidly in the coming years, and the opportunities for Asian companies to benefit from international branding will be larger than before. The growing emphasis on international branding will move up the boardroom agenda and branding will become one of the most prominent value drivers in Asia-Pacific in the next two decades.

Branding is discussed almost daily in the Asian media and at numerous conferences and seminars. Yet it is widely misunderstood. Most still believe branding activities refer to how a company uses logos, packaging, and advertisements, whereas branding activities actually comprise anything strategy-involved and execution from top to bottom of an organization. Whatever activity eventually contributes to the outstanding, differentiated customer experience must be considered branding.

A global brand and a company are two dramatically different entities. As this book has illustrated, branding is a boardroom agenda. The branding process cannot reach its logical conclusion unless the chairman and CEO accept it and allocate the required resources to it. But merely having knowledge will not suffice. Leaders need a holistic vision and an in-depth understanding of the discipline, as well as to be truly international, excellent business leaders and brand marketers.

Asian boardrooms have traditionally been the playing fields for technology, operations, and finance professionals. In the future, these capabilities alone will not be sufficient for sustained growth and enhanced shareholder value. With branding taking center-stage, it is crucial that the boardroom represents brand capabilities and experiences to ensure that brand guardianship is practiced at the highest level. This can be accomplished in two ways.

Firstly, educating and training boardroom directors can create a common understanding of the discipline, its opportunities, and its challenges. Secondly, the company can elevate people with strong marketing and branding backgrounds to the board. Ideally, companies can combine the above two ways to achieve optimum results.

Asian brands can indeed challenge global players, but this requires a new mind-set, resources, and capabilities. Asian boardrooms and their brands face new opportunities, as the following points illustrate.

Challenges for Aspiring Asian Brands

Low Cost Becoming a Commodity

Low cost, once the competitive advantage for a select few Asian companies, is now something that global companies can achieve. It has become the entry ticket into most markets today. In other words, low cost has become a commodity. Given these market dynamic changes, Asian companies must find alternative sources of sustainable competitive advantage. Adopting a more brand-oriented thinking and building strong brands would be a desirable way for Asian companies to increase growth opportunities and margins.

Asian cost advantages are diminishing. When Accenture asked 250 senior executives of Asian companies expanding overseas to compare their source of competitive advantage today with that of three years' time, 55 per cent cited high quality products and services, while 47 per cent cited high-value innovation. Only a small minority thought low-cost operations would be an advantage in three years' time.[1]

Price competition is the enemy of differentiation in a global marketplace. Companies must become great by getting better before they get cheaper; by emphasizing higher revenues and innovation over lower costs. With increased pressure on margins, companies must shift from the old paradigm (cost advantage) to a new paradigm (design and innovation) to grow.

Brands looking to expand outside domestic markets must become known for innovation. Panasonic, Samsung, and Toyota chose to do things better, not cheaper. This strategy, however, requires patience and persistence. Business leaders must have the courage to move from a volume-obsessed manufacturing paradigm toward a customer-value driven purpose.

XIAOMI — INNOVATION AS THE NEXT FRONTIER

Founded in 2010, Xiaomi has become the biggest smartphone maker in China and fourth biggest globally, behind Samsung, Apple, and Lenovo.[2] According to its founder, Lei Jun, Xiaomi is best known for its business model based on keeping costs to a minimum.[3] To most, however, Xiaomi is known for copying everything about Apple down to its handset designs, its founder's clothing, and its Apple-like product launches. In November 2014, Xiaomi accounted for 6 per cent of all smartphones shipped worldwide. It has not even started marketing to the West, exporting to only 10 Asian countries in 2014.[4]

Unlike Apple, Xiaomi targets emerging middle-class consumers and teenagers who want a comparable product at low cost, instead of premium customers. Xiaomi sells Android-based smartphones from US$100 to US$400 compared to more than US$650 for Apple's or Samsung's newest models. While performance admittedly does not live up to that of its higher-end competitors, the relative performance more than justifies the 40 per cent or more savings.

With a US$40 billion valuation – a market value three times that of Lenovo – and the goal of becoming a Fortune Global 500 company soon, Xiaomi is set for international expansion. But it must do so with innovation rather than replication to survive over the long-term.[5] If Xiaomi can nearly replicate the iPhone in four years, its own model can be copied even faster.

The Opening Chinese Economy

The opening Chinese economy offers tremendous opportunities, especially China's entry into the WTO and the Chinese government's policy to allow foreign investment in sectors controlled by the state. But an equally tough set of challenges ensues. As branding is still a fairly new concept in China, there will be a number of companies still competing on price alone, trying to undercut the value players. With this market structure brand-oriented companies will in the short term face an uphill task to both compete on price and maintain their focus on branding.

A case in point was Coca-Cola's pricing strategy in China to widen distribution. To compete against its many copycats, Coca-Cola started selling Coke at 1Rmb (US$0.12). As of 2014, the price of a 0.33 litre bottle of Coca Cola sells for 3.45 Rmb.[6] The initial strategy of having a very low price point to gain access to remote areas did put brand equity at risk. Colgate also testifies to the above point. A survey conducted in China showed a 30–50 percent price difference between premium and mass-market Chinese brands, forcing Colgate to slash prices to gain market acceptance while maintaining its core identity of cavity protection. In the future, many brands in various sectors will face this challenge.[7]

The Asian Trading Mind-set

Even today, most Asian companies still function with a trading mind-set, wherein the function of businesses is arbitrage – acquiring goods (or producing commodities) at lower costs and sell them at higher cost – rather than creating uniqueness via branding and innovation. In fact, the Chinese character for "business" is actually a combination of the Chinese characters for "buy" and "sell" – perfectly explaining what comes to mind when the Chinese think about "business."

Short-term sales and investments in tangible capital assets are often priority areas. A McKinsey study shows that tangible assets are becoming less relevant in Asia's battle for global success. It shows that the biggest Asian value creators have a 1:1 sales-to-asset ratio compared to a 1:4 sales-to-asset ratio in an average Asian company.[8] A conservative mind-set focused on tangibles, the short-term, and risk-minimizing business aspects has relegated branding to an optional, tactical tool. As such, Asian companies have not fully realized the strategic role of branding and corporate management, especially CEOs, in instilling branding as an organization-wide discipline.

Asian boardrooms must accept and support consistent investment in intangible assets like brands and brand building, the results of which will take a few years to accrue.

Dominance of Large, Diversified Conglomerates

The origin of many Asian businesses can be traced back to their founding families. Unlike many advanced Western economies, where founding families often gradually dilute their stake in the businesses and evolve into a mixed owner-structure, Asian economies are still dominated by family-owned/controlled firms. Given the huge stakes of family wealth in these companies, the conventional wisdom has been to minimize risk by diversifying.

Brand building costs a considerable amount. Global brands have been able to reap economies of scale by spreading branding expenses across many related business units. Asia, however, is still dominated by large conglomerates that have diversified interests in many B2C and B2B companies, hindering them from reaping any scale economies in branding investments.

A McKinsey study showed that 90 per cent of Asia's value creators derive more than 80 per cent of revenue by focusing in one industry sector. Moreover, these companies focus on intangibles, like fostering human capital, exploiting network effects, and creating synergies based on brands and reputation, rather than investing in physical assets.[9] Additionally, interests in diversified areas pose a great challenge, as creating and managing a consistent brand personality are much more difficult.

The Reliance group of India is a typical example of such a diversified conglomerate, with businesses in petrochemicals, financial advisory, telecommunications, and oil explorations. Furthermore, the Reliance Group split into two in 2005–2006, with ownership of specific businesses within the group going to the two brothers, Mukesh and Anil Ambani.[10] Branding different businesses across a wide array of sectors will prove to be resource-draining in the longer run. Small and medium-sized firms that aspire to build strong brands but have resource constraints will find branding especially difficult if their businesses are highly diversified.

Asia's Excess Capacity

China and India together are attracting the world with their rapidly expanding economies with large growth potentials, and their large populations. With an ever-increasing assault from global brands and home-grown companies, the markets are facing an overcapacity of products.[11]

In China alone, many industry sectors suffer from up to 30 per cent overcapacity.[12] This causes immense pressure on companies to turn over their stock regularly, resulting in slower growth and decreasing profitability, which worries global economists and Chinese policy makers. Overcapacity often leads to a dumping of products in the market, possibly leading to price wars. In such situations, it would be difficult for companies to sustain branding investments and cling on to the value proposition.

Intellectual Property and Trademark Protection

Apart from countries like Singapore, Hong Kong, South Korea, and Japan, Asian countries are not known for strong IP laws. With innovation, technological advancements, and branding becoming the center of business activity, strong IP laws become crucial.

When even local Chinese home-grown brands like Li Ning suffer the counterfeit burn (they have full-time employees tracking counterfeiters), there is additional pressure on Asian governments to enforce stringent IP laws and implement effective enforcement measures to ensure the smooth transition of Asia's potential succession to a higher position in the value chain.

The lack of stringent enforcement of protection of intellectual property has been a major challenge in building Asian brands. Many Asian companies face rampant infringement of IP rights in their own backyard.

L E N O V O ' S   G L O B A L   L E A P [13]

Lenovo Group, China's biggest computer manufacturer, achieved much publicity and recognition when it bought IBM's PC division in 2005. Part of the deal was the right to use the IBM Think brand for another five years.

Prior to this, Lenovo had learned the hard way that protection of trademarks is an important step to becoming successful when expanding internationally. Legend, as the company was called then, had already been trademarked in several countries by other companies.[14] That led the company to overhaul its marketing, change its brand name, and reduce its 40 sub-brands. In April 2004, the company renamed itself Lenovo Group. The new name had the advantage of starting with "L" and also being connected to the Chinese name "Lianxiang." It passed tests in different languages, had availability of website addresses, and was easy to pronounce and spell.[15] But most importantly, Lenovo passed trademark procedures in most countries.

In 2005, Lenovo acquired the PC division of IBM for a whopping US$1.75 billion. The logic was simple and straightforward – Lenovo would ride IBM's brand equity in establishing itself as a credible brand in the PC industry. This acquisition was splashed across global media as the beginning of the Chinese global brand takeover. Instantly becoming the world's number three computer maker after Dell and HP, Lenovo jumped to second in 2012, finally becoming the world's biggest in 2013, accounting for 16 per cent of PCs shipped worldwide.[16]

Lenovo replicated this strategy in two new business areas when the company spent US$5.2 billion[17] on M&A in 2014 to purchase IBM's low-end data storage and server unit[18] and the Motorola brand from Google. Although an after-thought, Motorola has remained a solid brand in emerging markets where most global growth in mobile is expected, putting Lenovo in third position behind Apple and Samsung in mobile hardware sales.

As an indication of its global ambition, Lenovo signed actor Ashton Kutcher as its first global brand ambassador toward the end of 2013.[19] Lenovo's growth in the smartphones sector has also been impressive, which makes the Motorola purchase a critical strategic move for the company as it increasingly expands its mobile phone business outside China. In the second quarter of 2014, Lenovo sold more smartphones (15.8 million) than PCs (14.5 million).[20] The company aims to become the number one smartphone maker globally.[21]

Lenovo now stands alone as the only major tech company with global product lines in consumer mobile, PCs, and tablets, as well as business servers.[22] As a brand leader in emerging markets, Lenovo has a strong chance of repeating its climb to global leadership via emerging market dominance in new business units.

The Global Brand Landscape Will Change Significantly

Emergence of a Large Asian Value Segment

Despite Asia's transition into the value economy, a considerable percentage of Asia's population still lives in poverty, with little education and inferior infrastructure and support systems – often referred to as the bottom of the pyramid.[23] This segment lacks purchasing power to buy global premium brands. For example, Hindustan Lever, Unilever's Indian subsidiary, introduced shampoo sachets at low prices, successfully addressing the needs of this segment. This huge value segment represents an enormous untapped potential. Global brands must adapt their offerings and plan appropriate brand extensions to suit this huge market segment.

A *Harvard Business Review* article took a critical overview of how to market to the bottom of the pyramid. Organizations must improve their margins by reducing variable costs and raising price points for single transactions. The article suggested a three-pronged framework for boosting margins: localizing base products sold as a bundle, creating an enabling service, and marketing through customer peer groups.[24]

Emergence of Complex Brand Systems

With more global brands entering the Asian market and Asian brands expanding internationally, there will be numerous alliances and joint ventures between Asian and global brands. This presents the difficulty and dilemma for global brands to strike a balance between standardized offerings and customizing locally. The dilemma for Asian brands will be to maintain their own brand despite tying up with a bigger global partner.

Brands Need to Build Resonating Stories (Myths)

With the tremendous proliferation of brands in the global market, brands must find innovative and forceful ways of conveying their value proposition. They should excite customers by creating lasting associations and resonant stories. To ensure enduring success it will be crucial for companies to weave their brands into the social fabric and make them a part of the community.[25] Tapping into popular culture and society are two main drivers of successful branding.

GUIDELINE: IDENTITY MYTHS AND STORYTELLING ARE KEYS TO BUILDING ICONIC BRANDS

Many companies aspire to build brands that eventually become cultural icons, but very few are able to achieve iconic status. Iconicity does not happen by chance – it has to be carefully planned and executed.

Identity myths and storytelling are keys to building iconic brands, but stories cannot substitute for great products and services. The strongest brands are first rooted in product and service performance. In all categories, a minimum standard of quality is necessary to even compete. Second, these quality products and services are differentiated to help defend their market positions – often with innovation as an integrated component of their company culture. Third, they are profitable and have very well-driven operations that stick to a long-term plan and do not deviate when times get tough. Assuming these prerequisite strengths of product quality, differentiation, and operations, one final element remains in order to truly elevate the brand: a strong emotional connection.

A look at some of the most historically iconic brands such as Coca-Cola, Harley Davidson, Giorgio Armani, Apple, Chanel, IBM, Giorgio Armani, L'Oréal, Louis Vuitton, Aman, and Singapore Airlines reveals some common characteristics. All have built and sustained strong emotional bonds with their customers and stakeholders that are far greater than their strengths in quality management, innovation, and operations. These brands have created an enduring mythology about themselves. They have mastered the art of storytelling and passed the responsibility of sharing that story to their brand communities who do it for them. For any brand to attain iconic status, it has to create an identity myth.

Create an identity myth

Brands that resonate and direct the masses through brand stories and activities become inscribed in our culture. By creating an identity for themselves, these brands provide identity to society. Brands today are not inanimate "things" but thriving entities with identities and personalities that allow customers to express themselves through consumption. To attract customers and make them participate actively to this end, brands should have a strong story that they can easily identify and relate to. Such a story would not only provide brand authenticity but also allow customers to express their unique sense of self through their purchase or association.

Humans are wired for narratives. We are naturally skeptical of sales pitches but let down our guard for stories because they are less intrusive and can capture our imagination. Although effective in the short term, the marketer's tools of promotion and price discounting do little to create true loyalty. Furthermore, they can be easily copied by competitors, creating a downward spiral of discounting and bundling that distract from a brand's truly authentic narrative.

Humans are creatures of evolution and storytelling defines how we share ideas that matter and build relationships for survival.

Great brand stories that resonate with consumers and touch their lives can be defined by a single word such as freedom (Harley-Davidson), power (BMW), design (Apple), elegance (Dior), imagination (Lego), beauty (Estée Lauder), or safety (Volvo). These brand stories give consumers a good reason to elevate the brand beyond a mere utilitarian role. While logic opens the mind, emotions open the wallet.

Sociological research demonstrates that when multiple brand elements such as images, stories, and associations leverage deeper meanings or shared values, people are less likely to switch brands.

Weave powerful brand stories

A compelling brand story begins with the brand's purpose. To build an iconic brand, a company's purpose must be a clear transcendent idea – something that aspires to do more than simply be a competitor in a particular market, gain market share, or become "the chosen provider of" an item. Vision and mission are the cornerstones of brand and boardroom strategy. The vision gives the brand a reason for being while the mission provides it with strategic objectives.

A company's first priority should be a clear perspective on the organization's sustainable competitive advantage. There is no competitive advantage in doing what others have done before. To create a meaningful proposition, senior leadership must first understand each of their stakeholders and decide the priority each audience should be given. Stakeholders include not only customers, but also employees, investors, partners, and suppliers – even the citizens of a country where a brand bases its operations.

Assuming a strong vision and mission, how does a brand become a story? The answer: People. Brands must carefully nurture the culture that perpetuates its brand story. Rewards, process, strategy, and structure must effectively support culture. Companies can only expect to provide a true brand experience by closely aligning and tying the hiring processes, compensation systems, training, recognition, and measurement schemes directly to the brand proposition and ideal culture.

Build strong brand communities

The objective of developing an iconic brand is not just the sharing, but the growth and strength of brand communities. A brand community is a group of loyal customers who are bound together by their loyalty to the brand and what it offers them. There is an intrinsic connection between members and a collective sense of difference from those outside the community.

Conclusion

When people believe a brand is worth buying for a reason far greater than its product, price, place, or promotion, that is, because of a transcendent narrative that resonates with a consumer's core values, businesses have the foundational element of an iconic brand.

Iconicity begins with a mission founded on the true spirit or history of the company and requires product and service performance and profitability, but it is ultimately defined by a strong emotion that allows customers to express their unique sense of self through their purchase. Companies whose brands eventually become woven into the cultural fabric of society and become enduring cultural icons have mastered the art of storytelling and nurture communities that perpetuate and contribute to their tale.

For a brand to attain iconic status, it has to create a myth-driven identity, first and foremost, with highest concern for its customers' emotional needs.

Fiji Water is a brand that has grown on the basis of a powerful story (myth) related to the mystique of an island situated far away from its target market. By weaving the story into customers' daily lives, it has been able to maintain excitement around the brand.

FIJI WATER: THE EXOTIC WATER BRAND

There are few product categories where branding activities make such a dramatic impact on competitiveness and differentiation as in bottled water. As many may agree, all water tastes the same. This means branding in this category is not product-focused, but story-focused. The company that can tell a better story and back it up with credible facts, thereby creating an exciting myth, wins the day.

Although the product's physical attributes cannot be differentiated, Fiji Water has become one of the stand-out examples of creating a powerful story around a commoditized product. Intelligent and genuine branding can elevate even the simplest commodity to celebrity status. Fiji Water seems to have understood this extremely well. In a category dominated by France's Evian, Coca-Cola's Dasani and PepsiCo's Aquafina, Fiji Water has come to occupy an ultra-luxury foothold in a growing global market within the short span of a decade.

Like the best luxury brands, Fiji Water has been able to build its iconic premium water status on three pillars: creating an exciting myth, precision marketing (including personal relationships and product placements), and a controlled distribution strategy.

Fiji's background & brand philosophy

David Gilmour, a businessman with interests in hotels, real estate, and gold mining, founded Fiji Water in 1988 in Basalt, Colorado.

The brand came into life in the early 1990s when Gilmour secured a 99-year deal with the Fijian government to tap the aquifer discovered by government-contracted geologists and market the water under the Fiji Water brand.[26]

Fiji is a 332-island nation in the South Pacific, very far from most markets and customers. This physical inaccessibility has allowed Fiji Water to create the story of this water being extracted from a virgin ecosystem far from acid rain, herbicides, pesticides, and other pollutants, and filtered naturally for years through layers of silica, basalt, and sandstone. This journey, from the atmosphere to bottling – something unique for consumers to take notice of – is communicated clearly through packaging and exquisitely on the company's website.

Complementing the story of the water, the Fiji brand has long been presented it as an unexploited land full of tropical forest surrounded by coral reefs, unpolluted by the modern world's necessary evils and protected by nature. These factors created a very strong myth about the brand amongst customers who, in turn, perpetuate the mythology.

Myth creation was backed by precision brand marketing. Fiji Water did not resort to the usual mass media advertising for its product launch. Up to today, Fiji does very little traditional advertising and continues to emphasize a two-pronged strategy – building strategic relationships and careful product placement.

Building relationships: The first prong of Fiji Water's communication strategy was to build personal relationships with the chefs of leading restaurants, resorts, and spas to promote the brand's buy-in.[27] Gilmour used his hotel industry contacts to pitch his product to the top-end hotels, resorts, and restaurants. By coming out with an award-winning slippery silver bottle design, Fiji water has been able to replace Evian in many of the top-end restaurants.[28]

Through this controlled distribution strategy, in line with its positioning of a high-end product, Fiji Water has ensured that it is available at the best hotels, resorts, and spas used by the leading stars and managed to get chef's recommendations. As is generally known, the bottled water category is notorious for its difficulty in making money. Fiji Water's pricing strategies offered distributors and retailers the opportunity to make profits in a category that they had become used to not making money in. Furthermore, because Fiji Water's bottles were often off the shelves due to their early inability to match huge initial demand, exclusivity was enhanced.[29]

Product placement: The second prong of communication was placing the product in leading Hollywood movies and other high-profile events to associate the brand with an elite community, attracting attention and creating buzz. Fiji Water has resorted to product placement as a major channel of promotion and brand building. By hiring Creative Entertainment Services, a Hollywood marketing consulting firm, Fiji has been able to fit Fiji Water bottles in many major Hollywood movie scripts. These brand exposures, combined with the exciting mythical story, have made the product noticeable. Fiji Water has also sponsored many local events such as golf tournaments, sailing regattas, and musical events.[30] It regularly serves as an official water sponsor and exclusive partner of events such as the Toronto International Film Festival, New York Fashion Week, and Screen Actors Guild Awards.[31]

A strong connection with film stars and other artists has even inspired new features such as a straw-cap, which was a minor, but meaningful innovation that came from observing how celebrities would modify their bottles to sip without messing up their makeup. With a brand community of loyal, highly visible customers, Fiji water bottles appear in magazines constantly and appears to be the chosen water brand of many stars without them having to sponsor it. Consumers are now the most powerful force in marketing.

Society contributions: Launched in 2007, the Fiji Water Foundation is a charitable trust funded and supported by the owners, employees, and corporate affiliates of Fiji Water. The Fiji Water Foundation is one of the largest philanthropic organizations in Fiji. It focuses its efforts and investments on three priority areas of development:

- Providing clean water access to rural communities
- Building educational facilities and infrastructure that benefit children, teenagers, and adults

- Providing access to healthcare services to underprivileged communities. Additionally, the Foundation offers disaster relief during floods and severe weather events that frequently impact the islands.

To date, the Foundation has funded projects touching hundreds of thousands of lives across the Fijian islands.[32]

Since 2009, Fiji Water has been a proud member of One Percent for the Planet, a growing movement of more than 1,000 companies that donate 1 per cent of their sales to a global network of organizations committed to the preservation and restoration of the natural environment. Through its membership in 1 per cent for the Planet, Fiji Water supports a variety of environmental causes in Fiji, the US and other parts of the world.

Future Challenges

The biggest challenge for Fiji Water moving forward is sustaining this level of interest in its brand. The problem of basing it heavily on a myth is that it does not create barriers for new entrants to come up with some other equally exciting myths. Given the low level of customer involvement in selecting water, customers would be willing to try out newer and more exciting brands as and when they come up. In this regard, Fiji Water should focus on formulating a strong customer loyalty and retention drive in light of impending competition. Although it has managed to get Forbes to include it in a list of things "worth every penny," it will need much more than a strong story to carry it through the future.[33]

Evian pioneered the idea in the bottled water category of elevating a commodity to iconic brand status. Looking back, Evian did things that Fiji Water is doing now – becoming successful with its marketing, storytelling, and distribution strategies. By following non-traditional methods of marketing, a distinct positioning, and high-end pricing, Fiji Water has been able to establish strong brand equity and iconic status amongst the top tier market segment including celebrities, Hollywood stars, and the best restaurants globally – without being distinctly different from its competitors in terms of core product.

Branding in the Asian Boardroom

Match Corporate Strategy to Branding Strategy

Asian companies have traditionally handled branding as a tactical function. In the future, this needs to change and companies must realize the strategic significance of branding. Branding should be aligned to the overall corporate strategy and formulated and managed at the board level. This would give CEOs a powerful instrument to enhance shareholder value.

Shift strategy from Sales Orientation to Brand Orientation

The biggest challenge for Asian boardrooms will be the shift in mind-set from a sales orientation to a brand orientation; a change from short-to long-term value creation. Corporate management must understand that branding is a long-term activity, with results that are not immediate. The board, led by the CEO, should create an atmosphere in which emphasis is more on the long-term and on sustaining competitive advantage. Despite its intangibility, corporate management should be oriented to understanding the positive implications of building a strong brand.

Prioritization of shareholders over customers, unfortunately, is where many brands fail from the start. While they may pay lip service to their consumers as the force driving the company's actions, many executives place a higher priority on the company's stock price. Today's best brands have wrapped the company goals and vision around their customers' needs, values, and emotions. They are in touch with their humanity and evoke emotions that are tied to both conscious or unconscious needs and desires. This does not mean that executives should not care about shareholder value – they absolutely should. But those who manage sustainably iconic brands understand that financial performance must be driven, first and foremost, by a greater concern for those who buy their products than those who buy their shares. Iconic brands must have a higher purpose – a promise to create a better world somehow.

Make Contribution to Brand Growth a Part of Performance Appraisal

Asian companies can build strong brands only when brand building processes are well implemented internally. A major onus on management is to create a company culture that is conducive for everyone to live the brand. Companies should enforce and motivate everyone to contribute to the brand's growth. This should become one of the most important measures for performance appraisal. By installing such measures, companies can reap the full benefits of brand management, as brand strategy objectives are aligned with staff interests.

Human intangibles create the difference between iconic brands and commoditized competitors. Therefore, HR should take primary responsibility for providing advice and direction for the organization's most important asset – its people. Since teamwork, passion, and engagement are such vital components for the development of a brand-centric culture, these softer aspects of chemistry must be quantified and rewarded. If a brand can accurately measure the characteristics of its high-performers, it can further unlock leadership potential and assemble higher-functioning teams whose individual talents combine to create a whole significantly greater than the sum of its parts.

Workforce analytics will also ensure that people feel that their growth in the organization depends less on politics and more on merit. Resources and rewards spent on people without a long-term future in the organization can be considered subsidies for direct competitors when these people eventually leave for greener pastures and take their experience with them.

One study has stated that 18 per cent of employees are so "actively disengaged" that they undermine the work of their colleagues, costing businesses up to US$550 billion annually. Tony Hsieh, the CEO of Zappos – regularly named one of the top 100 workplaces in the United States – once estimated that his bad hires and their resulting decisions have cost the company well over US$100 million. CFOs should surely be in favor of using all means necessary to improve retention and engagement, identify "bad apples," and make the right hiring and leadership decisions.

HR can participate in brand development with management training programs that teach the leadership skills necessary to create a powerful culture by inspiring and empowering people to deliver the brand promise. Research has found that companies fail to choose the right candidates for important roles 82 per cent of the time. Therefore, understanding the essence of brand leadership is vital for companies to identify and develop their future leaders and to avoid mistakes in promotion and hiring. HR should actively seek and promote those with a branding mind-set.

Build a Strong Talent Base

In the coming decade, Asia will see a war over talent, with major companies fighting for the best talent to improve their business success. The best Asian talent will become increasingly choosy about the fit between their expectations, personality, and the corporate culture. One of the ways for Asian companies to attract and retain talent is to have an impeccable corporate reputation, an open corporate environment, and strong brand names with which people feel proud to be associated.

Leadership constraints are a top business challenge faced by multinationals in China. Rapid growth over the last 20 years has created a huge imbalance in demand and supply of experienced managers and leaders, which has caused compensation for senior executives to skyrocket.[34]

Introduce Diversity in the Asian Boardroom

When assembling a board of directors, the primary consideration is diversity. The best boards are often the most diverse – not only in terms of skills, experience, and beliefs, but also in terms of gender, age, and ethnicity.

Too many boardrooms suffer from too much homogeneity – their members are overwhelmingly male with the same racial background, averagely aged 68, and all former CEOs and CFOs. In 2012, 58 per cent of directors in boards of S&P 500 organizations were active CEOs or COOs, with another 35 per cent being retired CEOs or COOs. In Asia Pacific, this homogeneity is even stronger, with most boards comprising individuals from the same ethnic group with some exceptions in Hong Kong, Malaysia, and Singapore.

A global brand's customers are a diverse group and the organization behind the brand should have a board that reflects this real world diversity to be sensitive to the needs and aspirations of a wider variety of demographic groups and opportunities, and be adaptable to the real environment.

Diversity also ensures a balanced risk-taking approach and greater shareholder dividends. Recent research among the largest global companies found that companies with at least one woman on the board of directors outperformed those with no women by an average of 26 per cent over a five-year period. Interestingly, organizations in Asia-Pacific with at least one woman on the board saw much greater outperformance than their American and European counterparts. Gender diversity can be a strong corporate performance driver.

Age is an important influence on decision making. As executives take fewer risks as they grow older, brands and boards need a more balanced leadership structure in terms of age demographic. Today, the average age of a board member is 68. Older CEOs typically invest less in R&D in favor of debt and risk reduction, which can become a danger for brands in a fast-moving world with empowered consumers and dissolving barriers to international competition. It has been measured that a 25 per cent increase in a CEO's age corresponds with an average decrease in R&D costs of 8 per cent and a reduction in leverage of 13 per cent, as well as the introduction of more varied business units and acquisitions of more diversified rather than specialized companies. As indicated by the stock price outperformance of organizations with younger peers in the most senior executive positions, the inclusion of younger senior leaders pays off for shareholders in the long term.

It is vital for a foreign brand to appeal to local consumers. Therefore, boards must begin to reflect a cross-section of cultures of their foreign markets. Beijing-based telecom security company NQ Mobile, for example, has created a separate headquarters in Texas for their developed market business, managed by an American co-CEO.

A strong example of how a lack of ethnic diversity impacted a global icon is the case of Toyota, the world's largest automaker. Following embarrassing safety defects in 2009, which severely tarnished their global brand image, Toyota recognized the need to appoint outside board members in order to avoid similar future crisis. It appointed non-Japanese CEOs in the US, Africa, Latin America, and Europe for the first time – a huge shift for the company, which had always followed traditional Japanese management practices. This is also true for a majority of Japanese organizations.

In terms of age, Japan has the oldest directors on boards, with 89 per cent from the baby boom generation. In contrasting, China is the opposite with the youngest directors on boards. Boards must include members who can outright disagree with one another and provide different viewpoints. While many think that a perfect board is one that is free of conflict, in reality the worst boards are those that are silent or are compliant. Diversity creates these vital discussion forums in which boardrooms must constantly test their strategies. The quality of board-level team dynamics, measured in terms of engagement, openness, solidarity, creativity, innovation, satisfaction, and shared influence is highly correlated with profitability.

Have a CMO on the Corporate Board

Brand management is a dynamic and continuous process. It requires consistent investment and support to succeed. As illustrated by Singapore Airlines, branding goes beyond the CEO. Singapore Airlines has stuck to its brand strategy despite having a couple of CEOs during its lifespan. Moreover, corporate management can better understand the significance of branding, and the financial implications of brand management can be better tracked.

The best way to combat this lack of brand-orientation in the boardroom is to include a consumer representative on the board – the Chief Marketing Officer (CMO). In 2014, less than 40 of the nearly 10,000 board seats available at Fortune 1,000 companies were filled by a CMO.[35] Moving forward in the consumer age, a board of directors assembled only from those with technology, operations, or finance backgrounds is insufficient for sustained growth and enhanced shareholder value. The CMO plays a crucial role in constantly updating the boardroom and the CEO about the latest customer preferences and how well the corporate resources are aligned to meet those evolving customer needs. Many boards of directors are notorious for being insulated from the customers' voice in their organizations.

Marketers, with in-depth market and customer knowledge, should be a major resource for strategy formulation. In all corporate strategy issues – what markets to compete in, what segments to target, what entry mode and strategy to adopt, which partners to strategically ally with – marketing offers substantial information. In order to convey these holistic perspectives, it is imperative that marketing is represented by an CMO in the corporate boardroom who can speak to the directors and the CEO in his or her language. A classic example of this need is the iPhone from Apple. Given the tremendously successful iPod and iMac, Apple could have become complacent. But its executives' marketing acumen recognized the need to constantly excite customers. Apple built its growth strategies on satisfying customers' unmet needs. Marketing played a crucial role in guiding Apple's corporate strategy.

The Chief Information Officer (CIO) must become a key partner to the CMO. The world's most admired businesses have customer-driven IT as part of their DNA and those behind the curve can expect their IT function to change significantly in upcoming years. How organizations embrace data and technology from a branding perspective will separate the winners from the losers. Companies that are more data-driven are 5 per cent more productive and 6 per cent more profitable than other companies.[36]

Consumers are dictating the terms of interaction and business with brands, and the majority of brands are falling short of expectations. Together, the CMO and CIO roles are poised to lead brands through this change if they embrace new responsibilities and are given the authority and voice within the organization to do so.

Cost Advantage is Meant for Investment – not Short-term Profit Making

Invest in Channel Management

In two of the largest Asian markets, India and China, the key to business success is still good distribution. Given the size of these two countries, it is increasingly important for global brands to reach every nook and cranny of the market. As personal relationships and trust are still chief factors driving the channel partners, any amount of brand planning for success needs many resources to cement these relationships. Moreover, these widespread channels act as multiple brand touch points. Companies must ensure that all these touch points are managed properly to deliver consistently on all brand promises.

Reverse the Asian Innovation Deficit

Asia has thrived primarily by adapting Western technologies to local markets. In the future, this needs to change if Asia wants to accelerate away from the low cost OEM trap. Asian companies must invest substantially more in R&D and come up with new and proprietary technologies to survive among impending competition. Huawei spent US$4.9 billion on R&D in 2012 (13.7 per cent of revenues)[37] while Samsung spent 6.3 per cent of its revenue on R&D in 2013.[38]

Since 2006, Samsung has risen from the 26th to the 3rd most innovative company globally according to annual rankings by Boston Consulting Group.[39] Xiaomi – a newcomer to 2014's list – ranked 35th. These are strong Asian companies which focus on innovation.[40]

Governments must participate in reversing this innovation gap across Asia. China, for example, accounts for 20 per cent of the world's population, 11 per cent of the world's GDP, 14 per cent of the world's R&D expenditure – but less than 2 per cent of the patents granted by any of the leading patent offices outside China.[41] One often-cited reason is that state-owned enterprises, which dominate the Chinese business landscape, receive preferential treatment when it comes to government grants, stifling the companies that may be more deserving.

Invest in Strategic Acquisitions

This is one of the three strategies mentioned in Chapter 6: for Asian companies to acquire brands to leapfrog into other markets. Asian companies should

WHO SHOULD INNOVATE?

Organizations of all sizes, in all industries, in all parts of the world must innovate to achieve sustained competitive advantage. As technological cycles compress and digital accelerates the free flow of ideas across the globe, the pace of innovation has quickened to a point where organizations who fail to consistently and creatively add value for their customers quickly find their future in jeopardy.

Monopolies and industry leaders: History has shown that monopoly control is never permanent. Structural realities in every industry have always and will continue to change. While business models of the early 20th century could remain stagnant for decades, business tools, legal frameworks, consumer preferences, and barriers to entry now evolve faster and more unpredictably than ever before.

The biggest reason for failed sustained category leadership is complacency. Satisfied executives often miss opportunities because they have no incentive to cannibalize sales when markets are booming. In 2013, Intuit's founder, Scott Cook, proclaimed "Success is a powerful thing, it tends to make companies stupid, and they become less and less innovative."[42] When management emphasizes execution of existing systems rather than challenging what helped them achieve success, they are already trending toward obsolescence.

Companies determined to stick to core competencies and customers: Traditional management theories have long advocated that brands focus on their core competencies and most valuable customers. But this assumes a company's unique strength will always be relevant and that today's most valuable customers will remain so in future. Incumbents easily overlook upstarts who gain trust with customer segments they have ignored while, over time, these segments may become the most dominant.

Cost-competitive and commoditized brands: Once brand differentiation is established on lowest price, cheap products must keep getting cheaper and less profitable or a brand will fail to keep its promise. There can be no sustained cost advantage when global economies are constantly moving through different developmental stages. A prime example of this can be seen over the last 20 years in Asia.

Asia's early economic development can be attributed to low-cost advantages that enabled companies to undercut global competition. Panasonic, Samsung, and Toyota started international expansion on lower production costs. But as economies developed, pressure on margins forced them to shrug off their low-cost origins and become known for innovation and premium products in order to survive. Only Asia's most innovative companies are represented among the advertising industry's most valuable global brand surveys.

Publicly traded companies: The focus of stock markets on quarterly returns has entrenched a management system – especially in the US – that discourages dramatic change. The result, according to a 2013 Harvard study, has been a disastrous decline in the global competitiveness of American companies since the late 1970s. Because game-changing innovations are risky and stock markets pound innovators, most firms gravitate toward safer, more gradual change. Different thinking is required from today's sustainable brand leaders.

A prime example of leadership in the face of market resistance is Amazon's founder, Jeff Bezos. On announcing its move into Kindle e-readers and cloud computing, Amazon's stock crashed. The result: sales more than tripled between 2007 and 2011. Such leadership tends to be the exception, rather than the rule for today's publicly traded companies.

Asian brands: Thriving in Asia requires several types of innovations as deregulation, trade liberalization, and social change continue to alter the competitive landscape for regional brands. The density of urban regions and sparsely populated rural regions pushes companies to redefine distribution networks while simultaneously addressing the cost needs of lower-income consumers. On the higher-value scale, a recent Nielsen study supports the theory that Asia-Pacific consumers are addicted to "newness." This requires brands to continuously reinvent their products or services.[43]

One of the most famous adaptive Asian innovations was Procter & Gamble's packaging in India. Although consumers could save money in the long term by buying products in larger sizes, poorer consumers showed less interest in larger cash outlays for bulk items. Shop owners, with limited inventory and shelf-space, were also unlikely to carry the larger "value sizes." Beginning with smaller-sized tins of Vicks Vaporub, P&G quickly followed with one-dose sachets of shampoo, laundry detergent, and other household products. This small, meaningful, and profitable innovation has now become a standard for entry in many parts of Asia and helped P&G establish a foothold.

Companies who lack R&D: Most enterprises believe significant R&D spending is required to innovate. Often, however, a spark for innovation comes from the simple act of listening to customers and encouraging creativity among employees. Established companies can also harness creativity though partnership agreements with hungry start-ups that not only provide strategic insight and an unbiased perspective, but also help keep an eye on future competitors. All of these activities can be just as productive as and more cost-effective than pursuing traditional R&D.

To complement its world-renowned athlete feedback philosophy, Nike has tapped up 10 emerging companies to join its Nike+ Accelerator program to develop a line of active-lifestyle products. By taking a stake in young companies, Nike gets a crash-course in an industry it intends to establish a foothold in and a closer look at its future competitors.

Companies reliant on R&D: Many leaders are beginning to realize that organizations where innovation resides exclusively among R&D teams are boring workplaces. Statistics are also beginning to prove the frailty of their growth. Innovation must permeate every single organizational level, allowing employees to feel like they are a part of future growth, and can actively participate in it. Sometimes a mere warehouse worker, not a person with "R&D" in their job description, can identify a problem and solution that reinforces brand differentiation. However, it takes a courageous CEO to listen to, act upon, and stand behind a lower-level employee's idea. Innovation problems are often leadership problems. Brands must ask themselves, who leads our company's innovation? Disruptive change is a question of mindset, not money.

Hierarchical organizations: During the manufacturing and early technological age, firms perfected operations as well-oiled machines. Although a chain of command promoting uniformity and controlling quality is vital for branding – ensuring consumers can rely on a brand promise – it can be detrimental to innovation as traditional hierarchies do not nurture ideas. When process and procedure are paramount, change is often discouraged. Yet all companies have employees sharing ideas under the radar. This talk often has a negative tone but can be tremendously positive if channeled correctly.

Because proactive innovation is integral to long-term viability, today's businesses must shift away from hierarchy toward "wirearchy" – a more networked structure that encourages a flow of constructive thinking. The leaders of this system must ensure that new ideas do not simply add to existing hierarchal layers, but challenge the firm's complexity itself.

Small companies: Small businesses have a tendency to believe business theories are intended for the largest and most successful industry competitors. But without innovation, there is no reason for small companies to exist. A small entrant that competes in the same way as a larger incumbent will eventually succumb to inefficiencies of scale unless it chooses to think and act differently. Small businesses must be niche in a way that larger competitors cannot be. There is a growing theory that mega-brands should purposely limit themselves to innovation because smaller companies have financial constraints driving them to make things easier, simpler, and cheaper for customers.

In summary, the above lessons apply to organizations of all sizes, in all industries, in all parts of the world. The constant pursuit of improvement through innovation has become a necessary condition for sustained competitive advantage in the 21st century.

consider investing their profits in identifying compatible brands and acquiring them, should the need arise to enter different markets, product categories, or business lines. The future is not about acquiring manufacturing plants and other tangible assets.

While most mergers are predicated on cost efficiency and economies of scale, the most meaningful mergers and acquisitions for brand building are those that truly add to a company's competitive advantage, not just their bottom line.

Gaining authenticity or changing personality: For a brand struggling for relevance in a competitive environment, the right acquisition can give it the authenticity that makes it credible in a new space. This is what Lenovo intended in 2005 when it acquired the PC division of IBM, instantly becoming the world's number three computer maker.

A gateway to foreign markets: Breaking into a new region – especially Asia's emerging markets that are not well understood by many Western brands – is commonly done by acquiring a local brand for its unique expertise and distribution network. Diageo, for example, acquired a traditional Chinese spirit (*baijiu*) maker as part of its strategy to achieve 50 per cent of sales revenues from developing economies within several years. Starbucks, taking a less direct route toward higher revenues from Asia, acquired Teavana, a worldwide chain of loose-leaf tea stores in 2012. Complementing its existing Tazo teabag brand, Starbucks intends to make tea a force in Asia, where the beverage is much more popular than coffee.

Acquiring talented people: One of a brand's most valuable assets is the people whose ideas and efforts drive the company each day. But it can be difficult to dramatically transform a workforce or inject new ways of thinking on a large scale with traditional human resource management. This challenge has given rise to the "acqui-hire" – a phenomenon when one company buys another, not for its products, but for its people. One key benefit is how this maintains harmony among employees while still having a material impact on the workforce. Firstly, it circumvents head-hunting and negotiation, which often requires a salary premium and may create resentment. But more importantly, it brings together teams who have a common purpose and understanding of each other.

Acquiring ideas: Acquiring a company strictly for its intellectual property can help a brand overcome its weaknesses and become a category leader. Because it is concerned only with a company's ideas – not its tangible assets such as buildings, factories or employees – it is a much cleaner acquisition process as well. In 2011 alone, Google acquired 54 companies for their patents and intellectual property, in the process becoming the most dominant web company globally. Buying or licensing intellectual property can also help highly innovative firms protect themselves from infringement lawsuits that may damage their brand. It can be a shrewd defensive maneuver to simply buy a competitor rather than get locked in a legal battle over the technology down the road – precisely the strategy Google employed when it bought Motorola in 2012, partly to fend off legal attacks on its Android platform.

Can the West Maintain its Branding Edge in Asia?

The rise of Asian brands means stiffer competition for global brands who have established a foothold of their own. Foreign sales account for 33 per cent of revenue for the S&P 500, with 8 per cent from Asia-Pacific.[44] In other industries, the importance of Asia is even more pronounced. A BCG report forecast that in the global pharmaceutical industry, more than 70 per cent of future business would originate from developing countries. GE expects more than 60 per cent of its growth revenue to emanate from emerging economies in the coming decade.[45]

Western Brands in Asia Need to Customize their Offerings

Brands are about personality, about relevance, and about resonating with customers.

Western brands entering Asia should be ready to adopt a two-pronged strategy. First, they should be responsive to the unique needs and preferences of customers in different Asian markets. Next, they should retain certain standardized features like attractive packaging, overall identity, and so on. Undoubtedly, the quest to grow in multiple foreign markets can be a double-edged sword for the brand portfolio. As brands enter new segments or expand product variants, they can create chaos if coordination among the different markets is not tightly implemented.

Brands must create strategic processes wherein the CEO and brand managers can effectively differentiate between core brand elements and other peripheral elements. Such a distinction would enable them to maintain consistency of the core elements while being more responsive to changes in the peripheral elements.

Western Brands Need to be More Culturally Sensitive

Despite globalization, each Asian region has its own culture, heritage, beliefs, and value systems. To be successful in Asia means to be sensitive to these subtleties, both internally to its employees, and externally to its markets and customers.

McDonald's shows how a global brand has successfully customized its offering and also built a personality reflecting local values and belief systems. IKEA, the world's biggest furniture retailer, opened the world's largest IKEA store in a suburb of Seoul in January 2015. IKEA showed its lack of cultural insight when it used a map on their website referring to the waters to the east of the Korean peninsula as the Sea of Japan. This did not go unnoticed in South Korea, which calls the area the East Sea.[46]

KEEP THE HERITAGE OR ADJUST?

When Giorgio Armani opened its Beijing retail store in 2001, the company installed a large red-lacquer door in line with traditional Chinese design and architecture. But the Chinese disliked it and it was replaced. In contrast, Vivienne Tam, a Hong Kong-born and New York-based designer, kept the same items she used outside China, featuring Asian design elements and kept labeling her clothing as "Made in China" in a new Shanghai retail store, despite opposition from local staff. Vivienne Tam said she looked forward to the day "when Chinese people have enough self-confidence to support their own luxury brands and stop buying stuff just because it comes from somewhere else."[47] There are around 10–13 million Chinese luxury goods customers, so luxury brands are keen to correct their brand strategies.[48]

Western Brands Need to Collaborate with Asian Brands to Gain a Foothold

In this fast-paced world, time is money. Asian countries bring with them a complex set of cultural sensitivities. With this combination in mind, it would be much easier for global brands to gain a firm foothold in hitherto uncharted territories by collaborating with local players who better understand the local market, customers, and competitors. In China, the Shanghai Volkswagen Automotive Company was formed as a result of collaboration between

Shanghai Automotive Industry Corp. and Volkswagen. In India, the collaboration between Japan's Kawasaki and India's Bajaj to form the highly successful Kawasaki Bajaj is another example.

Western Brands Need to Become Part of the Asian Community

As discussed earlier, companies must ensure they weave their brands into the social fabric and become part of the community. Western brands must respond to local tastes, spend on building local relationships, react to social needs, and be proactive toward corporate social responsibility (CSR), which will grow significantly throughout Asia in upcoming years. CSR will act as a powerful channel as it will showcase the brand's concern toward the society in which it operates.

Asia's Challenger Nations and the Future of ASEAN

There is Much More to Asia than China

When most marketers and strategists think of Asia, they first think of the largest emerging markets, such as China and India, and the developed economic powers like Japan, South Korea, and Taiwan. But other emerging nations, and their brands, opportunities, and challenges, cannot be ignored.

China gets most of the headlines, and deservedly so. It accounts for around 8 per cent of private consumption globally and contributed most to the consumption growth from 2011–2013.[49] But growth is stagnating while costs are rising and global brands are getting better at competing for the Chinese consumer. Other economists have more pessimistic forecasts and believe that corruption and the risk in centrally-planning one of the world's largest economies could mean a hard landing for the Chinese economy.

While China will continue to hold its place as the world's major manufacturing nation, some low value-added industries are already starting to relocate – particularly garment and footwear manufacturing, and even mobile phone assembly – to places where the cost of labor is a fraction of that in some parts of China. This transition in China is similar to the transition Japan once experienced. As a nation develops economically, there will always be countries that can produce cheaper.

The ability to produce cheaper is a good start for Asia's challenger nations. Economic opportunities provided by this unique advantage can enable them to become dominant world players and, eventually, home to iconic global brands of their own.

The rise of manufacturing and growth means greater exports globally. As companies become more global, they face stronger and more varied competition and new potential consumers. In this situation, a well conceptualized brand image can be a powerful differentiator for brands for "successor nations."

In an attempt to categorize and identify these nations, Stratfor came up with what they consider the Post-China 16, or PC16 – a group of nations that are at roughly the same developmental stage and, when taken together, have a total population of just over 1 billion people. With these inputs, Stratfor believes the collective region will succeed China as the world's low-cost, export-oriented economy hub.[50] Asian nations included on this list include Indonesia, Cambodia, Laos, Myanmar, Bangladesh, and the Philippines.

The next segment of Asian nations on the global stage is the Association of Southeast Asian Nations (ASEAN), which currently includes ten nations: Brunei, Cambodia, Indonesia, Laos, Malaysia, Myanmar, the Philippines, Singapore, Thailand, and Vietnam. By forging free-trade agreements globally with countries that include Australia, China, India, Japan, New Zealand, and South Korea, ASEAN countries have been able to join a megatrading bloc comprising more than three billion people, a combined GDP of about US$21 trillion, and some 30 per cent of world trade, something unachievable if each country had had to negotiate individually.

Huge opportunities exist for foreign brands outside of the better-known countries if they simply look to ASEAN as part of the big picture. According to McKinsey, an estimated 67 million households in ASEAN are part of the "consuming class" – a number that could almost double to 125 million by 2025.

ASEAN: FACTS AND FIGURES

- If ASEAN were a single country, it would be the seventh-largest economy globally, with a combined GDP of US$2.4 trillion in 2013[51]
- ASEAN is projected to rank as the fourth-largest economy by 2050[52]
- In 2013, ASEAN surpassed China in terms of FDI inflow with more than 30 per cent of all FDI between 2005 and 2010 going toward manufacturing[53]
- ASEAN includes 227 of the world's companies having more than US$1 billion in revenues, or 3 per cent of the world's total[54]

- It is predicted that ASEAN's economy will grow at 6.2 per cent in 2014 and 6.4 per cent in 2015, faster than the 6.1 per cent recorded in 2013[55]

In 2015, The ASEAN Economic Community (AEC) will come into effect, creating a single free-trade market encompassing 600 million people across 10 countries. The prospect of improved intellectual property rights, lower trade barriers, and harmonized legislation across the region is creating a sense of excitement and optimism, with 61 per cent of consumers feeling it will have a positive impact on their lives while the majority of domestic companies plan to enter new markets and create new products.[56]

SC GLOBAL: REFINING LUXURY PROPERTY BRANDS

SC Global is a Singapore-based luxury property developer founded in 1996 by former investment banker Simon Cheong. Having engineered big property deals, Cheong aspired to change and disrupt the high-end market for luxury property. As Singapore grew to become a leading Asian global hub, it has seen a steep rise in wealth, foreign capital, and residents since 2000. This has been the perfect backdrop for creating the SC Global brand with the tagline "Own the Original."

In early 1999, Simon Cheong started purchasing plots of lands in prime districts in Singapore with money from family and investors. He listed SC Global Developments Ltd later that year.

SC Global's first project in 2000 was branded The Ladyhill, and became the most expensively constructed residential development up to that time.[57] SC Global was the first developer to conduct viewings by appointment only, a different marketing approach that has now become a standard with high-end developers.[58]

Since then the brand has continued to develop high-end luxury condominiums for a very select affluent clientele. Brands like BLVD, The Lincoln Modern, Martin No. 38, The Marq (it made global headlines as the first apartment globally to be fully decorated by the French luxury brand Hermes), and Seven Palms (the only condominium on Singapore's Sentosa Island with beachfront access) are all SC Global developments. Several of SC Global's clients own more than one property.

SC Global has built its lifestyle concept brand on the basis of originality, design, and quality, with style, aesthetics, and authenticity as key drivers, and craftsmanship and quality materials and appliances as the focus.

Simon Cheong participates actively and takes leadership in the design detailing of each building. Famous for hiring top-notch architects with knowledge of Asian architecture, he spends considerable time designing and overseeing the projects.

SC Global has further elevated its brand positioning by using TV campaigns featuring Sean Connery and more recently Yo-Yo Ma. Focused on building client relationships through a portfolio of properties that consistently exceed the expectations of high and ultra-high net worth individuals, SC Global offers a relationship, and not just a property.

"LOCAL DYNAMOS" THAT ARE WINNING AT HOME

BCG has highlighted 50 emerging market companies defeating foreign competition in their home markets. Instead of using cheap labor and low production costs, these leaders focus on innovating and understanding rising middle class consumers better than their larger competitors, and finding creative ways to overcome local challenges that larger MNCs have difficulty replicating.[59]

According to the report, the revenues of these top 50 companies grew 28 per cent annually from 2009–2013, much faster than S&P 500 companies (5 per cent growth). These "local dynamos" include 27 brands from BRIC nations, six from Africa, and seven from Southeast Asia, including:

- Jia Duo Bao (China, herbal tea)
- Jiangsu Hengriu Medicine (China, pharmaceuticals)
- Xiaomi (China, smartphones and consumer electronics)
- Amara Raja (India, electronics)
- Flipkart (India, online retail)
- Micromax (India, consumer electronics)
- Masan group (Vietnam, food and beverages)

Conclusion

All the factors discussed in this chapter provide a blueprint of the Asian landscape up to 2020. The chapter serves as a useful guideline for both Asian and Western companies planning growth in Asia. It has explored the importance of Asian branding going forward and the challenges Asia faces in driving shareholder value by adopting a long-term branding perspective in the corporate world. Asian companies must understand that overcoming branding barriers and its implications is indeed possible.

The following case study on Banyan Tree Hotels and Resorts is testament to this. It describes Banyan Tree's brand journey and how it has evolved into a widely-recognized and well-managed international brand with a large potential. This case can inspire other Asian companies to tread the branding path with renewed vigor.

BANYAN TREE: BRANDED PARADISE

Since 1992, Banyan Tree Hotels and Resorts has grown into one of Asia's most successful hospitality brands, winning numerous international awards and accolades from publications like the prestigious *Condé Nast Traveler*. Banyan Tree is one of the youngest chains of up-market and privately-held luxury boutique hotels, resorts, and spas. By successfully blending environmental concern with unique Asian traditions and heritage and the concept of individual luxury villas offering an intimate experience, Banyan Tree has emerged as one of the leaders in the hospitality industry.

Branding has been the strategy from the start, and was born out of a necessity to differentiate a traditional overseas Chinese family business. Banyan Tree wanted to escape being overrun by cheaper competitors from Indonesia and China, and to distract from tough pricing.[60]

The company was successful in breaking away from an Asian commodity business and changing the focus to higher value-added revenues. The brand is led by a centralized team headed by corporate management and the promise illustrated in the tagline "Sanctuary for the Senses" is delivered throughout the organization as part of a dedicated business strategy that is centered on branding.

The Banyan Tree Company manages more than 37 resorts and hotels, 70 spas, 80 retail galleries, and three championship golf courses in 28 countries. With corporate headquarters in Singapore, the company is traded publicly on the Singapore Stock Exchange. Banyan Tree also manages and/or owns interests in other hotels and resorts and employs more than 12,000 people representing more than 50 nationalities globally. The company shows the importance of corporate management's involvement in investing, building, and driving the brand and all related activities.

Background of the Banyan Tree brand

Banyan Tree was founded by Singapore-based Ho Kwon Ping, who named it after Banyan Tree Bay – or Yung Shue Wan in local dialect, a small fishing village on Lamma Island in Hong Kong – where he and his wife Claire Chiang (former Member of the Parliament of Singapore) spent three idyllic years when he was a reporter and editor for the Asian magazine *Far Eastern Economic Review*.

Ho Kwon Ping returned to Singapore after his father fell ill. As the eldest son, he had to take on the responsibility of the family business as is often expected in Asian business families. Shortly after, Ho Kwon Ping was looking for new ideas to take his father's family-run business, Wah Chang Group, ahead and away from the traditional revenue streams into different areas, from property to manufacturing. The business was under pressure, competed primarily on cost, and was not dominant in any particular industry or market.

In 1994, the couple opened the first Banyan Tree resort in Phuket, Thailand, with some investors and Ho Kwon Ping's brother Ho Kwon Cjan as the architect. Banyan Tree was built upon an old abandoned tin mine. The owners decided to clean the acid-laden soil by planting more than 7,000 trees. This ecological wasteland transformed into the first environmentally-sensitive Banyan Tree resort.

There began the trademark pool villa concept, which was an innovation then and became one of the brand's signatures.[61] Today, the private pool villa concept has proliferated to other resort groups and is used as a benchmark in the hospitality industry.

After Banyan Tree Phuket's success, the brand owners decided to launch two other resorts on Bintan Island, Indonesia, and Vabbinfaru Island in the Maldives.

Background of Ho Kwon Ping

Ho Kwon Ping was born in Hong Kong in 1952 although his father, Ho Rih Hwa, a businessman and diplomat, was born in Singapore. Kwon Ping grew up and studied in Thailand and went on to Taiwan's Tunghai University, where his exposure to Chinese culture left a deep impact on him. After a year, he left for Stanford University in the United States. After returning to Singapore, he did his national service as a combat engineer. He later studied at the National University of Singapore.

He joined the family business in 1981. In 1994, after successfully rehabilitating an abandoned tin mine into Laguna Phuket, Asia's first integrated resort, he launched Banyan Tree Hotels and Resorts.

Banyan Tree: How was the brand established?

Ho Kwon Ping says, "There are only two advantages in life which are proprietary: technology and branding. Since I am not a technologist, I decided that whatever business I was going to do next had to have a strong brand."

Given the inevitable turmoil of the volatile hospitality industry, Ho Kwon Ping was convinced that a strong branding focus would give Banyan Tree a sustainable competitive advantage. Indeed, Banyan Tree withstood the repeated crises of 1997–1998, the events of September 11, and the Iraq War. During the SARS outbreak in 2003, the company still emerged profitable by achieving average occupancy rates of 65–67 per cent.[62]

Branding starts right from the Banyan Tree resort locations and is consistent through designs, facilities, and ambience. Aligning with the "romantic escape" theme, Banyan Tree places a strong emphasis on the locations as a key element of brand identity. The company has chosen exquisite locations with exciting surroundings and good transportation infrastructure as the main destination highlights.

The resorts offer a unique visitor experience by providing a luxury experience complete with self-indulgence and pampering experiences like the Banyan Tree Spas, which offer traditional treatments and fresh ingredients. The company operates a training academy in Phuket where all spa therapists attend 400 compulsory training hours – way above industry standards.

Banyan Tree believes in the value of a destination's local heritage, so guests can find a Banyan Tree Gallery exhibiting and selling indigenous artifacts and handicrafts in every resort.[63] Guests can extend the brand experience by taking home some products relating to the place where they have had memorable experiences. The company constantly ensures that everything is in sync with the brand theme of romance, intimacy, and rejuvenation. Banyan Tree has more than 80 retail galleries worldwide.

Banyan Tree and Sustainability

Ho Kwon Ping has stated that he intends to maintain the social responsibility standards practiced by Banyan Tree since its inception. He and his wife are interested in economic development and social activism as they both grew up during the Vietnam War years. According to Ho Kwon Ping, corporate social responsibility was an integral part of the Banyan Tree group right from the start. He says that, "Banyan Tree was a vehicle for us, using business as a means to create something we hope is beautiful and sustainable, but simultaneously using business as a means to enable many of the deep-seated beliefs we have about sustainable development."

He continues, "The core beliefs that inform the group's sustainability policies, which range from building and running resorts with as little environmental damage as possible to conducting community development and environmental projects at each resort, are more fundamental to us than the notion of building a Banyan Tree. So there is no way we could possibly lose that."

Concern for nature and the environment surrounding the resorts has always been a trademark of Banyan Tree, and is appreciated by many environmentalists. The company builds villas around trees and boulders rather than cutting or excavating them, and subjects resorts to certification to the leading design standard for sustainable tourism, EarthCheck. The company also engages in numerous projects like the Sea Turtle Protection program and has built health clinics, schools, and temples for communities in which its resorts are located.

True to its belief that environmentally-sustainable and socially-responsible tourism is compatible with profit-making, Banyan Tree has established the Green Imperative Fund mechanism and Banyan Tree Global Foundation to extend financial assistance to environmental conservation and community projects.

The Green Imperative Fund forms part of the Stay For Good program, which crowdsources micro-contributions from guests during their stay, with every dollar matched by Banyan Tree. Since the fund's inception in 2001, the Green Imperative Fund has raised more than US$7 million, disbursing over US$4.1 million in support of worthy social and environmental efforts whereby the primary beneficiary is external to Banyan Tree.

These have endeared Banyan Tree to the public and media, which often feature its resorts. The company also takes a keen interest in providing support for young people's education globally and sources most materials required for its gallery artifacts from Asian cottage industries.

When the Asian tsunami struck in December 2004, none of the properties were badly damaged from the disaster. As part of its continuing efforts to provide assistance to the local community, Banyan Tree decided to focus on medium- and long-term relief efforts aimed at rebuilding shattered lives. To address these concerns, the company set up the Tsunami Recovery Fund working with the local authorities to determine community needs. The staff voluntarily contributed 5 per cent of their salaries to the recovery fund run by the company. Additionally, resort guests could donate US$2 per room per night, which Banyan Tree matched.[64] With these funds, the company purchased boats for fishermen and building material for use in construction of houses and schools.

Banyan Tree also created the "Greening Communities Together around World Environment Day." During the first week of June every year, all their hotels around the world plant two trees per room night as a gesture of environment conservation and habit protection. These June tree planting efforts are in addition to Banyan Tree's Greening Communities initiative, which has challenged resorts to plant 2,000 trees per year since 2007 (and has planted more than 300,000 trees) in order to raise local awareness for climate change. "Feeding Communities Together around World Food Day" is run mid-October annually in all hotels and resorts globally to support and empower communities through food.

Banyan Tree has been very successful in creating a strong personality around these core values. Delivering all its promises and leading by example in social causes, Banyan Tree has built a brand with minimal advertising or traditional brand building methods and established premium-pricing power for its brand portfolio.

Banyan tree brand communications

Banyan Tree initially resorted to advertising to build awareness, but the budget for this was soon cut to save costs. In fact, the overall marketing budget of Banyan Tree is 7 per cent of total revenue, with 60 per cent allocated for trade and 40 per cent allocated for consumer promotions.[65] The entire brand communications strategy is based on third party endorsements, word-of-mouth, and public relations.

In its early years, Banyan Tree used an international advertising agency to create its marketing communications. The agency designed the Banyan Tree logo and came up with the tagline "Sanctuary for the Senses" together with the Banyan Tree management team. Extensive advertising was used to gain initial recognition when the Banyan Tree brand was first launched.

With its very first resort in Phuket, Banyan Tree won the coveted Ecotourism award for total environmental regeneration of Bang

Tao Bay. The entire hospitality industry took notice of the new entrant as the United Nations had previously declared the former mining site impossible to rehabilitate. Banyan Tree did extensive rehabilitation work costing a total of US$250 million.

A string of awards followed: Best Beach Resort, World's Best Spa Resort, and more from reputed magazines and organizations like Condé Nast Travelers UK, TTG Awards, World Travel Awards, The Indonesia Travels and Tourism Awards, Best Resort in China, Best Resort Hotel in Asia Pacific, and Tourism for Tomorrow Award (2012).[66] Banyan Tree and its portfolio brands have won more than 900 awards and accolades since the company was established in 1994.

This generated a lot of awareness and curiosity in the industry. Banyan Tree also uses public relations as an important brand building strategy. It regularly invites editors and writers of prestigious travel and leisure magazines to visit the resorts, ensures that high-quality photos are ready for use, and ensures that the resorts are portrayed in line with the brand promise.

Such media coverage has helped build the Banyan Tree brand portfolio's international awareness and credibility, and its overall brand equity.

Expanding the Banyan tree brand portfolio

The strong belief in branding has started to pay off, and the Banyan Tree brand equity has enabled new revenue streams. It has enabled a brand extension in the form of Angsana (launched in 2000), a contemporary destination playground designed to bring the adventure back into travel whatever your age.

Angsana operates 13 resorts in nine countries (November 2014) and stand-alone Angsana Spas. With the backing of the Banyan Tree brand and its strong recognition in the leisure industry, Angsana has been well-received globally.

In 2003, a line extension, Colours of Angsana, a sister chain of resorts under the Angsana brand, was made. The hotels were launched in more remote areas including UNESCO's World Heritage sites, and located in off-the-beaten track destinations like

Laos, Sri Lanka, and China. It was later discontinued and wrapped under the Angsana brand.

New Cassia brand: A hotel residence with a twist

In June 2014, Banyan Tree announced the launch of their new brand, Cassia, focusing on a new market. Banyan Tree had identified a niche in the hospitality market which they wanted to explore through their expertise in management, design, and innovation to create a new proposition in the serviced apartment industry. Cassia brings the Banyan Tree portfolio to three unique brands.

Cassia was created to bring together investment opportunities for the growing middle-class looking for affordable holiday homes and the opportunity to develop an innovative hotel product in the serviced apartment segment.

Globalization of the Banyan Tree brand portfolio

Banyan Tree Group's future strategy is described as "to string a necklace of resorts around the world." It is not about being everywhere, but having a presence in chosen places. "It is not about quantity but building quality jewels that form a chain," according to executive chairman Ho Kwon Ping.[67] The company plans to expand it across new regions to create a truly global brand. Banyan Tree also has extensive plans for China, an expected huge growth market due to booming domestic travel patterns and rising new affluent consumer groups seeking status and luxury experiences, and the enormous inbound tourism market.

The company has full ownership of its Asian resorts, but part of the strategy outside Asia is to establish partnerships and joint ventures with local partners. Banyan Tree will typically hold a smaller equity stake, do all in-house design and decoration, and manage the property. This ensures good alignment between brand promise and brand delivery, and enables effective control of the brand despite foreign partners. This is not always easy as the management's decision-making power runs the risk of getting diluted, thereby affecting crucial brand decisions.

The international strategy is also part of having more diverse revenue streams from separate regions and markets. The leisure industry is volatile and Banyan Tree is hedging against unexpected events and cyclical economies by having properties in different locations.

Banyan Tree will continue to provide its unique blend of romance, rejuvenation, and sensuality in multiple destinations globally as the lifestyle hospitality group expands further into the Middle East, Central America, Europe, and Africa.

The future Banyan Tree brand and business challenges

Distinctively Asian versus developing a global image: As Banyan Tree has already expanded way beyond Asia, the company faces the typical dilemma of any Asian brand in finding a balance between being distinctively Asian and developing a more globally-oriented image. Although the entire brand is based on the unique Asian touch and cultural heritage, Banyan Tree has to constantly evaluate its relevance and sustainability as it enters new territories. Generally, the Asian touch and feel that Banyan Tree provides are deemed both exotic and distinct in its properties outside Asia.

Banyan Tree can localize its offerings to suit local tastes and environments better, but it should be sensible about the extent of localization. If Banyan Tree were to keep localizing its offerings, especially in Western markets, this might ultimately affect its core brand identity and drain its main differentiating factor – its unique Asian heritage.

Consequences of brand extensions: The Banyan Tree brand portfolio has increased to comprise different business lines, target groups, and price segments. This is a challenge that goes to the very foundation of the company – brand management and resource allocation. Although Angsana has a lower price point and is targeted primarily toward family guests, these resorts still have much of the typical Banyan Tree feel. The challenge is to balance two distinct brands and differentiate them without diluting the leading brand Banyan Tree. With the ongoing company expansion, there will be a resource allocation trade-off sometime in the future.

The centralized marketing and branding team is overseeing resorts in different parts of the world, so successful brand portfolio management would be extremely challenging and requires stringent procedures and decisions for each of the brands to stay in touch with market dynamics.

Keep innovating and avoid copycats: The market is crowded with many entrants running similar branded resorts in at the upper end. This is particularly true in Asia-Pacific, where Banyan Tree has its stronghold and traditional base, and new entrants face only small barriers-of-entry other than huge capital requirements and availability of good locations, something Asia is not short of. A new entrant can always try to copy the "romance-intimacy-rejuvenation" theme and replicate the serene locations with beautiful villas, providing it can offer lower prices to gain foothold in the market.

Therefore, Banyan Tree needs to keep innovating and exceeding customer expectations, something that requires substantial resources, management focus, and brand portfolio control to stay relevant and competitive.

Angsana Ihuru, Maldives

Source: Courtesy of Banyan Tree Hotels and Resorts.

The brand portfolio managed by Banyan Tree

Source: Courtesy of Banyan Tree Hotels and Resorts.

Conclusion

chapter 11

Without action, the world would still be an idea.

— Georges Doriot, Founder, INSEAD

It is clear that this is going to be Asia's century. The opening of China, the rise of India, and the resurgence of the Asian tigers makes Asia the most vibrant global business playground with a slow but steady shift in the Asian business mind-set. Gone are the days when low cost and manufacturing prowess alone served as competitive advantages for Asian companies. Asian corporations are realizing the importance of moving up the value chain through creating strong brands. Besides serving as the main competitive advantage, branding also enhances shareholder value in the medium and long term. As has been argued throughout this book, this is easier said than done, given the dominant Asian business mind-set of trading and sales.

A substantial part of shareholder value in successful companies derives from their ability to successfully manage and leverage their most important intangible assets: their brands' equity. In turn, Asian companies must realize that branding is a dynamic and continuous process that must be led by the boardroom and corporate management. It is too important to be left to the marketing function alone.

Contrary to common Asian perceptions, branding is much more than advertising and marketing communications. Nice company logos or modern design identities are not key branding ingredients – only a tactical face. Instead, successful branding is strategic, involves all company functions and aspects and aligns around multiple touch points. This ensures a successful balance between brand promise and brand delivery. In the future, the Asian marketing function needs to become more cross-functional, manage and measure results through several marketing metrics, and work in teams to contribute to brand building.

As more global and local companies enter the market in all possible categories, there will be intense competition and overcapacity in the marketplace. This will exert immense pressure on companies to resort to price wars to capture the market on a short-term basis. But Asian boardrooms must strategically find a balance between short- and long-term financial performance. Corporations need to look beyond quarterly results, monthly sales figures, and factory turnovers. This will be highly valued by shareholders and financial markets, as shown. Financial resources spent on brand management must be treated as an investment rather than an expense. Boardrooms must invest in sustainable intangible assets through branding strategies for survival, sustenance, and growth.

As more Asian countries open up to global companies and attract foreign investment, building strong brands becomes not only an important strategy but also a matter of survival. In changing market dynamics, being a domestic market leader does not guarantee long-term success, as global players entering domestic markets can easily challenge local players with their business might. A McKinsey study has shown that the top ten Asian value creators derive on average more than 50 per cent of revenues from outside their home markets.

Many global brands have established strong local relations, invested heavily to build robust distribution networks, worked closely with local authorities to establish good working rapport, and recruited locals to gain crucial "Asian" knowledge. By leveling the ground for local and global brands in terms of local market and customer knowledge, Asian companies will increasingly come under pressure to defend their traditional comparative advantage. This again stresses the need for local Asian companies to invest in building resonating brands with compelling stories to compete with global brands and survive in the marketplace.

Asian brands like Singapore Airlines, Banyan Tree Hotels and Resorts, HSBC, Samsung, and Shiseido have demonstrated that Asian companies can build brands on a par with those of Western countries and that a strong brand will enable companies to survive difficult times and maintain financial robustness.

This book has provided in-depth discussions and recommendations to help companies build strong brands and prepare for the next round of competition. It has highlighted the importance of building successful brands to effectively capture higher financial value and emphasized the importance of corporate management's involvement and commitment in realizing this. A branding drive in Asia is finally emerging and will change the global landscape in the next few decades, if taken seriously and managed properly throughout entire organizations.

The pressure to manage brands will only intensify in the coming years. The time needed to build a global brand is shortening, thanks to a more globalized world, faster communications, more pervasive media, and the Internet. While Japanese companies took 40 years, and South Korean companies took 25 years, Chinese and Indian companies might only need 5–10 years. This shortening timeframe will add further pressure on Asian firms to manage brands competently.[1]

As the late management professor Peter Drucker once said, "Whenever you see a successful business, someone once made a courageous decision."

Asian cultures have always valued long-term aspects. Let this unique strength influence Asian branding efforts in upcoming years. Now it is up to Asian boardrooms to make courageous decisions.

Appendix A: Interbrand Brand Valuation

Overview

Compared to when Interbrand first pioneered brand valuation in the 1980s, global business leaders now widely accept the importance and value of strong brands – and the significant role they can play in enhancing business performance. Strong brands enhance business performance primarily through their influence on three key stakeholder groups: (current and prospective) customers, employees, and investors. They influence customer choice and create loyalty; attract, retain, and motivate talent; and lower the cost of financing.

There are three key components to all of Interbrand's valuations: an analysis of the financial performance of the branded products or services, the role brand plays in the purchase decision on segmentation, and, at the end of the process, the bringing together of these to calculate the financial value of the brand.

1. **Segmentation**

   Segments are typically defined by geography, business unit, product, service, or customer group. Why is segmentation important? A robust valuation requires a separate analysis of the individual parts (or segments) of a business to ensure that differences between those segments in terms of the three key components of the brand valuation (financial performance, role of brand, and brand strength) can be taken into consideration.

2. **Financial Analysis**

   Interbrand starts by forecasting the current and future revenue that is due to the branded products. They subtract operating costs (the cost of doing business) to arrive at the branded operating profit. Interbrand then apply a discount rate to the branded profit that is based on the capital a business spends, versus the money it makes. This gives them the brand's economic profit.

Financial performance measures an organization's raw financial return to the investors. For this reason, it is analyzed as economic profit, a concept akin to the standard accounting measure of Economic Value Added (EVA). To determine economic profit, we remove taxes from net operating profit to get to net operating profit after tax (NOPAT). From NOPAT, a capital charge is subtracted to account for the capital used to generate the brand's revenues; this provides the economic profit for each analyzed year. For purposes of the ranking, the capital charge rate is set by the industry weighted average cost of capital (WACC). The financial performance is analyzed for a five-year forecast and for a terminal value. The terminal value represents the brand's expected performance beyond the forecast period.

3. **Role of Brand**

Role of Brand measures the portion of the purchase decision that is attributable to the brand, relative to other factors (for example, purchase drivers like price, convenience, or product features). The Role of Brand Index ("RBI") quantifies this as a percentage. Customers rely more on brands to guide their choice when competing products or services cannot be easily compared or contrasted, and trust is deferred to the brand (e.g. computer chips), or where their needs are emotional, such as a statement about their personality (e.g. luxury brands). RBI tends to fall within a category-driven range, but there remain significant opportunities for brands to increase their influence on choice within those boundaries, or even extend the category range where the brand can change consumer behavior.

RBI determinations can be derived in three ways (and are described in order of preference below):

- Primary research. Specifically designed research, such as choice modeling (although other techniques are available), where RBI is statistically derived
- Existing research plus Interbrand opinion. Existing research addressing the relative importance of purchase drivers is combined with Interbrand's opinion on the extent to which the brand influences perception of how the product or service will perform against each driver
- Qualitative assessment. Based on management discussions and past experience. This is used where no market research is available

RBI findings are cross-checked against historical roles of brand for companies in the same industry. Finally, RBI is multiplied by the economic profit of the branded products or services to determine the earnings attributable to the brand ("brand earnings") that contribute to the valuation total.

4. **Brand Strength**

Brand Strength measures the ability of the brand to create loyalty and, therefore, to keep generating demand and profit into the future. Brand Strength is scored on a 0 to 100 scale, where 100 is a perfect score, and is based on an evaluation across 10 key factors (see below) that Interbrand believes make a strong brand. Performance on these factors is judged relative to other world-class brands. The strength of the brand is inversely related to the level of risk associated with the brand's financial forecasts (a strong brand creates loyal customers and lowers risk, and vice versa). A formula is used to connect the Brand Strength Score to a brand-specific discount rate. The brand-specific discount rate is used to discount brand earnings back to a present value, reflecting the likelihood that the brand will be able to withstand challenges and deliver the expected earnings into the future. This is equal to brand value.

Interbrand's experiences show that brands that are best placed to keep generating demand and profit into the future are those performing strongly (relative to competition) across a set of 10 factors, shown below. Four of these factors are internally driven, and reflect the fact that great brands start from within. The remaining six factors are more visible externally, acknowledging the fact that great brands change their world.

Internal Factors

- Clarity: Clarity internally about what the brand stands for and its values, positioning, and proposition. Clarity, too, about target audiences, customer insights, and drivers. Because so much hinges on this, it is vital that these are articulated and shared across the organization
- Commitment: Internal commitment to brand, and a belief internally in the importance of brand. The extent to which the brand receives support in terms of time, influence, and investment
- Protection: How secure the brand is across a number of dimensions: legal protection, proprietary ingredients or design, scale, or geographical spread
- Responsiveness: The ability to respond to market changes, challenges, and opportunities. The brand should have a sense of leadership internally, and a desire and the ability to constantly evolve and renew itself

External Factors

- Authenticity: The brand is soundly based on an internal truth and capability. It has a defined heritage and a well-grounded value set. It can deliver against the (high) expectations that customers have of it

- Relevance: The fit with customer/consumer needs, desires, and decision criteria across all relevant demographics and geographies
- Differentiation: The degree to which customers/consumers perceive the brand to have a differentiated positioning distinctive from the competition
- Consistency: The degree to which a brand is experienced without fail across all touch points or formats
- Presence: The degree to which a brand feels omnipresent and is talked about positively by consumers, customers, and opinion formers in both traditional and social media
- Understanding: The brand is not only recognized by customers, but there is also an in-depth knowledge and understanding of its distinctive qualities and characteristics. (Where relevant, this will extend to consumer understanding of the company that owns the brand)

5. **Brand Value Calculation**

   The parts come together so that the forecasted financial performance projects economic profits that are multiplied by the role of the brand to reveal branded earnings. These branded earnings, which are based on the brand strength, are discounted back to a present value and totaled to arrive at a brand value.

A strategic tool for ongoing brand management, the brand value calculation brings market, brand, competitor, and financial data into a single, value-based framework within which the performance of the brand can be assessed, areas for improvement identified, and the financial impact of investing in the brand quantified. This calculation is also used in a wide variety of Brand Value Modelling situations, such as:

- Predicting the effect on marketing and investment strategies
- Determining and assessing communications budgets
- Calculating the return on brand investment
- Assessing opportunities in new or underexploited markets
- Tracking brand value management

Source: Interbrand

Appendix B: Interbrand's 2014 Best Global Brands

2014 Rank	2013 Rank	Brand	Sector	2014 Brand Value (USD $billion)	% Change in brand value
1	1	Apple	Technology	118.863	21%
2	2	Google	Technology	107.439	15%
3	3	Coca-Cola	Beverages	81.563	3%
4	4	IBM	Business Services	72.244	-8%
5	5	Microsoft	Technology	61.154	3%
6	6	GE	Diversified	45.480	-3%
7	8	Samsung	Technology	45.462	15%
8	10	Toyota	Automotive	42.392	20%
9	7	McDonald's	Restaurants	42.254	1%
10	11	Mercedes-Benz	Automotive	34.338	8%
11	12	BMW	Automotive	34.214	7%
12	9	Intel	Technology	34.153	-8%
13	14	Disney	Media	32.223	14%
14	13	Cisco	Technology	30.936	6%
15	19	Amazon	Retail	29.478	25%
16	18	Oracle	Technology	25.980	8%
17	15	HP	Technology	23.758	-8%
18	16	Gillette	FMCG	22.845	-9%
19	17	Louis Vuitton	Luxury	22.552	-9%
20	20	Honda	Automotive	21.673	17%
21	21	H&M	Apparel	21.083	16%
22	24	Nike	Sporting Goods	19.875	16%
23	23	American Express	Financial Services	19.510	11%

2014 Rank	2013 Rank	Brand	Sector	2014 Brand Value (USD $billion)	% Change in brand value
24	22	Pepsi	Beverages	19.119	7%
25	25	SAP	Technology	17.340	4%
26	26	IKEA	Retail	15.885	15%
27	27	UPS	Transportation	14.470	5%
28	28	eBay	Retail	14.358	9%
29	52	Facebook	Technology	14.349	86%
30	29	Pampers	FMCG	14.078	8%
31	34	Volkswagen	Automotive	13.716	23%
32	30	Kellogg's	FMCG	13.442	4%
33	32	HSBC	Financial Services	13.142	8%
34	31	Budweiser	Alcohol	13.024	3%
35	33	J.P. Morgan	Financial Services	12.456	9%
36	36	Zara	Apparel	12.126	12%
37	35	Canon	Electronics	11.702	6%
38	37	Nescafe	Beverages	11.406	7%
39	42	Ford	Automotive	10.876	18%
40	43	Hyundai	Automotive	10.409	16%
41	38	Gucci	Luxury	10.385	2%
42	40	Philips	Electronics	10.264	5%
43	39	L'Oréal	FMCG	10.162	3%
44	41	Accenture	Business Services	9.882	4%
45	51	Audi	Automotive	9.831	27%
46	54	Hermès	Luxury	8.977	18%
47	44	Goldman Sachs	Financial Services	8.758	3%
48	48	Citi	Financial Services	8.737	10%
49	45	Siemens	Diversified	8.672	2%
50	50	Colgate	FMCG	8.215	5%
51	49	Danone	FMCG	8.205	3%
52	46	Sony	Electronics	8.133	-3%
53	59	AXA	Financial Services	8.120	14%
54	56	Nestlé	FMCG	8.000	6%
55	63	Allianz	Financial Services	7.702	15%
56	65	Nissan	Automotive	7.623	23%
57	47	Thomson Reuters	Media	7.472	-8%

2014 Rank	2013 Rank	Brand	Sector	2014 Brand Value (USD $billion)	% Change in brand value
58	60	Cartier	Luxury	7.449	8%
59	55	Adidas	Sporting Goods	7.378	-2%
60	64	Porsche	Automotive	7.171	11%
61	58	Caterpillar	Diversified	6.812	-4%
62	62	Xerox	Business Services	6.641	-2%
63	71	Morgan Stanley	Financial Services	6.334	11%
64	68	Panasonic	Electronics	6.303	8%
65	73	Shell	Energy	6.288	14%
66	76	3M	Diversified	6.177	14%
67	70	Discovery	Media	6.143	7%
68	66	KFC	Restaurants	6.059	-2%
69	74	Visa	Financial Services	5.998	10%
70	72	Prada	Luxury	5.977	7%
71	75	Tiffany & Co.	Luxury	5.936	9%
72	69	Sprite	Beverages	5.646	-3%
73	77	Burberry	Luxury	5.594	8%
74	83	Kia	Automotive	5.396	15%
75	84	Santander	Financial Services	5.382	16%
76	91	Starbucks	Restaurants	5.382	22%
77	79	Adobe	Technology	5.333	9%
78	81	Johnson & Johnson	FMCG	5.194	9%
79	80	John Deere	Diversified	5.124	5%
80	78	MTV	Media	5.102	2%
81	N/A	DHL	Transportation	5.084	NEW
82	89	Chevrolet	Automotive	5.036	10%
83	88	Ralph Lauren	Apparel	4.979	9%
84	85	Duracell	FMCG	4.935	6%
85	86	Jack Daniel's	Alcohol	4.884	5%
86	82	Johnnie Walker	Alcohol	4.842	2%
87	96	Harley-Davidson	Automotive	4.772	13%
88	97	MasterCard	Financial Services	4.758	13%
89	90	Kleenex	FMCG	4.643	5%
90	95	Smirnoff	Alcohol	4.609	8%
91	N/A	Land Rover	Automotive	4.473	NEW

2014 Rank	2013 Rank	Brand	Sector	2014 Brand Value (USD $billion)	% Change in brand value
92	N/A	FedEx	Transportation	4.414	NEW
93	93	Corona	Alcohol	4.387	3%
94	N/A	Huawei	Technology	4.313	NEW
95	92	Heineken	Alcohol	4.221	-3%
96	94	Pizza Hut	Restaurants	4.196	-2%
97	N/A	Hugo Boss	Apparel	4.143	NEW
98	57	Nokia	Technology	4.138	-44%
99	100	Gap	Apparel	4.122	5%
100	67	Nintendo	Electronics	4.103	-33%

Source: Interbrand.

Notes

Preface and Acknowledgments

1. http://www.wpp.com/wpp/marketing/brandz/china-100-2014/

1 Introduction

1. "Xiaomi muscles past Apple to take sixth place in China's smartphone market as Samsung stays on top," thenextweb.com, August 6, 2013.
2. "The rise of Xiaomi and Micromax – Asia's smartphone innovators that are taking on the world," *Business Insider*, April 10, 2014.
3. "Xiaomi faces bumpy road abroad," *Asian Wall Street Journal*, December 12, 2014.
4. Author interview with L Capital Asia and Charles & Keith Group.
5. "Uniqlo's parent presses to become world's top retailer," *Asian Wall Street Journal*, March 5, 2014.
6. "Uniqlo's brilliant strategy is to totally ignore fashion," *Business Insider*, October 11, 2012.
7. "Uniqlo poised to open flagships in drive to expand," *Financial Times*, November 2, 2006.
8. "How clothing chain Uniqlo is taking over the world," *Business Insider*, April 26, 2013.
9. "Global Economics Paper No: 208," *Goldman Sachs*, December 7, 2011.
10. "Growth journeys," *Accenture*, 2013.
11. "Business in Asia" *Economist* special report, May 31, 2014.
12. Author's interview with Lars Wiskum, a leading international consultant in the sports goods industry.
13. "Rankings," *Interbrand*, 2014.
14. "The world's largest companies: China takes over the top three spots," *Forbes*, July 5, 2014.

15. "Understanding the diversity of Indonesia's consumers," *McKinsey & Company*, April 2013, World Bank GDP.
16. "Business in Asia" *Economist* special report, May 31, 2014.
17. "China can't be a global innovation leader unless it does these three things," *Harvard Business Review*, November 8, 2013.
18. "2014 Global R&D Funding Forecast," *Battelle*, December 2013.
19. Would Intellectual Property Organization.
20. "China tops Europe in R&D intensity," nature.com, January 8, 2014.
21. "Understanding Asia's conglomerates," *McKinsey*, February 2013.
22. "Korean beauty firm rides K-Pop wave," *Asian Wall Street Journal*, September 28, 2014.
23. "Keeping the family fortune relatively intact," *Financial Times*, September 22, 2013.
24. "Leading growth in a family business: learning from Eu Yan Sang," *NUS Business School*, March 19, 2014.
25. "Keeping the family fortune relatively intact," *Financial Times*, September 22, 2013.
26. "$1.3 billion (84%) of counterfeit goods seized from China and Hong Kong," *Global Intellectual Property Center*, January 5, 2013.
27. "Counterfeit goods from China make up almost 2pc of world trade," *South China Morning Post*, April 16, 2013.
28. "Fakes! The global counterfeit business is out of control, targeting everything from computer chips to life-saving machines," Frederick Balfour and Carol Matlack in Paris, Amy Barrett in Philadelphia, Kerry Capell in London, *Business Week,* February 7, 2005.
29. MIT's Center for Digital Business.

2   Branding – The Driver of a Successful Business Strategy

1. For a more elaborate explanation of brands and brand cultures, see "Brands and Branding," Douglas Holt, Class discussion note, Harvard Business School, 2003.
2. "Luxury Brands step Down a Notch to Lure Buyers from Middle Class," *The Economic Times*, November 26, 2013.
3. "Rankings," *Interbrand*, 2014.
4. Frederick E. Webster, Jr. and Kevin Lane Keller, "A Roadmap for Branding in Industrial Markets," February 2004.
5. "Is Your B2B Brand Strong Enough To Keep You in the Game?," *Forrester*, November 12, 2013.
6. "How B2B Companies Talk Past Their Customers," McKinsey & Co, October 2013.
7. Grahame R. Dowling and Richard Staelin, "A Model of Perceived Risk and Intended Risk-handling Activity," *Journal of Consumer Research*, (21), 1997, pp. 119–134.

8. Scott M. Cunningham, "The major dimensions of perceived risk," in Donald F. Cox (ed.), *Risk Taking and Information Handling in Consumer Behavior*, Boston, MA: Harvard University Press, 1967, pp. 82–108.

9. "Asians Most Reluctant to Try Out New Brands: Nielsen," *Campaign Asia*.

10. Ibid.

11. http://www.twgtea.com/aboutus.html.

12. http://www.thenational.ae/business/retail/twg-brews-up-three-more-tea-outlets-in-uae

13. http://www.twgtea.com/aboutus.html.

14. Peter Doyle, "Value-based Marketing," *Journal of Strategic Marketing*, (8), 2000.

15. Tim Ambler, "Market Metrics: What Should We Tell the Shareholders?," *Balance Sheet*, Bradford, 10(1), 2002, 47.

16. Michael V. Marn, Eric V. Roegner and Craig C. Zawada, "The Power of Pricing," *McKinsey Quarterly*, (1), 2003.

17. Ambler, "Market Metrics," 2002.

18. "Winning Asian Strategies," *McKinsey Quarterly*, (1), 2002.

19. "How to Keep Roaring," *The Economist*, May 31, 2014.

20. "Explaining Variation in Market to Book Ratios: Do Corporate Reputation Ratings Add Explanatory Power Over and Above Brand Values?," *Journal of Finance and Accountancy*, 2, January 2010.

21. "Brands Matter: An Empirical Investigation of Brand-building Activities and the Creation of Shareholder Value," Working Paper, 02–098, May 2, 2002.

22. Richard A. Brealey and Stewart C. Meyers, *Principles of Corporate Finance*, 5th edn, McGraw-Hill, 1996.

23. "Lenovo Completes Acquisition of IBM's Personal Computing Division," *Press Release*, www.ibm.com, May 1, 2005.

24. "Interbrand's 15th Annual Best Global Brands Report," *Interbrand*, October 9, 2014.

25. Nirmalya Kumar, *Marketing as Strategy*, Harvard Business School Press, 2004, p. 5.

26. David Aaker, "Aaker on Branding – 20 Principles That Drive Success," Morgan James Publishing, 2014.

27. "The Business Life, Perfected," *Fortune Magazine*, (19), October 2003.

28. Perhaps a better source: "ILA Alumni," *The Performance Theatre*, 2014.

29. Fast Retailing Co Ltd, Bloomberg, December 17, 2014.

30. Fast Retailing, *Forbes*, May 2014.

31. "Fast Retailing Emerges as Top Asian Contender in Global Apparel," *Wall Street Journal*, April 6, 2014.

32. UNIQLO Business Strategy, Fast Retailing Website, July 11, 2014.

33. Results Summary, Fast Retailing Website, October 9, 2014.

34. Ibid.

35. "Fastest Gun in the East," *Barron's Asia*, January 25, 2014.

36. "Uniqlo's Success Outside Japan Prompts Owner to Predict Recovery," *Bloomberg*, October 10, 2014.
37. Ibid.
38. "The Best Performing CEOs in the World," *Harvard Business Review*, November 2014.
39. UNIQLO Business, Fast Retailing Website, February 12, 2014.
40. "Uniqlo's Brilliant Strategy Is To Totally Ignore Fashion," *Business Insider*, October 11, 2012.
41. Made For All, Uniqlo website, 2014.
42. "6 Reasons Why Uniqlo Is Winning," Prophet Consultancy Website, October 21, 2014.
43. "Uniqlo's Brand Differentiation Dilemma," *Labbrand*, April 25, 2014.
44. "How Uniqlo Plans to Become America's Top Retailer," *Racked*, April 8, 2014.
45. Ibid.
46. "Inside Uniqlo, The Japanese Company With Designs On Dressing The World," *Huffington Post*, January 22, 2014.
47. "Uniquely Positioned," *The Economist*, June 24, 2010.
48. Kumar, *Marketing as Strategy*, 2004.
49. "A Credibility Gap for Marketers," *McKinsey Quarterly*, (2), 2005.
50. Kumar, *Marketing as Strategy,* 2004.
51. "Use a Brand Council to Help Steer Strategy," *Harvard Business Review*, July 24, 2014.
52. Raj Srivastava and David J. Reibstein, "Metrics for Linking Marketing to Financial Performance," Working Paper, October 19, 2004.
53. "CEO Succession in the S&P 500: Statistics and Case Studies," *Harvard Law School*, April 25, 2014.
54. Ian Davis, "How to Escape the Short-term Trap," *McKinsey Quarterly*, web exclusive, April 2005.
55. Gail J. McGovern, David Court, John Quelch, and Blair Crawford, "Bringing Customers into the Boardroom," *Harvard Business Review*, November 2004.
56. Janamitra Devan, Anna Kristina Millan, and Pranav Shirke, "Balancing Short- and Long-term Performance," *McKinsey Quarterly*, (1), 2005.
57. "McKinsey Focusing Capital on the Long Term," *McKinsey & Co*, 2014.
58. "Focusing Capital on the Long Term," *McKinsey & Co*, December 2013.

3 Transforming How We Understand Asian Cultures and Consumers

1. "Understanding ASEAN: Seven Things You Need to Know," *McKinsey,* May 2014.
2. Jocelyn Probert and Hellmut Schütte, *De Beers: Diamonds are for Asia*, INSEAD Euro-Asia Centre, Case 599-011-1, 1999, p. 12.
3. "Luxury Brands Battle to Stay in Fashion in South Korea," *Financial Times*, June 22, 2014.

4. "50 McDonald's Menu Items Only in Japan," *tsunagu Japan*, July 7, 2014.

5. McDelivery, McDonald's Korea, 2014.

6. Interview with founder Kasper Leschly, November 2014.

7. Developed from company website and from an internal paper, Courtesy of Shangri-La Hotels & Resorts.

8. Shangri-La Employee Survey 2011.

9. Jim Aitchison, *How Asia Advertises: The Most Successful Campaigns in Asia-Pacific and the Marketing Strategies Behind Them*, John Wiley & Sons Asia, 2002.

10. "Shanghai Tang Mark Two Gets Ready to Retail," *New York Times*, September 29, 2013.

11. "Woman Sues SK-II over Skin Damage," *The Straits Times*, March 9, 2005.

12. Homepage, SK-II, 2014.

13. "AEC Presents Unprecedented Opportunity for SE Asia Brands," *Digital Market Asia*, December 3, 2013.

14. See Arjun Appadurai, *Modernity at Large: Cultural Dimensions of Modernity*. London and Minneapolis: University of Minnesota Press, 1996.

15. "Saris and Bhangra Rhythms: Ads in Asia Go Bollywood," *Asian Wall Street Journal*, December 17–19, 2004, pp. A5–A7.

16. "Groundbreaking Study by Institute on Asian Consumer Insight at NTU Reveals Asian Consumers' Psychological Make-up," *NTU Institute of Asian Consumer Insight*, August 22, 2013.

17. "Korean Wave to be Promoted in New Regions," *Korea Times*, March 17, 2005.

18. "Regional Strategy Holds Key to Effective Hallyu Promotion," *Korea Times*, May 1, 2012.

19. Youna Kim, *The Korean Wave: Korean Media Go Global*, Routledge, November 12, 2013.

20. Park Min-young, "Government to Expand Korean Wave and Overseas Cultural Exchanges," *The Korean Herald*, March 13, 2012.

21. Susie Mesure, "Move Over, Psy! Here Comes G-Dragon Style," *The Independent*, August 17, 2014.

22. Euny Hong, *The Birth of Korean Cool*, Simon & Schuster, 2014.

23. "Fashion's New Favorites: Korean Celebrities," *Women's Wear Daily*, September 10, 2014.

24. *LEX, Financial Times*, November 22, 2014.

25. "Hallyu Boosts Korea's GDP by 0.2 per cent," www.korea.net, May 4, 2005.

26. LEX, *Financial Times*, November 22, 2014.

27. "Hallyu Fuels Foreign Investment in Korea," *Korea Times*, August 31, 2014.

28. Ibid.

29. Kim Sung-jin, "Hallyu Boosts Korea's GDP by 0.2 per cent," *Korea Times*, May 3, 2005.

30. Yu Byungchae, *Korea's Tourism Branding & Communication Strategy*, Ministry of Culture, Sports and Tourism, June 3, 2013.

31. See W. Mazzarella, *Shoveling Smoke: Advertising and Globalization in Contemporary India*. Durham, NC: Duke University Press, 2003.

32. Seah Park, "Coming to a Theatre Near You?; South Korean Movie Exports Mark Shift Away from Manufacturing," *Wall Street Journal* (Eastern edn). October 3, 2003, p. A.10.

33. "Learn from South Korea: Its $9.16 Billion Gaming Market is Just $600M Less than China's and Double Japan's," *Bamboo Innovator*, October 30, 2013.

34. "L'Oréal Finds the Price-quality Sweet Spot," *Nikkei Asian Review*, November 6, 2014.

35. Anthony Giddens, *The Consequences of Modernity*. Stanford, CA: Stanford University Press, 1991, p. 54.

36. Murray Weidenbaum, *Greater China: The Next Economic Superpower?*, St. Louis: Washington University Center for the Study of American Business, 1993, pp. 2–3.

37. Wang Gungwu, *China And The Chinese* (2004); "The Impact of Japanese Popular Culture on the Singaporean Youth," *Keio Communication Review*, (26), 17–36; "The Consequences of Modernity Overseas," *Singapore Times*, 1993.

38. "Global Islamic Economy Growing Faster than Ever: Expert," *Asharq Al-Awsat*, September 10, 2014.

39. V.B. Srivastava, K.V. Singh, and N. Sharma, "Roadmap of Islamic Banking in India," 2014.

40. Homepage, www.mecca-cola.com, 2014.

41. LG Press Release, September 15, 2003.

42. United Nations Population Division, *The World at Six Billion*, 1999.

43. Living Alone: One-person Households in Asia, Conferences and Workshops, National University of Singapore, December 5–6, 2013.

44. "Driving Growth: The Female Economy in China and India," *BCG Perspectives*, October 25, 2012.

45. "China's Educated Women Power e-tailing," *warc.com*, February 5, 2014.

46. "Asia's New Key Segment: Powerful, Professional Women," *Harvard Business Review*, April 10, 2013.

47. "Women in Asia's Emerging Markets Take Reins on Household Finances: MasterCard Survey," *MasterCard*, March 27, 2013.

48. "Brands Note Changing Role of Asian Men," *warc.com*, November 20, 2013.

49. "JWT Asia Pacific Releases Report on the State of Asian Men in Singapore, Malaysia and China," *Campaign Brief Asia*, November 19, 2013.

50. "Understanding ASEAN: Seven Things you Need to Know," *McKinsey*, May 2014.

51. "The Accelerator Mindset," *BCG Perspectives*, September 4, 2012.

52. John Seely and John Hagel III, "Innovation Blowback: Disruptive Management Practices from Asia," *McKinsey Quarterly*, (1), 2005.

53. "Indian Rural Market," *India Brand Equity Foundation*, November 2014.

54. "Building Brands in Emerging Markets," *McKinsey*, September 2012.

55. "China Usurps USA as World's Largest Beer Market," *Euromonitor*, November 12, 2002.
56. "SABMiller is Hit by Weak Demand in China and Australia," *Wall Street Journal*, October 14, 2014.
57. "SABMiller Buys Seven Breweries Across China in £550m Deal," *The Telegraph*, February 5, 2013.
58. "Karsanbhai Patel – A Clean Sweep," *India Profile*, June 2002.
55. "Where is Nirma's Karsanbhai Patel?," *Forbes India*, October 19, 2010.
59. Niraj Dawar and Tony Frost, "Competing with Giants: Survival Strategies for Emerging Market Companies," *Harvard Business Review*, March–April 1999, 119–129.
60. "Asian Paints Reaps its Head Start," *Business Standard*, August 21, 2013.
61. *Local Knowledge: Further Essays in Interpretive Anthropology*. New York: Basic Books, 1983, p. 59.
62. "We Aren't The World," *Pacific Standard*, February 25, 2013.
63. Russell W. Belk, "Third world consumer culture," in E. Kumçu and A. Fuat Firat (eds), *Research in Marketing*, supplement 4, Greenwich, CT: JAI Press, 1988.
64. Hofstede, G. *Culture's Consequences: International Differences in Work-related Values*, Beverly Hills: Sage, 1980.
65. Yasusuke Murakami, "*Ie* society as a pattern of civilization: An introduction by Kozo Yamamura," *Journal of Japanese Studies*, 10(2), 1984, pp. 281–363.
66. Dae Ryun Chang, "The We-Me Culture: Marketing to Korean Consumers," *Cross Cultural Buyer Behaviour, Advances in International Marketing*, (18), 2007, pp. 141–157.
67. Michael Ashekenazi and John Clammer (eds), *Consumption and Material Culture in Contemporary Japan*, New York: Columbia University Press, 1999.
68. Homepage, www.lvmh.com, 2014.
69. "2013: Another Significant Year Of Revenues for LVMH, Hermes & Kering," *Luxury Society*, March 20, 2014.
70. Robert B. Cialdini, *Influence: Science and Practice*, Allyn & Bacon, 4th edn, 2001.
71. "Hello Kitty – Taiwan's Billion Dollar Fad," *Susan Fang*, accessed December 30, 2014.
72. Jessica Tan, "I'll Have that Snoopy Please," *The Straits Times*, October 4, 1999, p. 5.
73. Radha Chadha, *Luxury Brands in Asia*, Columbia University Press.
74. D. Tse, "Understanding Chinese People as Consumers: Past Findings and Future Propositions," in M.H. Bond (ed.), *The Handbook of Chinese Psychology*, Hong Kong: Oxford University Press, 1996. See also K. Leung, "The role of beliefs in Chinese culture," ibid., p. 249.
75. V. Worm, *Vikings and Mandarins*, Copenhagen: Munksgaard, 1997.
76. "The Party's Not Over for Luxury Brands in China," *Campaign Asia*, May 4, 2014.
77. "Survey Reveals Chinese Consumers Demonstrate Loyalty for Personalized Service, Not Points," *Campaign Asia*, March 20, 2013.

78. "Main Players Adapt to Slowing Sales," *China Daily*, April 12, 2013.
79. "6 China Luxury Trends to Watch in the Year of The Horse," *Advertising Age*, January 28, 2014.

4 Asian Country Branding

1. International tourists (overnight visitors) travelling January–August 2014 reached 781 million, 36 million more than same period in 2013. See http://www.unwto.org/ for latest figures.
2. "Made in: The Value of Country of Origin for Future Brands," *Futurebrand*, 2014.
3. "Made in: The New Meaning of 'Made in China'," *Futurebrand*, 2014.
4. See A. Tversky and Kahneman, "Judgment under Certainty: Heuristics and Biases," *Science*, (211), 1974, pp. 1124–1130; A. Tversky and Kahneman, "Availability: A Heuristic for Judging Frequency and Probability," *Cognitive Psychology*, (5), 1973, pp. 207–232.
5. C. Min Han, "Country Image: Halo or Summary Construct?" *Journal of Marketing Research*, (26), 1989, pp. 222–229.
6. Doug Holt, John Quelch, and E. Taylor, "How Global Brands Compete," *Harvard Business Review*, 82(9), 2004, pp. 68–75.
7. Zeynep Gurhan-Canli and Durairaj Maheswaran, "Cultural Variations in Country of Origin Effects," *Journal of Marketing Research*, 37(3), 2000, pp. 309–317.
8. Jill G. Klein, Richard Ettenson, and Marlene D. Morris, "The Animosity Model of Foreign Product Purchase: An Empirical Test in the People's Republic of China," *Journal of Marketing*, 62(1), 1998, pp. 89–100.
9. Iwabuchi Koichi, *Recentering Globalization*, Durham, NC: Duke University Press, 2004.
10. "Toyota Recalls 'offensive' Sports Vehicle Ads in China," *Straits Times*, December 5, 2003.
11. "Rankings across Industry Sectors," *Futurebrand*, 2014.
12. Ibid.
13. "Malaysia Country Report," *UNWTO*, April 12–14, 2013.
14. "Investing in Malaysia: Boost for Tourism," *Asia Inc.*, August 1, 2004.
15. "Malaysia Country Report," *UNWTO*, April 12–14, 2013.
16. "Malaysia is 10th Most Visited Country," *The Star Online*, August 6, 2013.
17. "New 'Amazing Thailand' Campaign Launched for 2014," *Tourism India*, January 2014.
18. Advertorial, *Thailand in Forbes*, December 2014.
19. "Political Advertising: The India Shining Campaign," A. Suman, ICFAI Center for Management Research, 2004.

20. Harish Bijoor, "Branding the Govt of India", The Hindu Business Line, February 19, 2004.
21. Edward Luce, "Rural India Humbles Vajpayee," *Financial Times (UK)*, May 14, 2004.
22. Suhel Seth, "Taking the Shine off India," www.india-seminar.com, accessed February 17, 2005.
23. Vir Sanghvi, "The Big Idea: Hubris at the Hustings," http://www.freeindiamedia. com, accessed February 18, 2005.
24. *Japan Times*, Editorial, accessed February 18, 2005.
25. "Ministry Invites Bids for Makeover of Incredible India Website," *Business Standard*, October 4, 2014.
26. "Creating a New Japan," *Cool Japan Advisory Council*, May 12, 2011.
27. "Japan: How Cool is That?," *Mission Network News*, December 1, 2014.
28. "Creating a New Japan," *Cool Japan Advisory Council*, May 12, 2011.
29. "Cool Japan Struts the Runways at Fashion Week in Tokyo," *Reuters*, October 22, 2013.
30. "Backgrounders," *Council on Foreign Relations*, 2014.
31. "Investment Schemes," *Cool Japan Fund*, 2014.
32. "News," *Cool Japan Fund,* 2014.
33. "Japan Spends Millions in Order to be Cool," *Time*, July 1, 2013.
34. "Chuck Chiang: Tokyo Tries to Counter South Korean Pop Culture with 'Cool Japan' Campaign," *Vancouver Sun*, June 29, 2014.
35. "Japanamerica: Why 'Cool Japan' is Over," *3:AM Magazine*, May 17, 2010.
36. "Japan: How Cool is That?," *Mission Network News*, December 1, 2014.
37. "'Cool Japan' Initiative to Use $1 Billion in Public Funds to Push Japanese Cultural Exports," *Japan Daily Express*, November 25, 2013.
38. "'Uncool' Cool Japan Video Goes Viral," *Wall Street Journal, Japan Realtime*, August 2, 2013.
39. "Takashi Murakami Blasts Japan's 'Cool Japan' via Twitter," *Complex*, January 7, 2012.
40. "Is Japan Losing its Cool?" *Christian Science Monitor*, December 8, 2012.
41. All figures on GMAT applications from www.gmac.com.
42. "Indians Sending Fewer GMAT Scores To U.S.," *Poets & Quants*, September 25, 2012.
43. D. Ging and Y. Feng (eds), *Chinese: Golden Sayings of Chinese Thinkers over 5,000 Years*. Beijing: Sinolingua, 1994, p. 55.
44. Homepage, INSEAD, 2015.
45. Jan-Benedict E. Steenkamp, Rajeev Batra, V. Ramaswamy, and Dana Alden, "How Perceived Brand Globalness Creates Brand Value," *Journal of International Business Studies*, 34(1), 2003, pp. 53–65.
46. "India's Global Ambitions," *Far Eastern Economic Review*, November 6, 2003.
47. "Global Medical Tourism Market Growth Driven by Asia Says a New Research Report," *PR Newswire*, July 4, 2014.

48. Department of Export Promotion, Ministry of Commerce, The Thailand Authority of Thailand.
49. "Get Well Away," *The Economist*, September 10, 2004.
50. "Thailand Medical Tourism & Forecast," *Market Reports Online*, 2015.
51. "Medical Tourism industry to touch Rs 10,800 cr by 2015: Assocham," *The Economic Times*, August 5, 2011.
52. "Cataract Surgery Costs, Complications Low at Aravind," *Modern Medicine Network, Ophthalmology Times*, May 6, 2014;
53. Country Brand Index 2014–2015, *FutureBrand*, Report published November 11, 2014.
54. "Heart Surgery in India for $1,583 Costs $106,385 in U.S.," Bloomberg, July 29, 2013.

5   Celebrity Branding in Asia

1. Hershey Friedman and Linda Friedman (1979), "Endorser Effectiveness by Product Type," *Journal of Advertising Research*, 19, October 5, 63–71.
2. LEX, *Financial Times*, November 22, 2014.
3. "K-Pop Attracts Louis Vuitton Investment," *Asian Wall Street Journal*, August 21, 2014.
4. Homepage, http://news.naver.com.
5. "Bachchan Brand Ambassador News," *NDTV*, 2015.
6. Joseph M. Kamen, Abdul C. Azhari, Judith R. Kragh (1975), "What a Spokesman Does for a Sponsor," *Journal of Advertising Research*, 15, 17–24.
7. Friedman and Friedman (1979), "Endorser Effectiveness by Product Type."
8. L. R. Kahle and P. M. Homer (1985), "Physical Attractiveness of Celebrity Endorser: A Social Adaptation Perspective," *Journal of Consumer Research*, 11, March, 954–961.
9. Paul Surgi Speck, David W. Schumann and Craig Thompson (1988), "Celebrity Endorsements – Scripts, Schema and Roles: Theoretical Framework and Preliminary Tests," *Advances in Consumer Research*, 15, 69–76.
10. "Star Marketing," *The Korea Economic Daily*, October 27, 2003.
11. "Alicia Keys Ends One-Year BlackBerry Deal: Inside The Troubled Partnership," *billboardbiz*, January 2, 2014.
12. "The World's Highest-Paid Soccer Players," *Forbes*, April 18, 2012.
13. Zafer B. Erdogan (1999), "Celebrity Endorsement: A Literature Review," *Journal of Marketing Management*, 15, 291–314.
14. Michael Alan Hamlin (2004), "Celebrity Branding," *Team Asia*, September 20, 2004.
15. "South Korean Actor Bae Yong Joon Arrives to Tumultuous Welcome," *Japan Today*, April 17, 2005.
16. "South Korean Star Sparks Tourist Boom," *CNN.com*, March 13, 2005.

17. "Adjusting McLuhan's Reception of Hot and Cool Media," *The Japan Times*, September 12, 2004.

18. "Address by Prime Minister Junichiro Koizumi At Dinner for International Conference on 'The Future of Asia'," Ministry of Foreign Affairs of Japan, June 3, 2014.

19. "Bae Yong-joon Wins Grand Prize at Japan's Hallyu Awards," *Yonhap News Agency*, October 21, 2013.

20. B. Zafer Erdogan (1999), "Celebrity Endorsement."

21. "Cadbury India Fined for Worms in Chocolate," *DNA India*, December 20, 2006.

22. "How much? Burberry Tightlipped on Romeo Beckham's Festive Fee," *The Guardian*, November 12, 2014.

23. "Cosmetics and Fashion Eye New Sales Front," *Financial Times*, November 8, 2014.

24. Grant McCracken (1989), "Who is the Celebrity Endorser? Cultural Foundations of the Endorsement Process," *Journal of Consumer Research*, 16, 310–321.

25. "The World's Most Valuable Sports Brands," *Forbes Asia*, November 2014.

26. "Beijing Yanjing Pays 150 million Yuan to Acquire Jinchuan," *China Daily*, January 7, 2011.

27. Peter Kafka, "Celebrity by the Share," *Forbes*, March 21, 2000.

28. Carolyn Tripp, Thomas D. Jensen, and Les Carlson (1994), "The Effect of Multiple Product Endorsements by Celebrities on Consumers' Attitudes and Intentions," *Journal of Consumer Research*, 30, 535–547.

29. "Wow! Yao!," *Bloomberg Businessweek*, October 24, 2004.

30. Hesseldahl, Arik, "Garmin Signs NBA's Yao as Pitchman," *Forbes*, April 13, 2004.

31. "Wow! Yao!," *Bloomberg Businessweek*, October 25, 2004.

32. Luo, Michael, "Yao Ming Boosts Ethnic Pride," *Times Union*, Albany, New York, February 9, 2003.

33. "Wow! Yao!," *Bloomberg Businessweek*, October 24, 2004.

34. "Bollywood Sets Sights on Wider Market," *BBC*, June 24, 2011

6 Asian Brand Strategy

1. "Luxury Brands: The Business of Selling Dreams," *European Business Review*, October 26, 2007.

2. Jennifer L. Aaker, "Dimensions of Brand Personality," *Journal of Marketing Research*, (34), 1997, pp. 347–356.

3. *McKinsey Quarterly*, (2), 2005, ibid.

4. "Fast Retailing Emerges as Top Asian Contender in Global Apparel," *Asian Wall Street Journal*, April 6, 2014.

5. *McKinsey Quarterly*, (2), 2005, ibid.

6. Homepage, http://www.lcapitalasia.com.

7. "LVMH Explores the Layers Below Luxury," *Financial Times*, September 10, 2014.
8. "K-Pop Stars Launch New Brands to Cash In on Chinese Consumers," *Wall Street Journal*, September 12, 2014.
9. "Factory," honda2wheelersindia.com, 2014.
10. "Jetstar Group," jetstar.com, 2013.
11. "P&G to Acquire Gillette for $57bn," *BBC*, January 28, 2005.
12. "Premji Builds Global FMGC Play," *Times of India*, January 19, 2013.
13. *Forbes Asia*, September 2014.
14. "The Philippines Richest 2012," *Forbes*, June 20, 2012.
15. "Jollibee Seeks to Double Earnings in 5 Years," *Asian Meat Magazine*, September–October 2014.
16. "The Philippines Richest 2012," *Forbes*, June 20, 2012.
17. "Philippines' Fast Food Icon Jollibee Sets Sights on Indonesia," *Wall Street Journal*, August 8, 2014.
18. Ibid.
19. Denise Lee Yohn, *What Great Brands Do – The Seven Brand-Building Principles that Separate the Best from the Rest*, Jossey-Bass, 2014.
20. "The Premier League, Sponsored by … Asia?" *Connected Asia*, February 15, 2014.
21. "Everton Paid Nil in Li Tie's Transfer?" *China Daily*, August 14, 2003.
22. "Chinese Phone Maker's Fancy Footwork," *BBC News*, October 27, 2003.
23. "Building Brands in Emerging Markets," *McKinsey*, September 2012.
24. David A. Aaker, *Building Strong Brands*, Free Press, 1996.
25. Alastair Gordon, *How Consumers Identify Good Brands*, AC Nielsen Paper.
26. Kevin Lane Keller, *Strategic Brand Management*, 2nd edn, Prentice Hall, 2003.
27. Douglas Holt, *How Brands Become Icons*, Harvard Business Press, 2004.
28. "The Consumer Decision Journey," *McKinsey Quarterly*, June 2009.
29. Jan Lindemann, "The Financial Value of Brands," *Brands and Branding*, The Economist/Bloomberg Press, 2004.
30. James A. Abate, L. Grant and G. Bennett Stewart III, "The EVA Style of Investing," *Journal of Portfolio Management*, Summer 2004.
31. Rajendra K. Srivastava, Tasadduq A. Shervani and Liam Fahey, "Market-based Assets and Shareholder Value: A Framework for Analysis," *Journal of Marketing*, (62), January 1998.

7 Successful Asian Brand Cases

1. Brand case developed through interviews with Singapore Airlines.
2. For further reference to iconic brands, see Douglas Holt, *How Brands Become Icons*, Harvard Business School Press, 2004.
3. AsiaWeek, "Paradise Regained," June 15, 2001.
4. Ralph Lauren Magazine, http://global.ralphlauren.com/en-us/rlmagazine/editorial/hol12/Pages/AmanResorts.aspx????ab=en_us_Archive_StoryNav_NextStory.

5. Author interview with Anil Thadani, co-founder of Aman.
6. Author interview with Anil Thadani, co-founder of Aman.
7. Author interview with Anil Thadani, co-founder of Aman.
8. "Living Legend," *Bespoke*, June 2007.
9. "Trouble in Paradise," *Fortune Magazine*, October 2014.
10. Brand case developed partly through interviews with Shiseido.
11. Core Values, Shiseido, 2014.
12. "How South Korea Drives Asia's Love Affair with Cosmetics," *CNN*, November 6, 2014.
13. "Cosmetics and Fashion Eye New Sales Front," *Financial Times*, November 9, 2014.
14. "Shiseido Expands Indonesia Operations with Joint Venture," *Business Wire*, April 10, 2014.
15. Andrew McDougall, "Shiseido Targets India's Masstige as it Looks to Expand," cosmeticsdesign-asia.com, 25 July, 2013.
16. "Shiseido Buys Manufacturer of Cosmetics," *New York Times*, January 14, 2010.
17. "Shiseido Hoping 'Stealth' Strategy in China More than Cosmetic," *Nikkei Asian Review*, February 13, 2014.
18. "Shiseido Breaks Ranks in Japan, Featuring Japanese Women in Ads," *New York Times*, August 28, 2007.
19. "Shiseido Announces Gold Medallist Hannah Teter as New U.S. Spokesperson," *PR Newswire*, September 30, 2013.
20. "Activities of the Advertising and Design Department," *Shiseido Group*, 2014.
21. "Foreign CEOs Face Challenges in Japan," *Financial Times*, April 29, 2012.
22. "Ranking," *Interbrand*, 2014.
23. "Samsung's Big Q4 2012: $52.4 Billion In Revenue Is Nice, But Operating Profit Surged 89% Year-Over-Year To $8.27 Billion," *Tech Crunch*, January 24, 2013.
24. "Samsung's Q4 2012 Financial Earnings: We Made Lots of Money," *Android Central*, January 24, 2013.
25. "History," *Samsung*, 2014.
26. "Samsung Launches Industry's First Tizen Smartphone – the Samsung Z," *Samsung*, 2014.
27. "Samsung Ranks Second in R&D Spending for 2013," *GSM Arena*, October 24, 2013.
28. "Samsung Looks to the Future with $4.5 Billion Investment in Five New R&D Centres," *Digital Trends*, July 4, 2013.
29. Ibid.
30. "Patenting by Organisations," United States Patent and Trademark Office, 1995–2013.
31. Assif Shameen, *Asia Inc*, June 1, 2004, op. cit.
32. Tobi Elkin and Beth Snyder, "Samsung's DigitAll Tag Takes a Democratic Turn," *Advertising Age*, 70(10), 77, May 2005.
33. Ibid.

34. "Samsung Debuts the GALAXY Note 3 and the GALAXY Gear With 'Design Your Life' Global Campaign," *Samsung*, September 11, 2013.
35. "Samsung Launches Biggest U.S. Campaign to Date for Galaxy S III," *Advertising Age*, June 20, 2012.
36. "CES 2014: What Does the Show Mean to Las Vegas?," *BBC*, January 10, 2014.
37. "The 2004 Olympic Torch Relay: The First Global Road Show, Samsung Gets Up Close and Personal," *M2Presswire*, August 5, 2004.
38. "Samsung Seals Wide-ranging NBA Contract," *SportsPro Media*, October 28, 2013.
39. "Samsung to Title Sponsor World Surfing Tour," *SportsPro Media*, February 21, 2014.
40. "Samsung Becomes RFUS Official Consumer Electronics Smartphone Partner," *Samsung*, October 16, 2014.
41. "Samsung Opts to Leave Time Warner Center," *The Real Deal*, December 6, 2011.
42. "1,400 'Samsung Experience' Shops in Best Buy Locations Spell More Bad News for HTC," *The Verge*, April 4, 2013.
43. "Samsung Takes on Apple with the Launch of 60 High-street Stores across the UK and Europe," *The Daily Mail*, January 29, 2014.
44. "Samsung signs X Factor Product Placement Deal," *campaign.live.co.uk*, September 27, 2012.
45. "Why Sony's Smartphone Woes Should Worry Samsung," *Bloomberg Businessweek*, September 18, 2014.
46. "IPhone 6 Recharges Apple's Growth," *Wall Street Journal*, 21 October, 2014.
47. "Samsung Battles on Two Fronts as Apple Readies iPhone 6," *Reuters*, 16 July, 2014.
48. "Why Sony's Smartphone Woes Should Worry Samsung," *Bloomberg Businessweek*, September 18, 2014.
49. "Samsung Overtakes Nokia as the World's Biggest Phone Manufacturer," *Gizmodo*, April 27, 2012.
50. "Samsung Electronics Heads for Annual Profit Fall After Weak Third-quarter Guidance," *Reuters*, October 7, 2014.
51. "S. Korea's LG Group Announces Record Investment Plan for 2013," *Reuters UK*, January 6, 2013.
52. David Aaker, *Building Strong Brands*, The Free Press, 1996.

8 Aspiring Asian Brand Cases

1. "South Korea Cosmetics Firms Look Good in Unattractive Market," *Wall Street Journal*, November 9, 2014
2. "Amore Pacific Aims to Become Top Brand," *Korea Times*, October 26, 2014
3. "Singers and Actresses Sprinkle Stardust on Korean Cosmetics," *Financial Times*, November 25, 2013

4. "Amore Pacific Aims to Become Top Brand," *Korea Times*, October 26, 2014
5. "Korean Beauty Firm Rides K-Pop Wave," *Asian Wall Street Journal*, 28 September 2014
6. "AmorePacific Sales Soar as Tourists Race to Jeju for Cosmetics," *Forbes Asia*, November 3, 2014
7. "MakeUp Your Life," *AmorePacific.com*, 2014
8. "Women's Perceptions of Beauty Products in 14 Asian Cities," *Global HABIT*, November 19, 2012
9. "Korean Cosmetics Become Global Standard," *Korea Times*, January 12, 2014
10. "Dramas, R&D Fuel K-Cosmetics," *Korea Times*, 4 March, 2014
11. "Asian Cosmetic Surgery Latest Statistics Explained – The Craze and Boom," *Advance Beauty Cosmetic Surgery*, 2014
12. "The Accenture Luxury Shopping Survey: Insights for the Holidays and Beyond," *Chain Store Age*, January 7, 2013
13. "Amore Pacific Aims to Become top Brand," *Korea Times*, October 26, 2014
14. "AmorePacific Sustainability Report, 2012
15. "AmorePacific on the Scent in China," *Financial Times*, March 25, 2011
16. LEX, *Financial Times*, November 22, 2014
17. LEX, *Financial Times*, November 22, 2014
18. "Amore Pacific Aims to Become top Brand," *Korea Times*, October 26, 2014
19. "Osiao: Estée Lauder's First Chinese Beauty Brand," *Time Inc*, September 26, 2012
20. "Singers and Actresses Sprinkle Stardust on Korean Cosmetics," *Financial Times*, November 25, 2013
21. "Chinese Counterfeit Cosmetics Raise Eyebrows," *Korea Times*, 3 June, 2014
22. "In Asia, Men Take a Shine to Skin Care Products," *Asian Wall Street Journal*, May 30, 2014
23. Ibid.
24. Substantial part of the case is based on the author's interview with the company management
25. Michael Richardson, "Disappearance of Jim Thompson: The Silk Magnate Mystery/30 year Puzzle," *International Herald Tribune*, March 26, 1997
26. Ibid.
27. "Mystery of Jim Thompson's Disappearance," *New Sunday Times*, February 1, 2004
28. "Inspired by Asian Cultures," *The Nation* (Thailand), December 23, 2002
29. Ibid.
30. "Alibaba's Banks Boost IPO Size to Record of $25 Billion," *Bloomberg*, September 22, 2014
31. "Alibaba's IPO Filing: Everything You Need To Know," *Wall Street Journal*, May 6, 2014
32. "The Alibaba Phenomenon," *The Economist*, May 23, 2013
33. "Alibaba Surges 38 percent on Massive Demand in Market Debut," *Reuters*, September 19, 2014

34. "Where Did Alibaba, the Brand Name, Come From?" *Wordlab*, October 15, 2007
35. "The World's Greatest Bazaar," *The Economist*, March 23, 2013
36. "Alibaba's Next Move: Grow Abroad, or Go Deeper into China?" Knowledge@ Wharton, Wharton University of Pennsylvania, October 1, 2014
37. Ibid.
38. "History and Milestones," *Alibaba Group*, 2014
39. "The World's Greatest Bazaar," *The Economist*, March 23, 2013
40. "Our Business," *Alibaba Group*, 2014
41. "Alibaba Breaks a Record for Deals on Single's Day," *Asian Wall Street Journal*, November 12, 2014
42. How Jack Ma Went From Being a Poor School Teacher to Turning Alibaba into a $160 Billion Behemoth," *Business Insider*, September 14, 2014
43. "Crocodile in the Yangtze," *Youtube.com*, August 20, 2012
44. "What the Core Values of Alibaba Can Teach Us," *Forbes*, September 30, 2014
45. "The True Cost of China's Fakes," *The New York Times*, June 9, 2014
46. "The Top 500 Sites on the Web," *Alexa.com*, Accessed December 21, 2014, refreshed daily
47. "Corporate Information," *Huawei*, 2014
48. McKinsey, 2009
49. "Corporate Information," *Huawei*, 2014
50. "Carriers name Cisco the Top Router and Switch Vendor in Infonetics Survey," *Infonetics Research*, 2014
51. "Washington Tests Beijing's Patience With Latest Anti China Business Move," *Forbes*, October 8, 2012
52. "Governance at Huawei," *Huawei*, 2014
53. "Gartner Says Smartphone Sales Grew 46.5 Per cent in Second Quarter of 2013 and Exceeded Feature Phone Sales for First Time," *Gartner*, August 14, 2013
54. "The Strategy and Aim of Huawei Global Social Activities," *Huawei.com*, 2014
55. "The 50 Most Innovative Companies," *rankingthebrands.com*, 2014
56. "US and China Drive International Patent Filing Growth in Record-Setting Year," *WIPO*, March 13, 2014
57. "Huawei's CEO: The Innovation Journey To 5G And Beyond," *Forbes*, August 26, 2013
58. Ibid.
59. Ibid.
60. "A Tiny Island In The Irish Sea Might Be Home To The World's First 5G Network," *Business Insider*, November 11,, 2014
61. "94 Huawei," *Interbrand*, 2014
62. "Huawei's 'Make it Possible' Campaign Aims to Beat Samsung and Apple," *brandingmagazine.com*, February 27, 2013
63. "Android Poised to Dominate the Developing World," *Forbes*, August 16, 2011
64. "Huawei Boss says US Ban 'not very important'," *BBC*, October 15, 2014

65. "Huawei is First Chinese Brand to Break into Global top 100," *The Telegraph*, October 9, 2014
66. "The Deal That Could Have Saved Nortel," *Forbes*, January 14, 2009
67. "Washington Tests Beijing's Patience With Latest Anti-China Business Move," *Forbes*, October 8, 2012
68. "Huawei Plans First U.S. Ad Campaign, 500 New U.S. Hires This Year," *Forbes*, 12 May, 2011"
69. "Huawei-Motorola Rumours Look Logical," *Forbes*, April 13, 2012
70. "Huawei is Rotating its CEO Every Six Months to Stay Fresh," September 30, 2013

9   Ten Steps to Building an Asian Brand

1. "The Romantic Advantage," *The New York Times*, May 30, 2013.
2. IndiGo Getter, *Forbes Asia*, October 2014.
3. "Jet Airways, SpiceJet stare at June Quarter Loss," *livemint.com*, July 21, 2014.
4. "IndiGo Reports Sixth Straight Annual Profit," *livemint.com*, October 7, 2014.
5. "What Keeps IndiGo's Profit Flying High?," *Business Standard*, October 9, 2013.
6. IndiGo Getter, *Forbes Asia*, October 2014.
7. About Indigo, IndiGo.in, 2006.
8. IndiGo Experience, IndiGo.com, 2006.
9. IndiGo Fleet, IndiGo.com, 2006.
10. "The IndiGo Brand Story," *CNN Travel*, February 17, 2011.
11. Ibid.
12. Ibid.
13. IndiGo Getter, *Forbes Asia*, October 2014.
14. "5 Reasons why IndiGo is Market Leader Today," *Firstbiz*, August 21, 2012.
15. "Indian Airline IndiGo Agrees Record 250 Airbus Jet Order," *Reuters*, October 15, 2014.
16. "Bhatias top Bidder for GMR Hotel," *The Times of India*, January 24, 2014.
17. "IndiGo Picks Six Banks for IPO of up to $400 Million – Sources," *Reuters*, 16 July, 2014.
18. "The Funnel is Dead: Long live the Consumer Decision Journey," *McKinsey on Marketing and Sales*, February 2014.
19. "L'Oréal Finds the Price-Quality Sweet Spot," *Nikkei Asian Review*, November 6, 2014.
20. "Exploring the Inner Circle," *IBM*, 2013.
21. "Capitalising on Complexity," *IBM*, 2010.
22. Richard Tomlinson, "The 2004 Global 500 – L'Oréal's CEO on Managing Globally," *Fortune*, December 7, 2004.
23. "Top Selling Energy Drink Brands," *Caffeine Informer*, September 5, 2014.

24. "Company Profile," Red Bull, 2014.

25. "The Company Behind the Can," Red Bull, 2014.

26. "The Republic of Red Bull," *Men's Journal*, January 28, 2014.

27. "Q: When Is a Cliff Dive Good For Sales? A: When It's Sponsored by Red Bull," *Bloomberg Businessweek*, May 25, 2013.

28. "Coca-Cola's Brand Building Initiatives Could Shoulder Sluggish CSD Sales," *Forbes*, April 2, 2014.

29. "Cisco Visual Networking Index: Global Mobile Data Traffic Forecast Update, 2013–2018," *Cisco*, February 5, 2014.

30. "Facebook Earnings Beat Expectations as Ad Revenues Soar," *The Guardian*, July 23, 2014.

31. "Twitter Skyrockets After Reporting Big Q2 Revenue Of $312M, Profit Of $0.02 Per Share," *Tech Crunch*, July 29, 2014.

32. "Learning and Development," *HSBC*, 2014.

33. Homepage, Shangri-La Hotels and Resorts, 2014.

34. *Forbes Asia*, September 2014.

35. "Top Five Focus Areas for Improving Sales Effectiveness Initiatives," *Accenture*, 2013.

36. DDB Needham booklet.

37. "Gulliver Moves HSBC Away from 'World's Local Bank' Tag in Review," *The Independent*, May 12, 2011.

38. Author interview with the company management.

39. "Connecting Marketing Metrics to Financial Consequences," *Knowledge@ Wharton*, November 17, 2004.

40. Ibid.

41. Gail J. McGovern, David Court, John A. Quelch and Blair Crawford, "Bringing Customers into the Boardroom," Gail J. McGovern, David Court, John A. Quelch, and Blair Crawford, *Harvard Business Review*, November 2004.

42. "'Smart analytics' can Tap up to 20% of Lost ROI," *The Economist Group*, November 13, 2013.

43. "Corporate Governance Guidelines," *Nike*, 2014.

44. "CMOs in Asia Pacific have a Higher level of Preparedness than their Global Counterparts, Accenture study Finds," *Accenture*, May 13, 2013.

10 Asian Brands Toward 2020 – A New Confidence in the Boardroom

1. "Growth Journeys," *Accenture*, 2013.

2. "How Tight Is Smartphone Market? Xiaomi Joins Samsung, Apple in Top 3 for Only a Few Hours," *Bloomberg*, October 31, 2014.

3. Zhang Maiwen and Zhang Dan, "Leaders in Innovation," *Fortune Magazine*, May 19, 2014.

4. "Xiaomi Moves Into Third Place In Global Smartphone War," *Business Insider*, October 30, 2014.

5. "The Chinese Smartphone Company that Copies Apple is Looking at Raising New Funding at A $40 Billion Valuation," *Business Insider*, November 4, 2014.

6. "Cost of Living in China," *Numbeo*, January 2015.

7. "Research: Marketing to China," *Brand Strategy*, February 7, 2005,.

8. Tobias C. Hoschka and John Livingston, "Winning‹Asian Strategies," *McKinsey Quarterly* 2002 (1).

9. Ibid.

10. "Mukesh Ambani vs Anil Ambani," *Lawyers Club India*, September 11, 2010.

11. "Overcapacity Threatens China Growth," *Bloomberg Businessweek*, December 11, 2013.

12. "China's Power Brands," *Bloomberg Businessweek*, November 8, 2004,.

13. "Lenovo and IBM: East Meets West, Big-Time," *Bloomberg Businessweek*, May 9, 2005.

14. Kerry A. Dolan, "Taking it Haier," *Forbes Global*, May 13, 2002.

15. Evan Ramstad, "How Legend became Lenovo," *Far Eastern Economic Review*, April 8, 2004.

16. "Bow Down Before Your New Chinese Overlords: Lenovo Passes HP as World's Top PC Maker," *Tech in Asia*, July 11, 2013.

17. "Lenovo Swallows Motorola, Indigestion Coming?" *Forbes*, January 30, 2014.

18. "Lenovo Buying IBM's Low-End Servers Would Be The Biggest Ever Chinese IT Deal," *Business Insider*, January 21, 2014.

19. "Ashton Kutcher Straps On His Thinking Cap for New Lenovo Gig," *Brandchannel*, October 30, 2013.

20. "The World's Largest PC Maker Now Sells More Smartphones than PCs," *The Verge*, August 14, 2014.

21. "Lenovo Sets Global Push for Phones," *Asian Wall Street Journal*, November 7, 2014.

22. "Lenovo Aims to Build Global Tech Brand to Rival Samsung, Apple," *Brandchannel*, January 30, 2014.

23. C. K. Prahalad and Kenneth Lieberthal, "End of Corporate Imperialism," *Harvard Business Review*, August 2003.

24. "Reality Check at the Bottom of the Pyramid," *Harvard Business Review*, June 2012.

25. Douglas B. Holt, "How Brands Become Icons," *Harvard Business School Press*, 2004.

26. "Fiji Brand Gains on Evian as Bottled Water Hip to Sip – Closely Held U.S. Firm Proves the World's Simplest Drink Still can be Touted as Trendy," *Asian Wall Street Journal*, August 17, 2004.

27. Candice Choi, "Bottled Water Brand Uses Celebrity Exposure to Ring up Sales," *Daily News*, Los Angeles, Knight Ridder/*Tribune Business News*, September 1, 2004.

28. Susan Reimer, "Fiji the New Hotbed of Cool Water," *Baltimore Sun*, November 4, 2004.

29. "Island Water Floats on Luxury and Prestige (Fiji Natural Artesian Water)," September 1, 2000, *Beverage Industry*, 70, 91(9).

30. "Fiji Brand Gains on Evian as Bottled water Hip to Sip – Closely Held U.S. Firm Proves the World's Simplest Drink Still can be Touted as Trendy," *Asian Wall Street Journal*, August 17, 2004.

31. "Events," *Fiji Water*, 2014.

32. "About us," *Fiji Water*, 2014.

33. Susan Reimer, "Fiji the New Hotbed of Cool Water," *Baltimore Sun*, November 4, 2004.

34. "Strengthen Your Leadership Bench in China," *Frontier Strategy Group*, April 30, 2013.

35. "Why More CMOs Are Wanted as Board Directors," *Advertising Age*, May 20, 2014.

36. "Getting the CMO and CIO to Work as Partners," *McKinsey Quarterly*, August 2014.

37. "Huawei Ready to Outspend Ericsson in R&D Race to Woo Clients," *Bloomberg*, July 3, 2013.

38. "Top Tech Spenders," *Apps Run the World*, 2014.

39. "The Most Innovative Companies: An Interactive Guide," *BCG Perspectives*, October 28, 2014.

40. "Samsung Electronics – As Good as it Gets?," *The Economist*, January 15, 2005.

41. "China Can't Be a Global Innovation Leader Unless It Does These Three Things," *Harvard Business Review*, November 8, 2013.

42. "INTUIT FOUNDER: 'Success Makes Companies Stupid'," *Business Insider*, February 25, 2013.

43. "DATA POINTS: Asia Open to New Products," *Campaign Asia*, March 13, 2013.

44. "Here's How Much Business S&P 500 Companies Generate Outside Of The US," *Business Insider*, October 10, 2014.

45. "New Strategies for a Changing Global Landscape," *Martin Roll*, March 2014.

46. "Poäng! IKEA Hits Headwinds in Korea," *Korea Realtime, Asian Wall Street Blog*, November 18, 2014.

47. Clay Chandler, "Luxury Brands are Rushing into China's Red-hot Market," *Fortune*, July 26, 2004.

48. "Business: Luxury's New Empire; Conspicuous Consumption in China," *The Economist*, June 19, 2004.

49. "China Loses its Allure," *The Economist*, January 25, 2014.

50. "The PC16: Identifying China's Successors," *Stratfor*, July 30, 2013.

51. "Understanding ASEAN: Seven Things you Need to Know," *McKinsey*, May 2014.

52. Ibid.

53. "What Does The Rise of Manufacturing in ASEAN Mean for Multinationals?," *Frontier Strategy Group*, April 2014.

54. "ADB Sees Steady Growth for Developing Asia," *Asian Development Bank*, April 1, 2014.
55. Ibid.
56. "ASEAN Consumer and the AEC," *JWT Asia Pacific*, 2015.
57. "Build it, they're coming," *Forbes*, August 2010.
58. "Simon Makes Good his Vision," *Business Times*, April 12, 2011.
59. "How Companies in Emerging Markets are Winning at Home," BCG Perspectives, July 2014.
60. "From a Little Banyan Grows a Big Brand," *Far Eastern Economic Review*, November 2003.
61. Ibid.
62. "Banyan Tree Branching Out," *Ming Wu*, www.brandchannel.com, November 2003.
63. "Paradise Promised," *Straits Times*, November 20, 2003.
64. "Public Listing no Longer Banyan Tree's Top Priority," *Straits Times*, January 10, 2005.
65. "Banyan Tree Resorts and Hotels: Building an International Brand from an Asian Base," *INSEAD*, Singapore, 2003.
66. "Accolades," *Banyan Tree*, 2014.
67. "Tree's Company," *SilverKris*, *Singapore Airlines' In-flight Magazine*, January 2005.

11 Conclusion

1. "Brand and Deliver – Emerging Asia's new corporate imperative," *Economist Intelligence Unit*, 2010.

Index

Printed and bound in Great Britain by
CPI Group (UK) Ltd, Croydon, CR0 4YY